# I BUY HOU$ES

## The Property Investor's Handbook

# Paul Do

Wrightbooks

First published 2009 by Wrightbooks
an imprint of John Wiley & Sons Australia, Ltd
42 McDougall Street, Milton Qld 4064

Office also in Melbourne

Typeset in 10.5/12.6 pt New Baskerville

Reprinted September 2009

National Library of Australia Cataloguing-in-Publication data:

| | |
|---|---|
| Author: | Do, Paul. |
| Title: | I buy houses : the property investor's handbook / Paul Do. |
| ISBN: | 9781742168494 (pbk.) |
| Notes: | Includes index. |
| Subjects: | Real estate investment – Australia. |
| Dewey Number: | 332.63240994 |

Google Map: © 2008 Google – Data Map © 2008 Map Data Sciences Pty Ltd, PSMA

Cover image: © Shutterstock/Matt Trommer

Cover design by Brad Maxwell

Microsoft Excel charts reprinted with permission from Microsoft Corporation

Printed in China by Printplus Ltd

10 9 8 7 6 5 4 3 2

**Disclaimer**

The material in this publication is of the nature of general comment only, and does not represent professional advice. It is not intended to provide specific guidance for particular circumstances and it should not be relied on as the basis for any decision to take action or not take action on any matter which it covers. Readers should obtain professional advice where appropriate, before making any such decision. To the maximum extent permitted by law, the author and publisher disclaim all responsibility and liability to any person, arising directly or indirectly from any person taking or not taking action based upon the information in this publication.

# Contents

To my parents, Anthony and Wendy Do,
who instilled their values in me.

## Acknowledgements

My sincere thanks go to the team from John Wiley & Sons and their business partners. In particular, I would like to thank Kristen Hammond, my acquisitions editor, who not only knows a good thing when she sees it, but provided valuable feedback on the draft and project managed the book. Thanks also to Michael Hanrahan, who worked tirelessly to edit and lay out the book.

Finally, and most importantly, special thanks go to Amy Thai for being my biggest supporter and encouraging me to get published.

# Introduction

I wrote *I Buy Houses* because family and friends were always asking me for real estate advice: 'Should I get into the property market now?', 'How do I buy a property?' and 'How much should I pay?' When you look at the approach that most people use to buy a property, they attend open inspections every weekend for months on end, and eventually they get fed up and buy anything. They spend a lot of time and effort, but it is the wrong approach. I spend the bulk of my time at my desk; I focus on research, not inspections, and achieve a more effective outcome while expending much less time and effort. In this book I'm going to show you how you can do this too.

In addition, there are the things that family and friends should have asked me about real estate but didn't. Most people do not understand how real estate works as an investment or how to make money with it. They think the way to make money in real estate is to buy below market value, or buy a run-down property and then renovate it and flip it for a profit. No, I make money in real estate by spending time in the market, and augment my returns by timing the market.

## Who is this book for?

The people who will find this book useful are divided into two groups. Firstly, there are the people looking to buy their first home. None of the real estate investing books provide a detailed 'how to' guide to buying a property. I include a step-by-step guide to the buying process—with a comprehensive example of one of my recent purchases—to address this gap. The second group are property investors, both new and experienced. Other real estate investing books mostly focus on finding motivated sellers or positive-cash-flow properties. However, the market conditions for these strategies no longer exist. Instead, I explain my value approach to investing in real estate, a strategy that is universal, timeless and makes common sense, but also requires hard work. When I say 'hard work', I mean that it is not palatable work for many people. In terms of physical effort, it actually requires much less time and effort than most other strategies.

## Who am I?

What are my credentials for writing this book? Well, I don't have a rags-to-riches story to tell. What I do have is nearly 20 years of experience investing successfully in the real estate and stock markets, combined with the rigour of a corporate background in pricing and financial analysis. Why is this important? Well, firstly I am equally successful investing in the real estate market and the stock market, therefore I do not preach real estate all the time. As you will see later on, this is very important because there is a right time to buy real estate and there is a wrong time, and the difference can mean having a profitable portfolio of properties working for you or struggling to hold and service an overpriced property.

Secondly, I am a property-investing expert. I have bought and built many houses, in different states and over a number of cycles. So I know the boom times when most novices mistake luck for skill, and the down times when they question the merits of investing in real estate, and how to deal with both.

Thirdly, because I have invested successfully in the real estate market for so long, I know what works and what doesn't. For example, I have found that if you cannot get a standard loan then you are probably better off renting rather than buying a property.

Finally, I was a senior manager in a large corporation and I have an MBA, so I know how to manage businesses profitably, and investing in real estate *is a business*. For example, I explain how it is usually the boring things that make me money, while the 'sexy' things often cost me money. In addition, my background in pricing and financial analysis has helped me to understand how real estate price cycles work, how to manage them and how to take advantage of them, and I will show you how to do this too.

## I buy houses ...

*I Buy Houses* is divided into five parts. 'Real estate basics' forms the foundation for the rest of the book and will bring new readers up to speed with the fundamentals of real estate. Next, I explain my **SYSTEM T™** investment framework that forms the foundation of every buying and management decision I make with my real estate portfolio. Then I go through 'The buying process' in detail (with a comprehensive example provided in the appendix). I follow this with a section on 'Managing your properties', which covers property management, renovation, some advanced material on property development, and selling. Finally, I wrap up with 'Making money in real estate', including the common real estate investing strategies, how I make money in real estate using the value approach, and the stages of development of a real estate investor.

I started writing this book 10 years ago when I began to make some decent returns in the real estate and stock markets. As I grew, so did the book, and it has been a work in progress ever since. Over time I found that investing became quicker and easier, and it was then that I realised that I had mastered the principles of successful investing in the real estate market. These principles form the basis of my **SYSTEM T™** framework, my buying process and how I manage my properties, and they will act as guideposts on your investment journey.

I wish you all the best with your investing.

Paul Do
Sydney
December 2008

# Part I:
# Real estate basics

Real estate has created more millionaires than any other form of investment because it provides high returns over the long term and most people have a significant investment in it. Australians have one of the highest rates of home ownership in the world, and as a result many are becoming millionaires as their homes increase in value.

I have included the basics on real estate in this section as this forms the foundation for the rest of the book. Even if you are familiar with some of the material, I recommend that you still go over it for completeness. Here I cover the advantages and disadvantages of investing in real estate, the different characteristics of the real estate market, and the important concept of median prices.

# 1 Advantages and disadvantages of real estate

Over the years, I have found that the easiest way to make money from real estate is to maximise its advantages and avoid the disadvantages (where possible). The main advantage of real estate is that it allows you to borrow a lot of money to fund the purchase due to its high security. Real estate also offers high returns over the long term, and there are many other advantages that we are also going to look at in this chapter. The main disadvantages are high transaction costs, high holding costs, low liquidity and lumpiness, which mean that taking a long-term view with real estate is essential.

> The main advantage of real estate is that it allows you to borrow a lot of money to fund the purchase.

## Advantages of real estate

The advantages of real estate include high returns combined with high security that allows investors to borrow more. Let's have a look at these and the other advantages of real estate.

### Leverage

You can borrow more to fund real estate than you can any other asset because of its high security. This allows you to have a bigger asset working for you, so you can achieve your financial goals faster.

## Returns

Over the long term, real estate has returned around 10 per cent per annum in capital growth and rental yield, before holding costs (see 'High holding costs' in the next section). This return is comparable to shares but is more than bonds, cash and inflation. It is important that the long-term returns from real estate are higher than the returns from bonds and cash, because it means that the returns from real estate exceed your borrowing costs over the long term. It is also important that returns from real estate exceed inflation so that you can at least maintain your standard of living.

## Security

Unless you overextend yourself, it is very difficult to go bankrupt with real estate because there will always be demand for shelter. It is this security that affords high leverage.

## Familiarity

An often-overlooked advantage of real estate is that everyone is familiar with it as an owner, renter or boarder. The more familiar we are with real estate as an asset class, the more likely we are to invest a meaningful amount of money in it for the long term. Most people are less familiar with shares and, therefore, have less money invested in this way.

## Forced saving

Another advantage of real estate is that it forces disciplined saving through leverage. People with a large mortgage tend to refrain from splurging on things they do not need until they have reduced or paid off the mortgage. When you start on your investment journey, the amount you save is more important than the returns you make. Over the long term, the returns you make become more important than the amount you save. Through the power of compounding (see below), investors who start early can invest less but still be in a much better position financially than those who start later.

Table 1.1 shows the power of compounding when you start early. Mary invests $100 each year from the age of 21 to 28, a total of $800. John, on the other hand, invests $100 each year from the age of 28 to 65, a total of $3800. Assuming that both Mary and John are able to earn a return of 10 per cent per annum, at retirement Mary will have a portfolio worth $2730 more than John's ($42 775 versus $40 045), despite investing $3000 less than John. The reason for this is that by age 28 the return from Mary's investment exceeds the investment and return John makes each year ($114 versus $110, and then $126 versus $121, and so on). So in effect Mary is investing more each year than John is.

Table 1.1: the power of compounding

| | MARY | | | JOHN | | |
| Age | Investment ($) | Return ($) | Proceeds ($) | Investment ($) | Return ($) | Proceeds ($) |
| --- | --- | --- | --- | --- | --- | --- |
| 21 | 100 | 10 | 110 | | | |
| 22 | 100 | 21 | 231 | | | |
| 23 | 100 | 33 | 364 | | | |
| 24 | 100 | 46 | 511 | | | |
| 25 | 100 | 61 | 672 | | | |
| 26 | 100 | 77 | 849 | | | |
| 27 | 100 | 95 | 1044 | | | |
| 28 | 100 | 114 | 1258 | 100 | 10 | 110 |
| 29 | | 126 | 1384 | 100 | 21 | 231 |
| 30 | | 138 | 1522 | 100 | 33 | 364 |
| 31 | | 152 | 1674 | 100 | 46 | 511 |
| 32 | | 167 | 1842 | 100 | 61 | 672 |
| 33 | | 184 | 2026 | 100 | 77 | 849 |
| 34 | | 203 | 2229 | 100 | 95 | 1044 |
| 35 | | 223 | 2451 | 100 | 114 | 1258 |
| 36 | | 245 | 2697 | 100 | 136 | 1494 |
| 37 | | 270 | 2966 | 100 | 159 | 1753 |
| 38 | | 297 | 3263 | 100 | 185 | 2038 |
| 39 | | 326 | 3589 | 100 | 214 | 2352 |
| 40 | | 359 | 3948 | 100 | 245 | 2697 |
| 41 | | 395 | 4343 | 100 | 280 | 3077 |
| 42 | | 434 | 4777 | 100 | 318 | 3495 |
| 43 | | 478 | 5255 | 100 | 359 | 3954 |
| 44 | | 525 | 5780 | 100 | 405 | 4460 |
| 45 | | 578 | 6358 | 100 | 456 | 5016 |
| 46 | | 636 | 6994 | 100 | 512 | 5627 |

| Age | MARY | | | JOHN | | |
|---|---|---|---|---|---|---|
| | Investment ($) | Return ($) | Proceeds ($) | Investment ($) | Return ($) | Proceeds ($) |
| 47 | | 699 | 7693 | 100 | 573 | 6300 |
| 48 | | 769 | 8463 | 100 | 640 | 7040 |
| 49 | | 846 | 9309 | 100 | 714 | 7854 |
| 50 | | 931 | 10240 | 100 | 795 | 8750 |
| 51 | | 1024 | 11264 | 100 | 885 | 9735 |
| 52 | | 1126 | 12390 | 100 | 983 | 10818 |
| 53 | | 1239 | 13629 | 100 | 1092 | 12010 |
| 54 | | 1363 | 14992 | 100 | 1211 | 13321 |
| 55 | | 1499 | 16492 | 100 | 1342 | 14763 |
| 56 | | 1649 | 18141 | 100 | 1486 | 16349 |
| 57 | | 1814 | 19955 | 100 | 1645 | 18094 |
| 58 | | 1995 | 21950 | 100 | 1819 | 20014 |
| 59 | | 2195 | 24145 | 100 | 2011 | 22125 |
| 60 | | 2415 | 26560 | 100 | 2223 | 24448 |
| 61 | | 2656 | 29216 | 100 | 2455 | 27002 |
| 62 | | 2922 | 32138 | 100 | 2710 | 29813 |
| 63 | | 3214 | 35351 | 100 | 2991 | 32904 |
| 64 | | 3535 | 38887 | 100 | 3300 | 36304 |
| 65 | | 3889 | 42775 | 100 | 3640 | 40045 |
| Total | 800 | | | 3800 | | |

## Value add

Real estate has the added advantage (that shares do not) of allowing you to add value through refurbishment. For the experienced investor, cosmetic renovations as simple as tidying up the yard and repainting can add thousands of dollars to the value of a property. This can be important when you are starting out and have limited funds and the value of your time is lower. However, I have found that this advantage tends to be overrated because people forget to take the opportunity cost of their time into account.

# Disadvantages of real estate

Real estate also has some disadvantages, the main ones being high transaction and holding costs and lumpiness.

## High transaction costs

The round trip cost of buying and selling a property can be around 10 per cent of the property's value (see 'Transaction costs' in chapter 4). This is significantly more than the cost of buying and selling shares, which — depending on the size of the order — is only around 0.2 per cent for a round trip.

## High holding costs

The holding costs of investing in real estate can be around 20 to 30 per cent of the rental income each year (see 'Holding costs' in chapter 4). In contrast, the costs of investing in shares are much lower, and are mainly research-based.

## Lack of liquidity and lumpiness

The lack of liquidity and lumpiness are significant disadvantages of real estate. It can take weeks or months to buy or sell a property, as opposed to a few seconds for blue-chip shares. In addition, real estate is hindered by its lumpiness — you have to buy or sell the whole property, and not just, say, one bedroom. These disadvantages can be mitigated by planning ahead and taking a long-term approach, such as adopting a buy-and-hold strategy as opposed to a flipping (or trading) strategy.

## Inefficient market

The real estate market also has the disadvantage of being inefficient, unlike the stock market. In an efficient market, prices reflect all available information. This does not happen in the real estate market for two reasons. Firstly, information on specific properties is not widely available. Two-tier marketing, where out-of-area investors are charged a much higher price than locals, is an example of this. Secondly, even if the information were available, many buyers (especially owner-occupiers) would still transact with their hearts instead of their heads.

Since the real estate market is inefficient, the buyers that do the most research will achieve the better returns. This is one of my two key investing principles, the other being you should only buy real estate when market values are less than intrinsic values (see 'Fundamental analysis' in chapter 6).

# 2 Characteristics of the real estate market

The real estate market can be described in a number of different ways. Each characteristic provides an insight into how the market works and how to participate in it. The most commonly considered characteristic of property is location. The real estate market can also be classified according to land, houses and apartments, type of ownership, property age and architectural style of houses.

Let's have a look at each.

## Location

Unlike the stock market, the real estate market is location-dependent. The state economy drives the property market in each state. For example, while the Sydney real estate market peaked in 2003, then declined and moved sideways until 2008, the Perth market rose strongly off the back of the mining boom during this period. Furthermore, different states have different stamp duty and land tax rates (see chapter 9), and council rates vary from suburb to suburb.

Most of Australia's population resides in the capital cities in each state. The biggest capital cities are Sydney, Melbourne and Brisbane on the eastern seaboard. Perth, on the western seaboard, is catching up rapidly due to the strength of the mining boom, although this slowed down in 2008. Sydney is the most expensive Australian city measured on a house-price-to-income multiple, as it is a global coastal city that dominates its geographic location, like New York and London.

Within a capital city, properties are divided into concentric rings radiating out from the central business district: the inner, middle and outer rings. Prices typically start to rise in the inner ring, and then this ripples out to the outer rings. Satellite cities are suburbs within a capital city with significant business districts. In Sydney, they include Parramatta to the west, Chatswood to the north, Hurstville to the south and Liverpool to the south west. In Melbourne, they include Dandenong to the south east and Werribee to the south west. Satellite cities provide job opportunities, which is a significant driver of house prices. Outside of the capital cities are the regional areas.

**Start with the big picture**

One of the first things I did when I started investing in real estate was to get a foldout map of my capital city from the local motoring association and stick it onto the wall to get a bird's-eye view of the suburbs and their proximity to the central business district, satellite cities, transport, schools and shops. As I diversified my investments interstate, I did the same with the other capital cities.

## Capital cities vs regional areas

The majority of Australia's population lives in the main capital cities:

▸ Sydney has a population of over four million people, and is the corporate and financial capital of Australia. It contains the headquarters of more than half of Australia's top companies and the headquarters of many multinational corporations.

▸ Melbourne has a population of almost four million people and also houses the headquarters of many of Australia's largest companies and multinational corporations.

▸ Brisbane's population is just under two million. It is the headquarters of some medium-sized and smaller Australian companies, although most major companies have offices in Brisbane.

▸ Perth has a population of around one and a half million people, and is at the heart of the China-led mining boom, controlling around 80 per cent of Australia's mining and energy projects.

- Adelaide has over one million people, and its economy is based on manufacturing and defence.

- The remaining capital cities contain over half a million people combined: Canberra has a population of over 300 000, followed by Hobart with over 200 000, and Darwin with over 100 000.

Apart from location, the key difference between the capital cities and the regional areas is that they support different industries. Services and manufacturing dominate the capital cities, while the regional areas are usually supported by either agriculture or mining. Over the last century, there has been a significant shift in the composition of Australian industry, from agriculture and mining to services and—to a lesser extent—manufacturing. The percentage of persons employed in Australia in agriculture and mining shrunk from 26 per cent and 6 per cent respectively to 5 per cent and less than 1 per cent respectively over the last century.[1]

As a result, there has been a significant population shift in Australia over the last century from the rural areas to suburbia and the coast (from the bush to the block and the beach). Government projections show that the population of most inland areas is expected to fall further over the next 25 years, mainly due to the loss of working-age people to the cities. The rental yields on properties in the regional areas are higher than in the cities to compensate for the lack of growth. However, out-of-area demand over the last decade has pushed down rental yields and many of these properties are now negatively geared.

When you are starting out you will not have much money. It is very tempting to invest in the regional areas because property prices are so much lower. However, investing in the regional areas is a risky long-term strategy that could prove to be false economy. Properties in regional areas, like small-capitalisation stocks, are less efficiently priced than those in the capital cities because there is less attention from buyers, so you might be able to pick up a bargain. The downside is that you do not have local knowledge and could end up buying the lemons that the locals avoid. However, even if you manage to buy a bargain, you could find that a bargain in a declining market will still underperform an average investment in a strong market (see 'Sell if long-term demand declines' in chapter 20).

A less risky approach that I took to get into the property market was to buy a house in the outer suburbs of a capital city. Not only are prices more manageable, but the properties in the outer ring pay a higher rental yield (offset by lower growth), which helps you to service the loan. However, unlike the regional areas, the outer suburbs of a capital city are unlikely to experience future population decline. The people who live in the outer suburbs do not generally work in the CBD but in the satellite cities. While they have to spend more on petrol and there are fewer facilities, this is more than offset by cheaper housing costs.

**Investing in the regional areas could prove to be false economy**

Warren Buffett, the legendary investor who has returned over 20 per cent per annum over 50 years, bought his home in Omaha, Nebraska, in 1957 for $31 500. In 1971, he bought a beach home in Laguna Beach, California, for $150 000. When commenting on property taxes in 2003, he estimated the Omaha home to be valued around $500 000 and the beach home around $4 million. The capital growth of the Omaha home was 6.2 per cent per annum, while the capital growth of the Laguna Beach home was 10.8 per cent per annum. Although Omaha's economy is much stronger than most regional areas in Australia, the capital growth of the Omaha property was just over half of the Laguna Beach property.

Another attractive alternative I considered was buying an apartment in the middle suburbs. This has the same characteristics of a house in the outer ring: affordability combined with high rental yield. Furthermore, unlike the regional areas, the middle suburbs of a capital city are unlikely to experience future population decline.

# Land

Put your money in land, because they aren't making any more of it.

*Will Rogers*

Will Rogers is right. For example, Sydney is bordered by the Pacific Ocean to the east, national parks to the north and south and the Blue Mountains to the west. When the available land runs out, the only recourse is to increase the density of the land use by building townhouses and apartments in place of houses on big blocks of land. With demand constantly increasing due to population growth, investing in land would seem a sure thing.

### Land has the highest capital growth because they aren't making any more of it

In 1974 an investor paid $184000 for the corner piece of land of the Optus building in North Sydney. He sold it in 1988 for $7.2 million for a return of 30 per cent per annum.

The problem is that on the income–growth spectrum, land is to the extreme right. It has the highest capital growth but generates no income. This creates three problems. Firstly, there is no rent to cover the interest cost. Secondly, because land does not generate any income, you cannot deduct any expenses incurred in holding land against other sources of income. Therefore, you have to fund all of the out-of-pocket expenses yourself, instead of having the tenant and the Tax Office chip in. Thirdly, lenders are usually reluctant to lend against vacant land, so you have to put up most or all of the funds yourself.

The best returns from vacant land occur when there are zoning changes or subdivisions of land. Property developers either land bank (buy undeveloped land) or use options to acquire land in advance of their actual need to keep prices from increasing and to minimise their holding costs. These strategies are out of reach for ordinary investors in terms of both cost and opportunity. Investors can participate in the growth potential of land by investing in houses—which have high land content—instead of apartments.

### Do your research beforehand

I was young and inexperienced when I bought my first property. Having had some success with shares, I decided to consult a few financial planners to see if they could add anything to my wealth-creation strategy. They all suggested that I diversify my investments and invest in new apartment developments to maximise my tax deductions. I only realised later that the reason the financial planners did not recommend investing in established houses was that there was no developer to pay them a commission. I had never lived in a unit before and felt uncomfortable with the lack of land content, so I decided not to follow their advice.

As an alternative, one financial planner suggested buying land and then building a house on it. For introducing me to the builder, the builder paid the financial planner $2000, which was included in the building price. The financial projections the financial planner produced looked good on paper, but I knew that it was only as good as the assumptions supporting the projection. Remember, garbage in, garbage out. I checked the key assumptions such as the cost of similar-sized land and the rental yield of established properties around the neighbourhood. Once I was satisfied with these assumptions, I decided to go ahead with the arrangement. Fortunately, I got first pick from a land parcel that had just come onto market and chose the middle block on the top of a hill in a quiet cul de sac as it had the most frontage.

The land developer delayed the exchange of contracts for the land by eight months because he wanted to defer the income to the next financial year. However, the price was locked in. This was a blessing for me, because during this time the price of the land rose by 50 per cent based on recent sales. While waiting for settlement, I decided to go and see the other house designs my builder had available. After browsing for a few minutes, I found the design of my investment property. When I added up the cost, I was shocked to find out that the financial planner had overcharged me by $12 000 ($14 000 less the $2000 commission). I asked the sales manager to explain the discrepancy. She could not, and offered to write out another building contract for me.

I learnt two valuable lessons that day. Firstly, do all of your research thoroughly *beforehand*, and secondly, *always get at least a second quote*. Getting a second quote is especially important for new investors who do not have a feel for reasonable prices and can easily be ripped off. Apart from being inexperienced, the reason I was so blasé about doing my research was that the key performance indicators were good. The relative rental yield was high and the total cost (land and construction cost) was comparable to the surrounding established properties.

# Houses vs apartments

The real estate market is commonly divided into houses and apartments. Around 75 per cent of all dwellings in Australia are detached houses, which is high by international standards. This proportion is gradually declining, with semi-detached buildings and apartments making up one-third of all new dwellings completed each year. The distinguishing feature of apartments is that they do not have their own private grounds but usually share a common entrance foyer, stairs, lifts and grounds. New South Wales has by far the highest proportion of apartments, with around two-thirds of all new housing construction being medium and high density, followed by Victoria and Queensland, and then Western Australia and South Australia.

Houses and apartments cater to different types of people. High-rise apartments are suitable for singles and couples with no children. They are usually located in the inner city and near railway stations, close to cafes, restaurants and business districts. Maintenance is low because apartments do not usually have any private grounds. Houses located in the suburbs are more suited to young families, with plenty of space for the children to run about. Most of the people who live in apartments are renters, while most who live in houses are owner-occupiers.

## Land content

When considering a house or an apartment you must take into account the land content. This is important because only the land component appreciates over time. This is due to increased demand over time from population growth for a fixed supply of land. Buildings depreciate over time through wear and tear. Houses have the most land content, followed by duplexes and townhouses, and then apartments.

Land appreciates, buildings depreciate.

Another advantage of houses due to their high land content is the scope for higher use (subject to council approval), such as dual occupancy and redevelopment into apartments. As we run out of land, the only solution to meet increasing demand is to increase the density of the land by converting houses into townhouses and apartments. When this happens the house owner usually makes a windfall gain. However, this is a long-term phenomenon, and even in the inner city it might take many, many years for the land to be rezoned.

### The higher use of land can result in windfall gains

An aunt of mine was fortunate to benefit from the higher use demand for her land. In 1997, she and her husband bought a run-down house for $174 000 in an area surrounded by units. That was all they could afford at the time. The block was later rezoned, and in 2002 a developer paid my aunt and her neighbours $600 000 each for their properties to consolidate the land and build new apartments. The market price for similar houses was only around $350 000 without the rezoning premium.

## Growth vs yield

There is an inverse relationship between capital growth and income yield. That is, the higher the income yield, the lower the capital growth that can be expected from an investment, and vice versa. Houses have higher land content and therefore have higher capital growth over the long term. Since apartments have lower land content and therefore lower capital growth, they are priced to provide a higher rental yield than houses (see figure 4.9 on p. 61). The advantage of a higher yield is that it allows the buyer to service a higher loan, and hence purchase more assets.

Due to their different locations, it is possible for apartments by the seaside to achieve greater capital growth than houses in the outer suburbs. However, the comparison is only valid if you compare the capital growth of houses and apartments in the same location. The results will not be meaningful if you do not compare apples with apples because of the interaction of other factors. Some areas in the inner city and near the coast only contain apartments. Where there are restrictions on further development, these apartments will achieve the same capital growth as houses. Unfortunately, they will also be priced like houses, resulting in a low rental yield.

## Price

Apartments have the advantage of being cheaper than houses, allowing investors to get into the real estate market earlier. This can be a significant benefit when you take into account the power of compounding (see table 1.1 on p. 5).

## Maintenance and value add

High-rise apartment facilities such as lifts, gyms, pools and tennis courts are much more expensive to maintain than houses, and this is reflected in strata levies of around $2000 to $2500 per quarter. It is very difficult to recoup this cost in extra rent. On the other hand, most apartments are newer than houses, and so require less maintenance. Houses are detached, which gives the investor more scope to add value to the property. In addition, maintenance and improvements are easier to carry out for houses. Most changes to apartments require approval from the owners' corporation, and it can be a pain to get the agreement from the many owners in high-rise apartments.

## Tax

Apartments are usually newer than houses and have a greater proportion of their value in the building, and therefore enjoy greater depreciation tax benefits (see 'Non-cash expenses' in chapter 9). This is one of the main reasons why apartments attract more investors than houses. Apartments also incur less land tax due to their small land content, and hence small land value.

## Competition

One of the disadvantages of apartments is that there is more rental competition, especially in large complexes which tend to be bunched together. In addition, the tenants who live in apartments (often young singles) tend to be less stable than those who live in houses (generally families). The supply of new apartments also dampens the price of older apartments and restrains rents. In contrast, the building of new houses is usually only in the outer suburbs and does not affect the price or rent of established houses.

### Watch out for hidden agendas

Although real estate seminar spruikers explain that it is the land that appreciates while the building depreciates, they do not explain why they only spruik new apartments and townhouses (a small minority also sell house and land packages on the fringes of the city), and seminar participants never ask. The reason is that the developers of new apartments and townhouses pay them a marketing commission for each property they sell to their clients. If they recommended established houses and apartments, then they would not earn a cent, as the properties purchased would only earn a commission for the real estate agent.

Potential buyers are provided with a 'comprehensive' due diligence pack, but make sure you do your own independent due diligence before participating in any deal. The most *basic* would include asking local real estate agents the price of comparable established properties, whether there was any demand for the extra inclusions and upgrades, what the resale values of the spruiked properties were likely to be, as well as the rental demand and likely rents (without the guarantees). You want to make sure that you are familiar with both the pros and cons of any potential investment. You will hear all the pros from the spruikers, so let the local real estate agents balance them out with the cons. After all, it is in their interests to sell an established property.

During the downturn in the apartment market in the Sydney and Melbourne CBDs in the early 2000s, the price of apartments sold through financial planners and property seminar promoters dropped the most because the selling prices were set without any reference to comparable properties and were often inflated. Apartments sold through agents, on the other hand, fared better.

## Horses for courses

The most appropriate type of property depends on the buyer's circumstances. Buyers who have limited funds but want to get into the property market should consider older apartments that are more affordable. Buyers looking for strong growth should consider houses or apartments with unique characteristics such as proximity to the CBD and water. New apartments are advantageous for high-income investors who get maximum benefit from the tax deductions. Using the same logic, new apartments are less valuable to owner-occupiers, who cannot take advantage of any of the tax deductions. Owner-occupiers who buy a new apartment are in effect paying an inflated price because they do not have the benefit of the tax deductions.

You should also buy a property that is appropriate for the area (see 'What to buy' in chapter 12). In the outer suburbs, four-bedroom houses are the norm and the most appropriate for the area. The families who live out there are unlikely to consider renting an apartment. On the other hand, in the inner city most of the young professionals are single and used to apartment living. They probably could not afford to rent a terrace house for example, and so this would not be appropriate for many of the suburbs in the inner city.

Another consideration is the *relative* value of houses compared to apartments. When there is excessive demand for one type of property over another, buy the less fashionable one because there is more scope for capital growth. For example, in the early 2000s strong demand for apartments in the Melbourne CBD and Docklands pushed up prices.

Many of the apartments were bought off the plan to avoid paying stamp duty. The market became oversupplied and prices eventually dropped sharply, in many cases by 20 or 30 per cent. Five years later, some of the apartments are still worth less than what they were bought for. Houses near the CBD bought during the same period have fared much better, with most showing a respectable return.

In the past there was greater demand for two-bedroom apartments over one- and three-bedroom apartments. However, with the increase in rents over the last few years and higher interest rates, there is now strong demand for one-bedroom apartments. A good rule of thumb is to buy only units that do not need a lift, in small complexes with no more than three or four storeys. The percentage of owner-occupied units is usually high so there is less rental competition, and owners are more likely to take care of their apartments and the common areas than tenants, which improves rents and re-sale values. In addition, strata levies will be lower due to lower maintenance costs.

> A good rule of thumb is to buy only units that do not need a lift.

The ownership title of apartments can be either strata title or company title. You should only focus on strata title apartments, which give you the most flexibility. Avoid the less common and restrictive company title apartments because the company title owner does not have a title in any real estate like a strata title owner does. Instead, they own the shares in the company that owns the building, and have a right to occupy a unit in the building. The directors must approve purchasers and whether the apartment can be rented out, to whom, and under what conditions, which restricts the size of your market. Lenders are also more reluctant to lend against company-titled apartments.

### Houses have higher capital growth than apartments

In the early 2000s, one of my friends bought three units and a townhouse. When high-rise units were all the rage, he bought a unit on the ground floor with a courtyard that sold at a discount to the other units in the complex. Subsequently, buyers in the same complex paid a premium for ground floor units with a courtyard. In 2004, he moved to London to work, and decided to sell most of his units. The supply of new apartments in the area reduced his capital gains to nearly breakeven after transaction costs. With hindsight, he says that he should have

> bought houses instead for their capital growth. He kept the townhouse though, which is in the inner city and has a lot of growth potential.

## Buying off the plan

Buying off the plan involves entering into a contract to buy a property before it has been built. You only have the plans and a schedule of specifications (and perhaps a three-dimensional architectural model) to go by. It is attractive to speculators and people without much money or equity due to the high level of leverage possible, since usually only a 10 per cent deposit is required when contracts are exchanged, with the balance of the purchase price due on completion. Deposit bonds can be used to increase leverage even more by deferring the full amount of the purchase price until settlement for the cost of 1 to 3 per cent of the purchase price.

The advantages of buying off the plan are:

▸ Buying next year's property at today's prices, hence benefiting from any price appreciation before completion. You can either keep the property or on-sell it before settlement for a profit.

▸ Deferred settlement. Only the deposit needs to be paid until completion, providing you with more time to save and organise your finances.

▸ The property might be sold at a small discount to the market to achieve strong pre-sales so the developer can get financing for the project.

▸ Stamp duty savings. In Victoria, stamp duty is only payable on the proportion of construction commenced at the time of purchase, which can result in savings of tens of thousands of dollars (see 'Stamp duty' in chapter 9).

The disadvantages include:

▸ The selling price is sometimes inflated, especially when there are significant marketing costs (advertising and sales commission) of 10 per cent or more. There are no free lunches in life, so guess who ends up paying for the marketing costs? In addition, off-the-plan sales are a bit like IPOs (initial public offerings) in the stock market: it is difficult to establish market value because there are no comparable sales to benchmark prices. If the developer provides a rental guarantee or some other frill, then this might be an indication that the property is overpriced.

▸ Off-the-plan sales usually occur towards the end of the property cycle, when prices are booming. Hence, prices could fall between signing the contract and completion due to the combination of inflated selling price, declining market prices and the oversupply of new properties.

▸ Lenders could tighten lending conditions due to the oversupply of new properties, making it difficult to get financing for the property.

▸ The quality of the finishes could be below your expectations. You should make sure that every detail is specified in the contract, down to the particular brand and model of fixtures.

▸ If the developer goes bankrupt, you potentially could lose your deposit. You should only buy from established developers with a track record, and make sure your deposit is held in a trust and not by the developer. You might also want to include a clause that allows you to be released from the contract with your deposit refunded if the property is not completed by a specified date.

Timing the market is critical to successful off-the-plan buying. You should only buy off the plan at the start of the property cycle, and only if you can buy at market value. This strategy is consistent with my value approach to investing in real estate (discussed later). Any off-the-plan purchase that satisfies these two conditions can produce spectacular returns in a short time frame. Buying off the plan at any other time is risky, and the later you buy in the property cycle the more likely you could end up with a dud.

### You should only buy off the plan at the start of the property cycle

In 2003 (the top of the Sydney real estate cycle), an investor bought a unit off the plan in an inner city suburb of Sydney for $600000. In 2005, the same developer advertised similar units in the next stage of development for $450000. Facing a 25 per cent loss, the investor took legal action to be released from the contract because the height of the building had been reduced from 18 to 14 floors, and in Chinese the number 8 sounds like wealth and fortune, while the number 4 sounds like death.

This example highlights the dangers of buying overpriced real estate. Firstly, the investor faced a large capital loss. Secondly, the fall in prices made financing the property much more difficult. Assume that she paid a 10 per cent deposit or $60000 when contracts were exchanged and was hoping to borrow the rest near completion ($540000). If the property was only worth $450000 at that time, then at most the bank would lend 90 per cent of $450000, or $405000. She would have to find *another* $135000 (600000 − 90 per cent × 450000 − 60000) to cover the difference between her purchase price and the bank loan and her deposit. However, the glut of new apartments and weaker prices could cause the banks to tighten their lending conditions, perhaps to 60 per cent loan-to-valuation ratio (LVR). In this case, she has to find *another* $270000 (600000 − 60 per cent × 450000 − 60000).

However, her problems do not end there. Thirdly, because she paid so much for the property, her cash flows will be heavily negative, and her out-of-pocket costs will be much higher. The net rent is the same irrespective of how much you pay for a property, so the more you pay for a property, the more you have to borrow and the higher the interest cost relative to the net rent, and hence the higher your out-of-pocket costs. Fourthly, we have not considered transaction costs. If the investor cannot service the property and is forced to sell, she will incur further losses due to transaction costs.

## Owner-occupiers vs investors

Another way of looking at real estate is by the type of ownership. Approximately 70 per cent of Australian dwellings are owner-occupied, which is high by international standards. Investors, half of whom have a mortgage, own the remainder. A high proportion of owner-occupied properties dampens the big swings in market cycles. In boom times, investors will buy in the expectation of higher prices, causing prices to overshoot their long-term values. When prices retreat, investors that are unable to service their properties are forced to sell. Owner-occupiers, on the other hand, live through the cycle and effectively put a floor under property prices. As a result, real estate prices tend not to correct on the downside like shares do. For example, the Australian stock market dropped by over 50 per cent from its high in 2007 to its low in 2008, while the Sydney property market (as measured by median three-bedroom houses) dropped by just over 10 per cent from its high in 2003–04 to its low in 2006.

The key difference between owner-occupiers and investors is that owner-occupiers have to fund the property themselves, while investors are assisted by tenants and the Tax Office. So all other things being equal, investors can withstand higher interest rates than owner-occupiers. Therefore, a good time to buy real estate for investors is when interest rates are high because many owner-occupiers are forced out of the market and so there is less competition. Another consideration for investors is to avoid the areas where there is a high concentration of investment properties due to the competition for tenants (and sales if you need to sell). Furthermore, the upkeep of these areas is poorer, which restrains property values.

# New vs old

The real estate market can be divided into new and old properties. New properties increase the existing stock by approximately 2 per cent each year. In the larger capital cities, a large proportion of new properties are apartments due to the shortage of land. New apartments are usually built near the CBD and in high-demand areas such as the coast and near train stations, while new housing estates can be found on the urban fringe.

New properties attract higher rents and are easier to rent out than older properties in the same area, but they cost more to purchase. They have a much greater depreciation allowance than older properties. Depreciation expenses are non-cash costs that allow you to reduce tax from other sources of income and boost cash flow (see 'Non-cash expenses' in chapter 9). Moreover, new properties require no work to be done and need less maintenance over time, and are ideal for high-income (who can benefit most from the depreciation benefits), time-poor investors.

Investors are also attracted to new properties because they can speculate and buy them off the plan with little initial outlay. As a result, the prices of new properties, especially apartments, are usually more volatile than established properties. In addition, financial advisers and seminar promoters push their clients into new properties, citing higher rents, low vacancy rates and maintenance costs and high depreciation tax benefits.

What they usually neglect to mention is that they will only earn a marketing commission from new properties (paid by the developer), which could lead to a conflict of interest. The commission is similar to that received by real estate agents when they sell an established property. To avoid this potential conflict of interest, ask whether the financial planners and seminar promoters are prepared to be paid a flat fee for their service to source you the best value property (new or established). If they say that established properties are too difficult to understand, you know why.

> It is difficult to get a man to understand something when his salary depends on his not understanding it.
>
> *Upton Sinclair*

While new properties are easier to rent compared to older properties in the same area, they are usually located near other new properties, such as in a new block of apartments or a new estate. In the short to medium term, it might be harder to rent out these new properties than older properties in established areas with less rental competition. In addition, the new properties will experience some price weakness as new completions come onto the market and increase the supply. Therefore, new properties usually take longer before they show any capital gains.

The advantage of an old property is that you can quickly increase its value through renovation. For example, by just tidying up the garden, applying a new coat of paint and changing the carpets you can increase the rent on an old house by $20 or more per week, and increase the value of the property by tens of thousands of dollars. In addition, unlike new properties, the supply of old properties is fixed, and therefore old properties should see steady capital gains. Older properties are also found in the inner and middle rings, where the rental demand is stronger than in the outer suburbs.

### Established properties are less likely to be overpriced

One of my friends bought an old two-bedroom apartment in a small complex on the North Shore in 2002 because it was much more affordable than the new apartments for sale. Within two years she had a leak in her bathroom, which flowed into the bedroom of the unit below. In addition, gas leaked from her stove. Unable to find the source, she took the opportunity to replace the kitchen completely. Just when she thought things could not get any worse, one day she looked up from her parking space and saw concrete cancer in the support above her. Despite all of these problems, her returns were better than

**Established properties are less likely
to be overpriced (cont'd)**

if she had bought one of the many overpriced new apartments
for sale at the time because the value of her apartment never
reduced to the extent of the new apartments after the peak.

# Architectural styles

Houses can be classified by architectural styles that give an indication of the period in which they were built. Many of the houses of the early styles were constructed of double brick, and may have subsequently been bagged and painted, renovated and extended. Later houses were built out of fibro and brick veneer. The building costs for double-brick houses can vary from $300000 to $700000, while the building costs of brick veneer houses are around half, ranging from $150000 to $300000.

Following are some of the more common architectural styles in Australia from the last 150 years that are still commonly found nowadays. Except for the Victorian terraces, they are all free standing.

## Victorian terrace (1840–1900)

Victorian terraces were built before Federation in rows of attached houses. They are found in the inner ring suburbs such as Paddington, Bondi Junction, Glebe, Darlinghurst and Surry Hills in Sydney and Middle Park, Albert Park, East Melbourne, South Melbourne and Carlton in Melbourne. The houses are long and narrow and usually contain two storeys on a very small block of land (around 100 m²). A terrace typically has the living areas located downstairs, with the kitchen and bathroom at the back, the bedrooms on the first floor, and a small court-yard at the back. Terraces are an alternative to apartment living in the inner city.

# Federation house (1900-20)

Federation houses were built around the turn of last century, of deep red brick and terracotta tile with a distinctive timber veranda on large blocks of land (600 to 1000+ m$^2$). In Sydney they are found on the North Shore such as in Roseville, and in the inner west such as in Haberfield. The decorative style includes leadlight windows, high ceilings and ornate plasterwork. They are mainly single storey, and many now have first-floor additions and extensions opening up the house to the backyard.

# Californian bungalow (1915-40)

Californian bungalows were built after World War I of liver-coloured brick in Sydney and red brick in Melbourne and terracotta tiles on large blocks of land (600 to 1000+ m$^2$). They are distinguished by two or three roof gables and a brick veranda supported by brick or masonry pillars. To reduce costs the houses were reduced in size and most of the decorative features of Federation houses were removed, including lowering the ceilings. They were originally built as single-storey houses, and a number have been extended to the rear. They are found throughout the inner and middle ring suburbs.

### Red brick house (1945-70)

Small red brick houses were built after World War II of red brick and terracotta tiles on large blocks of land. They are distinguished by an austere look and are found in the middle and outer ring suburbs.

### Fibro cottage (1950-mid 1980s)

Fibro cottages became popular after World War II in Housing Commission developments. The walls and roofs were made from fibrous cement sheets, with some having tile or sheet metal roofs. Fibro cottages are found in the less affluent middle and outer ring suburbs.

### McMansion (1990s-present)

'McMansions' are brick veneer double-storey houses cheaply and quickly built to standard designs. A distinctive feature of McMansions is the double garage at the front of the house. Early McMansions

were built on medium-sized blocks (and included single-storey houses), but with the shortage of land block sizes have shrunk to around 400 m² in Sydney, making single-storey houses impractical. McMansions are found in new developments in the outer suburbs such as the Hills District and the south western suburbs of Sydney, and these areas are often connected by new motorways such as the M2 and M5.

# Median prices

A widely used price reference for real estate is the median price and rents of three-bedroom houses and two-bedroom units for each capital city. For example, table 2.1 shows the median prices of three-bedroom houses and two-bedroom apartments for the capital cities of Australia at June 2008, and for Australia as a whole. This is different from the median price quoted for a suburb, which is not restricted by the number of bedrooms.

The median is the middle value of a series of numbers arranged from lowest to highest. The median price is a better indicator than the average or mean price because it is not skewed by a small number of very high priced properties. For example, suppose five houses were recently sold for $200 000, $300 000, $300 000, $400 000 and $1 000 000. The median price is $300 000. The average price of $440 000 is not representative of the prices of the houses sold because it is skewed by the price of the million-dollar house.

Table 2.1: median prices at June 2008[2]

|  | 3-bedroom houses | 2-bedroom apartments |
| --- | --- | --- |
| Sydney | 542 000 | 364 000 |
| Melbourne | 451 000 | 370 075 |
| Brisbane | 420 300 | 356 000 |
| Perth | 443 000 | 374 000 |
| Adelaide | 366 000 | 276 000 |
| Hobart | 325 000 | 260 000 |
| Darwin | 423 299 | 328 950 |
| Canberra | 450 000 | 353 000 |
| Australia | 459 216 | 357 358 |

However, even the median price can be skewed by an increase in sales in a particular price range. Continuing with the above example, suppose only the $400 000 house was sold the next year for the same price. The median price increases by 33 per cent to $400 000, even though the price of the property sold did not change from last year. Therefore, some median prices are calculated from repeat sales to provide a more accurate picture of price changes. For example, the median house price in Surry Hills increased by nearly 30 per cent in 2007. However, this was skewed by the increase in sales of bigger and more expensive houses.

Problems can also arise when the pool from which the median price is calculated changes. For example, in 2007 the median price of Chatswood houses fell by nearly 10 per cent despite a strong rise in North Shore median house prices, which includes Chatswood. In fact, the market for Chatswood house prices was very strong as measured by the high percentage of listings that sold before auction. The reason for the fall in median house prices was due to Willoughby Council expanding the boundaries of Chatswood to include cheaper houses that were formerly in Chatswood West, while at the same time moving some of Chatswood's former expensive houses to Roseville.

Another problem with the median price is that it does not take into account the *capital injection* by investors for renovation and building costs, which artificially increases capital gains. New building costs have a greater effect on the price of apartments, while renovation and extension costs affect houses more. For example, if the median price of established apartments is $200000 and a number of new apartments are completed and sold for $300000, then there is an automatic increase in the median unit price that does not correspond with the natural price increase of established apartments over time.

Similarly, if you buy a house for $500000 and spend $200000 to add a second storey and subsequently sell it for $700000, the $200000 capital gain is due to your capital injection, rather than the natural growth in value of the property. This is why the capital returns from real estate measured by the increase in median prices are unrealistically high. Median prices calculated from repeat sales that cover the 'secondhand' market (properties that have sold at least twice) is a partial solution to this problem because it only addresses new building costs.

The capital returns from real estate measured by the increase in median prices are unrealistically high.

# PART II: **SYSTEM T**™

**SYSTEM T**™ is the investment framework that I used to build my real estate portfolio. It forms the foundation of every buying and management decision I make with my real estate portfolio. You can incorporate it into your decision-making process by systematically assessing the impact of each component. **SYSTEM T**™ stands for:

▸ **S**ecurity—my *first* aim is to avoid losing money (which is why security is first on the list). Real estate has high security, which allows high magnification.

▸ **Y**ield—my second aim is to make money. With real estate, this comes from capital growth and rental income.

▸ **S**pread—I started with my first investment property many years ago and gradually built up a diversified real estate portfolio from there by spreading the properties over different states. In addition, real estate provides spread for the rest of my investment portfolio, which includes other asset classes such as shares and cash.

▸ **T**ime—over the long term, the yield from real estate exceeds the interest cost by a small margin, which I earn by spending time in the market. However, I augment my returns by timing the market and only buying when market values are less than intrinsic values.

▸ **E**quity—I use the increase in equity in my real estate portfolio to add to my real estate and share portfolio.

▸ **M**agnification—the *key* advantage of real estate is that it allows me to leverage my equity more than any other investment. This magnifies my yield but also reduces my security, so I use it conservatively.

▸ **T**ax—while important, this is my *last* investment consideration (which is why tax is last on the list). I maximise my after-tax yield by buying high-capital-growth properties and never selling them.

Each one of these steps is covered in its own chapter in part II.

# 3 Security

With real estate, your first goal is to avoid losing money, and your second is to make money—not the other way around. That is, your first goal is to ensure the security of your investment. It is why security appears first in my **SYSTEM T™** framework. The security of your investment has two parts: the return *of* investment and the return *on* investment.

There are a number of threats to the security of your investment. These are also known as risks or the chance of loss, and include:

▸ declining long-term demand

▸ operational risks

▸ overextending.

You can improve the security of your investment by avoiding and mitigating these risks and, where possible, by taking out insurance to transfer the risks to someone else.

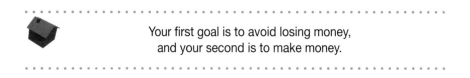

Your first goal is to avoid losing money,
and your second is to make money.

# Return *of* investment

Most people are enamoured with real estate because of the perceived high security from the tangibility of bricks and mortar. After all, they can drive by and touch their investment. In addition, they have full control of it, unlike shares, over which they have no control. In fact, the security is due to real estate's high return *of* investment. While a company can go bankrupt and its shares become worthless, the risk of bankruptcy of ungeared real estate is negligible. Even highly geared real estate is secure over the long term, since the population is always increasing, which supports demand and hence prices.

This high security allows high leverage of real estate. This is most apparent when you go to the bank and ask for a loan. It is much easier to borrow against real estate to buy shares than to borrow against shares to buy real estate. Moreover, you can borrow much more using real estate as security. The typical loan-to-valuation ratio for real estate is 80 per cent, and you can borrow even more with mortgage insurance. In contrast, the typical loan-to-valuation ratio for blue-chip shares is 50 per cent, and 0 per cent for smaller capitalisation stocks. The real security lies in the land content, which appreciates over time, and not the structure, which depreciates over time from wear and tear.

# Return *on* investment

The return *on* real estate is also more secure than shares, for two reasons. Firstly, real estate prices are less volatile due to infrequent valuations. Shares are valued by the market every day, while real estate is usually only valued when it is bought and sold every couple of years. Secondly, investors only own around 30 per cent of all real estate. The rest is owned by owner-occupiers who need a place to live, thus dampening fluctuations in price. Irrespective of whether prices rise or fall, owner-occupiers just sit on their investment. It is the speculative property investors that cause property prices to overshoot their long-term trend. Furthermore, rents are more stable than dividends, although real estate can be subject to prolonged vacancy periods, which is equivalent to when a company cuts or cancels a dividend.

While infrequent valuations encourage a long-term view, the downside is that buyers can be deluded by their financial position and are less concerned with overpaying for real estate. People who buy at the top of the market can suffer capital losses of hundreds of thousands of dollars, but might not be fully aware of this because they do not 'mark to market' the value of their property by putting it up for sale (or getting a valuation). It is like buying a share that has fallen 20 per cent or more and refusing to check the latest price.

# Declining long-term demand

In real estate, the biggest threat to your return of investment is the decline in long-term demand due to a declining population. When this happens, your property gradually reduces in value, so that when you come to sell the property you will incur a capital loss. Furthermore, the decline in long-term demand will also reduce the return on your investment. Weakening demand results in high vacancy rates, which drives down rents as landlords compete to tenant their properties.

# Operational risks

Real estate is subject to operational risks that affect both the return of and return on investment. For example, structural problems due to termites, concrete cancer or weak foundations can cost tens or hundreds of thousands of dollars to rectify, and even small problems such as a faulty air conditioner compressor can take weeks to resolve. In an economic downturn, properties can remain vacant for months, and it can also take just as long to evict problem tenants who do not pay the rent or damage the property.

The real estate market also has greater exposure to political tampering than the stock market because it has a more direct impact on voters. For example, in the cities of some countries rental properties are subject to rent control. This restrains capital growth and provides no incentive for property investors to maintain their properties. In 2004 the New South Wales Government imposed vendor stamp duty and stamp duty on buyers of luxury homes and changed land tax calculations to include all investors. After the backlash from mum-and-dad property investors the vendor stamp duty and land tax changes were withdrawn.

# Overextending

The greatest risk with real estate is usually self-created by inexperienced investors who overextend themselves. Instead of buying just one property or one off-the-plan apartment with one deposit bond at a time, some investors become greedy and gear to the hilt to make up for lost time and simultaneously buy two properties or three off-the-plan apartments with three deposit bonds. These novices usually compound the problem by being greedy right at the top of the cycle. When their circumstances change or interest rates rise, they are unable to service the loans on their properties and suffer heavy losses from the fire sale of their properties.

The greatest risk with real estate is usually self-created by inexperienced investors who overextend themselves.

# Protecting your wealth

As you build up your real estate portfolio, you will need to protect yourself and your dependants against unforeseen circumstances with insurance. It is important to remember than you have not lost anything if you do not make a claim. What your premium purchases is peace of mind.

There are seven types of insurance to consider.

## Life insurance

Life insurance protects your dependants if you do not have many assets. It pays your dependants a fixed lump-sum benefit on death, illness or disability. The lump sum can be used to pay off a mortgage or to provide a capital base to generate future investment income. Term life insurance is the best option for most people because of its affordability and transparency; it only covers life insurance and does not include any savings component. You do not generally need life insurance if you are single and have no dependants. Similarly, older people with sufficient assets that provide an income stream for their dependants do not usually need life insurance, especially since premiums increase with age. Superannuation funds usually provide some form of life cover, but this might not be sufficient for your needs.

## Income protection insurance

Most people insure minor things but forget to insure their most valuable asset: their income-producing ability. Income protection insurance provides a replacement income of up to 75 per cent of your pre-tax income if you are unable to work due to sickness or injury. You may even receive a benefit if you can only work at a reduced capacity. Until you have achieved financial independence, it is important to have income protection insurance to cover your expenses if you fall ill or become injured. The premiums vary with the level of coverage, waiting periods and benefit periods, and are tax deductible. Your superannuation fund might provide income protection cover, but it usually only lasts for two years. If this is the case, you can take out separate income protection insurance and select a two-year waiting period.

## Health insurance

There are two types of health insurance cover. Hospital insurance covers the costs of hospital treatment as a private patient, such as doctor's charges and hospital accommodation. This provides choice of doctor, hospital and access time. Ancillaries cover includes the cost of services such as dental, optical and physiotherapy treatment not covered by Medicare. Premiums vary with the extent of cover. Hospital cover is genuine insurance, while ancillary cover is more akin to a savings plan. If you can only afford one, it's usually best to take out hospital cover.

Not having hospital cover can be very expensive if you require medical treatment, especially for complex procedures. Furthermore, the government has created two initiatives that increase the cost of not having hospital cover. Lifetime Health Cover is designed to encourage young people to take out private health insurance. People who did not have hospital cover prior to 1 July 2000 are charged an extra 2 per cent over the normal premium for every year they are aged over 30 when they first take out hospital cover. High-income earners have an additional incentive; they have to pay an additional 1 per cent surcharge on top of the Medicare levy if they do not have hospital cover. It is also important to take out travel insurance to provide health insurance cover when travelling overseas, as medical costs can be substantial in countries such as the United States.

## Property insurance

Property insurance provides replacement of your possessions in case of damage or loss and is essential to maintain your wealth. Property insurance includes building and contents insurance on your home, motor insurance on your vehicles and building insurance on your investment properties. Make sure you are not underinsured (this is when you only have cover for a fraction of the value of your possessions), because the insurer will only pay out the proportion of the claim equal to the proportion you insured.

## Liability insurance

Liability insurance covers you against your negligence that results in property damage or bodily injury. It is even more important than property insurance because, at worst, without property insurance you can only lose everything you own. Without liability insurance, you could lose everything you own *and* be in debt as well. So make sure you have adequate liability insurance with your building insurance, and as a minimum take out third-party property damage insurance and compulsory third party insurance for your car. Also, it can be a good idea to take out workers compensation insurance if you have anyone working in your home.

## Landlord insurance

Landlord insurance covers you against damage to the property by the tenant, legal expenses and loss of rent if the tenant defaults or leaves without sufficient notice. When starting out, I suggest you take out landlord insurance to provide yourself with security of cash flow and to avoid unnecessary costs. As your property portfolio grows you might want to self-insure against this risk (that is, bear the risk yourself). For example, if you own five properties and the average landlord insurance premium is $200, the total cost of your premiums is $1000 a year or $5000 every five years. If your average loss is only $3000 every five years, you are better off self-insuring. If you have a good property manager that conducts detailed reference checks on new tenants and manages tenant arrears effectively, this is further incentive to self-insure.

## Home warranty insurance

If you have any building work done to a property valued at more than $12 000, make sure the builder or tradesperson has home warranty insurance to cover you against incomplete work, structural defects for six years and non-structural defects for two years after completion of the work if the builder dies, disappears or becomes insolvent.

# Excesses

Having adequate insurance coverage can be expensive. If you are starting out, the way to reduce your costs is not to underinsure or self-insure, but to take out a higher excess or deductible or co-payment for health insurance, where you pay the first few dollars of every claim. You only need insurance to cover catastrophe-type losses, not small claims that are an administrative hassle for everyone. When you take out a higher excess, you signal to the insurer that you are a better risk since you are willing to put some of your own money on the line. The insurer usually responds by reducing your premium more than proportionately.

# 4 Yield

The yield, or total return, on a property is how much money you made on that property in the past. The yield can be expressed as a dollar amount, but it is usually calculated as a percentage of the purchase price each year. The yield on a property comprises the capital growth of the property and the net rental income. The capital growth is the increase in price of the property, while the net rental income is the gross rent less all holding costs. A high yield is nice to have by itself, but is much more effective when combined with the power of compounding through reinvesting. You can achieve a better feel of the yield by using the Rule of 72 to link it to time.

Over the long term, the yield from real estate has averaged around 10 per cent per annum. This is comparable to the return on shares, and is more than bonds, cash and inflation. Capital growth is determined by the interaction of demand and supply, which in turn are driven by population growth, immigration, wages, interest rates, inflation and building approvals. For a particular property, capital growth is also determined by its location and other specific factors, and the transaction costs incurred. There are also significant holding costs that reduce the gross rent by up to 30 per cent.

The inverse relationship between capital growth and income states that a property with more of one will have less of the other. High-capital-growth properties provide a higher after-tax return, but are harder to service in the short term, especially with rental yields so low compared to interest rates.

The Australian Dream of owning your own home makes less sense when rental yields are low because renting is more attractive than buying a property. However, unless you diligently save the difference and invest in comparable growth assets such as shares, I encourage you to try to buy your own home.

# The power of compounding

Your investments will grow much quicker if you combine a high yield with the power of compounding through reinvesting. Compounding is the earning of a return on the return. When you invest an amount of money, you receive a return on it at the end of the period. When you reinvest the proceeds of the first period, you will receive a return on your initial investment *and* the return in the first period. For example, if you invested $100 at 10 per cent per annum compound interest, at the end of the first year your investment turns into $110, consisting of your original $100 investment and $10 interest. At the end of the second year the $110 turns into $121, consisting of your $110 investment at the start of the year and $11 interest. The $11 interest in the second year consists of the $10 interest on your original $100 investment and $1 interest on the $10 interest you earned in the first year.

Table 4.1 shows the power of compounding, and the results are shown in figure 4.1 (on p. 40). Compounding is such a miracle that Albert Einstein called it the eighth wonder of the world.

The keys to remember with compounding are:

▸ Increasing your investment increases your proceeds proportionately.

▸ Increasing the rate of return on your investment increases your proceeds exponentially.

▸ Increasing the term of your investment increases your proceeds exponentially.

Increasing the rate return on your investment or the term of your investment increases your proceeds exponentially.

## Table 4.1: the power of compounding

1. If you invest $100 at 10 per cent for 10 years and didn't reinvest the interest (this is called simple interest), your proceeds will be:

Proceeds = $100 × (1 + 0.1 + 0.1 + 0.1 + 0.1 + 0.1 + 0.1 + 0.1 + 0.1 + 0.1 + 0.1)

= $200

---

2. If you invest $100 at 10 per cent compound for 10 years, your proceeds will be:

Proceeds = $100 × 1.1 × 1.1 × 1.1 × 1.1 × 1.1 × 1.1 × 1.1 × 1.1 × 1.1 × 1.1

= $259

> $200

Compound interest increases your proceeds exponentially compared to simple interest, which only increases your proceeds linearly.

---

3. If you invest $200, instead of $100, at 10 per cent compound for 10 years, your proceeds will be:

Proceeds = $200 × 1.1 × 1.1 × 1.1 × 1.1 × 1.1 × 1.1 × 1.1 × 1.1 × 1.1 × 1.1

= $519

= 2 × $259

Doubling your investment only doubles your proceeds.

---

4. If you invest $100 at 20 per cent compound instead of 10 per cent, your proceeds will be:

Proceeds = $100 × 1.2 × 1.2 × 1.2 × 1.2 × 1.2 × 1.2 × 1.2 × 1.2 × 1.2 × 1.2

= $619

> $519 (= 2 × $259)

Doubling the rate of return on your investment *more than doubles* your proceeds.

---

5. If you invested $100 at 10 per cent compound for 20 years instead of 10, your proceeds will be:

Proceeds = $100 × 1.1 × 1.1 × ... × 1.1 (20 times)

= $673

> $519 (= 2 × $259)

Doubling the term of your investment *more than doubles* your proceeds.

Figure 4.1: the power of compounding

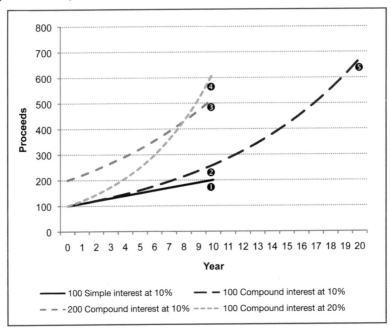

Most investors do not understand the power of compounding, and how easy it is to take advantage of it. To take advantage of compounding:

▶ Save and invest as much as possible. You can also increase the size of your investment by judiciously borrowing other people's money.

▶ Maximise the return on your investments using **SYSTEM T™**.

▶ Maximise the term of your investment by starting to invest as early as possible and holding on to the investment for as long as possible.

## The Rule of 72

The Rule of 72 is a useful rule of thumb linking yield and time. You can use the Rule of 72 as a party trick, but I find it much more valuable as a check of the yield of a potential investment. The Rule of 72 states that:

It takes T years at y per cent per annum for an investment to double in value, where $y \times T = 72$

If your investment earns 7 per cent per annum, you will double your investment in roughly 10 years ($7 \times 10 = 70$, which is approximately 72).

If your investment only earns 6 per cent per annum, you will double your investment in 12 years (6 × 12 = 72). If your investment earns 10 per cent per annum, you will double your investment in roughly seven years (10 × 7 = 70, which is approximately 72).

### From $25 000 to $1.5 million in 40 years

A friend of mine mentioned that her friend's parents recently sold a property in Balmoral that they bought 40 years ago for just $25 000. Being near the water, I estimated that the property's capital return would be close to 10 per cent per annum, offset by a low rental yield. Based on the Rule of 72, the property's value doubles every seven years at 10 per cent per annum, and in 40 years it would have doubled in value nearly six times (40 ÷ 7 is nearly 6) — $25 000 doubled six times gives $1.6 million ($25 000 ⇨ $50 000 ⇨ $100 000 ⇨ $200 000 ⇨ $400 000 ⇨ $800 000 ⇨ $1 600 000). When I told her that I thought the property was worth around $1.6 million, she was stunned. She told me it sold for $1.5 million.

# Capital growth

The capital growth of a property is the increase in its value over time. In my experience, the key to achieving financial independence is to find and buy properties that grow strongly over the long term. The income should take care of itself down the track. Most people think that the capital growth of their property is the difference in the sale price or valuation price and their purchase price. This is not necessarily the case, as the true capital growth needs to take into account any capital injections you have made.

For example, if you bought a two-bedroom house for $200 000 and added a third bedroom at a cost of $20 000, and sold the next year for $230 000, your return is not 15 per cent (230 ÷ 200 − 1) but 4.55 per cent (230 ÷ 220 − 1). You need to take into account the capital injection of $20 000 in the cost base. The increase in median house prices does not take into account new building costs (unless it is measured on established properties), or the costs of alterations and additions. The value of these construction costs as a percentage of the total value of Australia's housing stock is approximately 1 per cent per annum.[1] Note that this does not include maintenance expenses, which are included in the net rental yield calculation (see 'Net rent' later in this chapter).

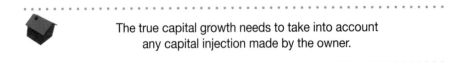

The true capital growth needs to take into account
any capital injection made by the owner.

Figure 4.2 shows that the median Australian house price has increased
by around 45 times over 45 years. This is equivalent to a capital growth
rate of 8.5 per cent per annum. However, approximately 1 per cent
per annum of this is due to the capital injection by investors for new
buildings, alterations and additions. Therefore, the true capital growth
over this period is around 7.5 per cent per annum. Interestingly, this is
similar to the capital growth on the Australian stock market over this
period.

Figure 4.2: Australian median house prices over the last 48 years[2]

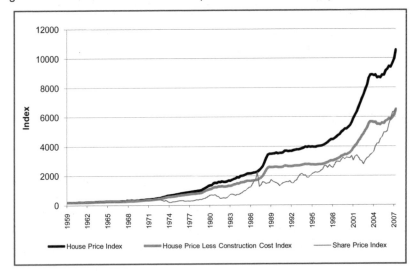

Table 4.2 summarises the increase in median house prices in Australia
by decade. It shows that house prices increase strongly with high
inflation (1970s and 1980s), while share prices were adversely affected
by high inflation (1970s). The real (after inflation) increase in house
prices is approximately 3 per cent per annum. With the Reserve Bank
targeting an inflation rate of 2 to 3 per cent, future property prices
are unlikely to increase as fast as they did in the 1970s and 1980s when
inflation was around 10 per cent per annum. The future capital growth
of median houses will probably be around 5 to 6 per cent per annum
(2 to 3 per cent inflation plus 3 per cent real return).

The future capital growth of median houses will probably be around 5 to 6 per cent per annum.

Table 4.2: capital growth of median houses[3]

| Period | Increase in houses prices | Increase in share prices | CPI | Real increase in houses prices | Real increase in share prices |
|---|---|---|---|---|---|
| 1960s | 5.5% | 7.2% | 2.5% | 3.0% | 4.8% |
| 1970s | 13.3% | 1.4% | 10.1% | 3.3% | -8.7% |
| 1980s | 11.7% | 13.1% | 8.3% | 3.4% | 4.8% |
| 1990s | 3.6% | 6.7% | 2.3% | 1.3% | 4.4% |
| to 2007 | 9.9% | 9.6% | 3.2% | 6.6% | 6.4% |

The strong growth in house prices in the 2000s seems to be an aberration because this increase ran away from the increase in average earnings (see figure 4.6). That is, house prices are overpriced compared to average earnings (wages). As a result, the future increase in house prices will probably be lower than the increase to 2007. Furthermore, except for Sydney where house prices have been weak since 2003, the capital growth in the other capital cities will probably be flat for the next few years, before resuming their uptrend.

Another reason why we are unlikely to see the level of past price increases is that rents have only increased slightly above inflation over the last 28 years. If house prices increase at a much faster rate than rents, eventually the rental yield will fall to ridiculous levels. As rental yields fall lower than interest rates (see figure 4.9), renting becomes a more attractive option than buying, which reduces the demand for houses and moderates price increases. Despite the strong increase in rents in 2007 and 2008, rental yields are still at historical lows relative to interest rates (see figure 4.9).

Figures 4.3 (overleaf) and 4.4 (on p. 45) show the increase in median three-bedroom house and median two-bedroom apartment prices and rents in each capital city over the last 28 years. Note that the price and rental data were only collected recently for some of the smaller capital cities. The prices are in thousands of dollars and the rents are in dollars per week. When the prices in thousands of dollars are in line with the rents per week, the properties are providing approximately a 5 per cent per annum rental yield. For example, in Sydney in 1995 the median three-bedroom house cost around \$200 000 and achieved a rent of \$200 per week, giving a rental yield of 5.2 per cent per annum (200 × 52 ÷ 200 000).

## Figure 4.3: median house prices and rents[4]

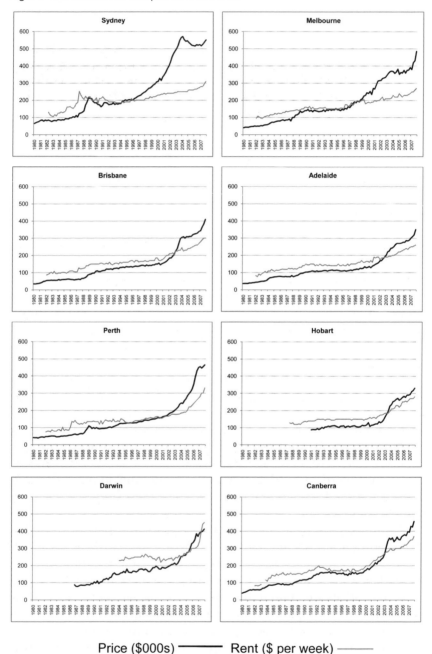

Price (\$000s) ——— Rent (\$ per week) ———

Figure 4.4: median apartment prices and rents[5]

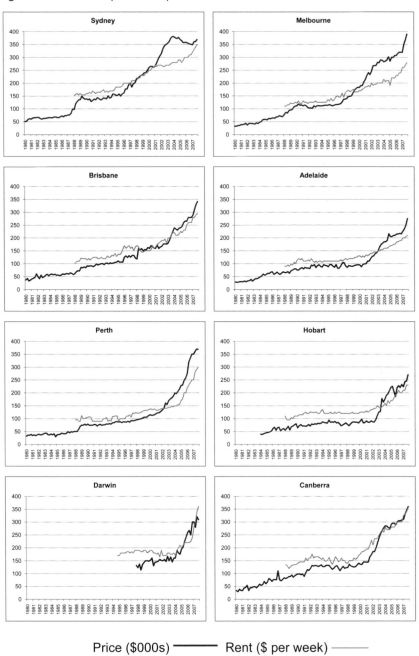

Price ($000s) ——— Rent ($ per week) ———

From 1995 onwards, house prices in Sydney and Melbourne pulled away from rents, while they moved in parallel for the other capital cities. From a value perspective, these two capital cities appear more expensive than the smaller ones. However, buyers have bid up prices in these two cities in anticipation of a higher rate of capital growth in the future. The analogy with the stock market is that Sydney and Melbourne are equivalent to the high P/E stocks, such as Macquarie Bank in the banking sector, while the other capital cities are equivalent to the high yielding, lower P/E stocks, such as the big four banks in the banking sector.

The last uptrend in Sydney and Melbourne property prices started in the late 1990s, and after 2000 for the other capital cities. Sydney property prices reached a peak in 2003 and have since pulled back, while the prices of the other capital cities have continued to rise. Apart from Melbourne, this has mainly been driven by the commodities boom and rotation away from the Sydney and Melbourne property markets. In the past, Sydney property prices were significantly higher than the other capital cities, including Melbourne. However, over the last few years property prices in the other capital cities—Melbourne and Perth in particular—have started to catch up. This could indicate that value is returning to the Sydney property market.

## Demand

Like any other good, the interaction of supply and demand drives real estate prices, and hence capital growth (see figure 4.5). Demand increases over time due to population growth, household formation and affordability. Supply is increased by expansion on the urban fringes and through higher density living. The cyclical fluctuations in real estate prices result from the lag in supply responding to increased demand.

The interaction of supply and demand drives real estate prices, and hence capital growth.

Population growth and the reduction in household size drive the growth in demand for the number of dwellings.[6] There are around eight million dwellings in Australia.

Figure 4.5: house prices are determined by demand and supply

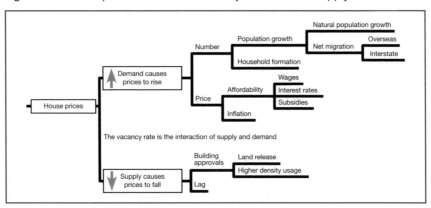

The number of dwellings needed is determined as follows:

Number of dwellings needed = Population ÷ Average household size

Over the last 15 years, the number of dwellings needed in Australia has increased by approximately 1.8 per cent, or approximately 150 000 each year. Two-thirds of this is driven by population growth, with the remainder due to the reduction in household size.

Australia's population growth rate of 1.5 per cent per annum is driven by the rate of natural population growth and net immigration, at a ratio of around 50:50 lately.[7] Employment growth drives overseas immigration, which augments Australia's slowing natural population growth. Over the last 25 years, Australia's net immigration intake has been around 80 000 to 120 000 persons each year, fluctuating with government policy and economic conditions. Most migrants settle along the eastern seaboard, with approximately 40 per cent settling in Sydney and 25 per cent in Melbourne.

Interstate migration increases or reduces the population growth in each state. Relative house prices and the strength of the economies in each state drive interstate migration. Most of the interstate migration has been from Sydney and Melbourne to South-East Queensland. The net population growth of Sydney and Melbourne are in line with the national average, while Brisbane's is approximately 50 per cent higher. More recently, the commodities boom has driven the interstate migration to Western Australia and Queensland.

Demographic changes—such as the ageing population, the increasing incidence of family breakdown and later marriages—drive the reduction in average household size, which increases the demand for housing. The average Australian household size reduced from 4.5 in 1911 to 4.0 in 1933, 3.0 in 1981 and 2.6 in 2001.[8] The sharp rise in rents in 2007 and 2008 has resulted in a temporary reversal of this trend, with many young adults moving back home to save money (the 'boomerang kids').

## Wages

Apart from population growth and the rate of household formation, wages also drive the demand for real estate. Even if population growth were negligible, as incomes rise the demand for better quality housing in more desirable areas would still push real estate prices up. On the flip side, wages constrain property prices through affordability. There are many definitions of housing affordability, such as the ratio of:

▸ average household income/wages to average loan repayments

▸ median house prices to average wages.

The best measure of affordability is the second one: the ratio of median house prices to average wages (also known as average earnings), because it measures the price of real estate in terms of its intrinsic currency—how much we earn. Measuring affordability by the number of times average household income or average wages covers average loan repayments can be misleading because it is affected by the extent of indebtedness as well as the level of interest rates (the cost of the debt), which fluctuate around a long-term trend.

. . . . . . . . . . . . . . . . . . . . . . . . . . . . . . . . . . . . . . . . . . . . . . . . . . .

Wages constrain property prices through affordability.

. . . . . . . . . . . . . . . . . . . . . . . . . . . . . . . . . . . . . . . . . . . . . . . . . . .

Figure 4.6 compares Australian median house prices and male average wages from the same level in 1959. It shows that median house prices increased *in line* with average wages from 1959 to 1986. In 1987 and 1988 there was a sharp spike in median house prices, and then prices increased *in line* with average wages again until 1998. Prices have risen since then, and are *double* what they should be if house price increases were constrained by the increase in average wages. The pullback in prices in 2004 due to the fall in Sydney property prices allowed wages to catch up. However, this was only momentary as the increase in property prices in the other capital cities pushed Australian median property prices up even further.

The ratio of median house prices to average wages measures how many years of gross wages it takes to pay for a median house. Figure 4.7 shows that this ratio hovered around 4 from 1959 to 1987–88. It then fluctuated around 5 until 1998, and since then has steadily risen to 8.[9] Figure 4.7 also shows that the cost of finance—the standard variable rate—fell dramatically in the 1990s. However, this does not necessarily justify a higher price-to-wage ratio, since current interest rates are still above the 1960s level, when the price-to-wage ratio was only 4. (The early 1960s was a great time to be buying real estate. Although taking out a loan was much harder back then, the standard variable rate was just 5 per cent and house prices were only four times average wages!) Part of the reason for the increase in the house-price-to-wage ratio is the increase in household income due to the increase in the number of dual-income households. In 1954, 29 per cent of women in Australia were employed, while in 2007 this had risen to 65 per cent.[10]

Figure 4.6: Australian median house prices vs average wages[11]

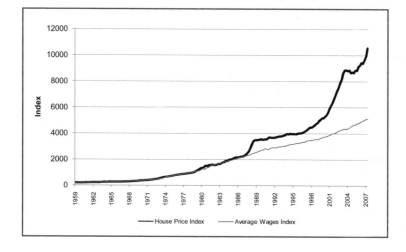

Figure 4.7: Australian median house price ÷ average wages, and interest rates[12]

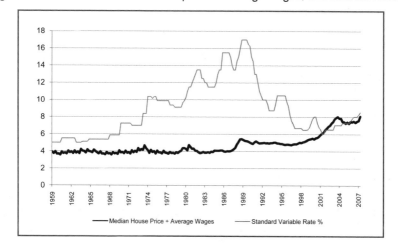

The house-price-to-wage ratio is a measure of value. Clearly, you get more value buying a *median* house for four times average wages than eight times average wages. That is, median houses that cost eight times average wages are twice as overpriced compared to median houses that cost only four times average wages. With median Australian house prices at such a high multiple of average wages (higher than most other Western countries), the most likely future scenario is that house prices will move sideways for a number of years while average wages catch up, before prices take off again.

The house-price-to-wage ratio is a measure of value.

Note that this analysis is for Australian houses as a whole. The situation is different for each state. For example, average wages in New South Wales are slightly higher than in Victoria (slightly less for males, about 10 per cent higher for females), but until recently median house prices were one and a half times higher in Sydney than in Melbourne. Therefore, Sydney houses were relatively more expensive than Melbourne houses. The strong rise in Melbourne house prices in 2006–07, combined with weak Sydney house prices, has brought prices for both cities back in line with average wages. However, this does not allow for the attractiveness of Sydney as a global city.

## Interest rates

Interest rates are the cost, as a percentage, of borrowing money. Interest rates drive real estate prices in two ways. Firstly, a significant part of the real estate owned by owner-occupiers and investors is funded by debt, so a reduction in interest rates reduces the cost of finance. This increases affordability by allowing buyers to service more debt, which in turn increases demand and drives up property prices. Secondly, interest rates are an opportunity cost of investing in real estate. If interest rates fall, then the returns from real estate are relatively more attractive than the returns from debt investments, all other things being equal. This results in greater demand for real estate from investors, which drives up prices and forces down rental yields.

Over the 1990s, interest rates fell by a half, sending the property market into a bull run that lasted from 1997 to 2003 for Sydney and longer in the other smaller capital cities. Not only did the opportunity cost of investing in real estate fall by a half, but it also allowed investors to borrow twice as much. Novices who bought real estate in Sydney in 2003 and 2004 in the expectation that prices would continue to increase like the past seven years were in for an unpleasant surprise. The large reduction in interest rates only supports a *once off* increase in real estate prices. Unless interest rates continue to fall, further increases in real estate prices will only be supported by population growth and growth in average wages. Sometimes interest rates also increase, which causes property prices to fall.

> A large reduction in interest rates only supports a *once off* increase in real estate prices. Further increases will only be supported by population growth and growth in average wages.

Note that the inverse relationship between real estate prices and interest rates does not necessarily apply in the short term. For example, between March 1988 and March 1989, the standard variable rate rose from 13.5 per cent to 16 per cent, while median Sydney house prices increased from $138 000 to $210 000. Then from June 1989 to September 1994, the standard variable rate almost halved from 17 per cent to 9.5 per cent, while the median house price fell from $210 000 to $195 000. In fact, real estate prices sometimes rise after higher interest rates deflate a stock market boom as investors switch their funds from shares to real estate.

A consequence of a reduction in interest rates driving up real estate prices is that it pushes gross rental yields down. Over the long term, gross rental yields move in line with the level of interest rates, because rents are an important source of funds for servicing loans. This can be seen in the reduction in rental yields over the 1990s and early 2000s in line with the significant falls in interest rates. Similarly, rents rose sharply in 2007 after a number of increases in interest rates.

Interest rates also affect different areas in different ways. For example, in Sydney in 2007 property prices in the eastern suburbs, inner west and North Shore rose strongly despite numerous interest rate rises over the previous two years. In contrast, property prices in Sydney's west remained weak. This discrepancy is due to the effect of interest rates on the buyers in the two areas. High-income earners who target the inner suburbs are less sensitive to interest rates than first home buyers in the outer suburbs.

## Subsidies

The First Home Owner Grant (FHOG) scheme was introduced on 1 July 2000 to offset the effect of the GST on home ownership. Nowadays it is seen as a subsidy for first home buyers to alleviate the national housing affordability crisis. The First Home Owner Grant is a $7000 tax-free grant to home buyers who have never owned a property before.

For contracts made between 14 October 2008 and 30 June 2009, an extra $7000 for buying an established home or $14 000 for buying or building a new home is payable under the First Home Owner Boost Scheme, in addition to the $7000 First Home Owner Grant. The states and territories also provide concessions on stamp duty for first home buyers. For example, in New South Wales no stamp duty is payable on homes up to $500 000. See <www.firsthome.gov.au> for more details.

Unfortunately, all the subsidies do is increase the demand for real estate, which in turn pushes property prices up if the supply of housing stock remains the same. Doubling or tripling the subsidies will have the same effect, pushing up the prices of the cheapest property by the same amount.

## Inflation

Inflation is the sustained increase in prices. High inflation is positive for real estate, unlike shares. Inflation drives wages growth, which increases housing affordability and hence house prices. Inflation also increases the cost of building materials and labour. Over the 1970s, when inflation was very high, share prices only increased by 1.5 per cent per annum while real estate prices increased by over 13 per cent per annum. However, the high inflation of the past is now less likely to occur with the Reserve Bank focused on keeping inflation within its target range of 2 to 3 per cent. Over the last 45 years, the real rate of growth (that is, the rate of growth in excess of inflation) of house prices in Australia has been around 3 per cent per annum.[13] Therefore, the total (or nominal) increase in house prices is likely to be only 5 to 6 per cent per annum in the future.

## Supply

While the supply of land is fixed, infill and higher density developments, developing new land on the urban fringes and reducing block sizes can increase the supply of dwellings. The number of building approvals provides a gauge of the increase in supply, although you need to take into account the lags between approval, commencement and completion. It can take a number of years to convert raw land into dwellings due to the need for council approval, developing the supporting infrastructure and then construction. The housing boom in the early 2000s saw over 150 000 new dwellings built in Australia each year.

Property prices move in cycles driven by the interaction of demand and supply:

1   Over time, population growth causes vacancy rates to fall. (The vacancy rate measures the number of vacant rental properties as a proportion of the total number of properties available for rent.)

2   This pushes up property prices and attracts new construction with higher profits. It usually takes two to three years before supply can respond to the increase in demand, resulting in a sharp rise in property prices over a few years.

3   Eventually supply exceeds demand and vacancy rates rise, causing prices to level off and fall.

4   Construction slows down and property prices move sideways for a number of years while demand absorbs the excess supply.

The cycle usually takes seven to ten years, and then repeats itself.

> Property prices move in cycles driven by the interaction of demand and supply.

It would be handy to have a chart of house price cycles to guide your investment decisions. The problem is that all house price charts are backward-looking. To forecast house prices, it is necessary to keep track of supply and demand factors. Fortunately, there is an easier way. All you have to do is to monitor the vacancy rate, which measures the interaction of all demand and supply factors (see 'Technical analysis' in chapter 6).

> The vacancy rate measures the interaction of all demand and supply factors.

## Location, location, location

I previously looked at location from a helicopter view in terms of capital cities versus the regional areas and highlighted the risks of investing in the regional areas. Within the capital cities, the properties located close to the CBD and water are in limited supply and have strong demand, and will achieve stronger capital growth than other locations. A rule of thumb that highlights the importance of location in Sydney is that a $1 million property in the upper North Shore (for example, Wahroonga) would fetch $2 million in the lower North Shore (for example, Mosman) and $4 million in the eastern suburbs.

Figure 4.8 (overleaf) shows the increase in median house prices from 1992 to 2002 (from the dotted line to the solid line) for various distances from the CBD. In Sydney, prices in the inner suburbs more than doubled, while further out prices only increased by 50 to 75 per cent.

The differences are even more extreme for Melbourne. Prices in the inner ring increased by around 150 per cent, over three times the increase of the outer suburbs.

Figure 4.8: capital growth vs location[14]

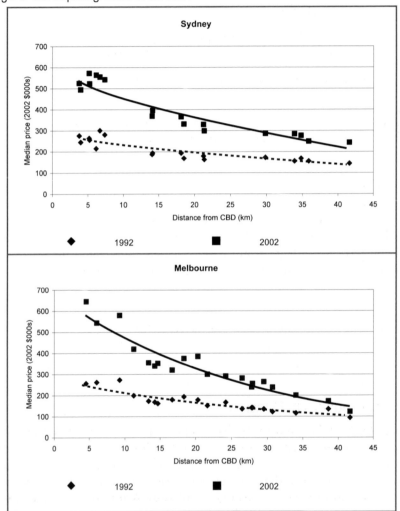

However, there is an inverse relationship between capital growth and income yield. Properties near the water and CBD that have high capital growth also have a low rental yield. Properties in the outer suburbs have lower capital growth but higher rental yield. My preference is high-capital-growth properties, provided you can service the loan in the short term (and they are not overpriced relative to high-rental-yield properties). This is because the after-tax returns are higher due to the more favourable treatment of capital gains tax over income tax (see 'The effect of tax' in chapter 9).

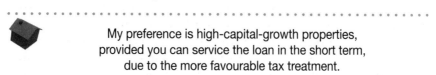

My preference is high-capital-growth properties,
provided you can service the loan in the short term,
due to the more favourable tax treatment.

The most important location requirement is access to employment and transport. Transport includes rail, busses and motorways into the central business district in a capital city or a satellite city. There is strong demand for these locations, which have high population and wages growth, which in turn are the key drivers of real estate prices over the long term. With the development of satellite cities and better transport facilities and the rise in telecommuting, it is not necessary to be located within the inner ring of a capital city to maximise the benefits of location.

### The most important location requirement is proximity to employment and transport

When I first started investing in real estate, I was unsure about the prospects of a particular suburb that was nearly 50 kilometres out from the CBD, where I worked. However, when I spoke to a local real estate agent, I found out that there was an express train service that stopped at only four stations before the suburb, making it much quicker to get into the city than a number of closer suburbs. Moreover, only a small percentage of the population in the suburb worked in the CBD; the rest were employed in two nearby satellite cities that were only 10 and 20 minutes away by train.

Apart from employment and transport, other important location considerations include schools, hospitals, shopping centres and other amenities. For example, Killara High on the North Shore is one of the top non-selective government schools in New South Wales, with an outstanding Higher School Certificate performance. Enrolment is restricted to students that reside in the local enrolment area, so there is very strong demand for properties that fall in the catchment area, especially from Asian parents. On a different note, the strong demand for suburbs such as Leichhardt and Surry Hills in the inner city and

Crows Nest in the North Shore is due to their abundance of cafes and restaurants.

Owner-occupiers should also consider unique properties with proximity to water (harbour or river) and the CBD. These properties are rare and in constant demand, and have the highest growth rates. They command premium prices and are out of reach for most investors. The prices of these properties are also very volatile, typically fluctuating up and down with the economy. If you buy at the wrong time, you could lose a lot of money. Furthermore, the low rental yields and high land tax bills of these properties make it very difficult for investors to service them in the short term.

An important feature of location is that real estate prices usually increase in the more expensive areas first, and then ripple out to the other areas in a concentric circle. This feature can also extend from the main capital cities to the smaller ones. High Sydney property prices are one of the main drivers of interstate migration from Sydney to South-East Queensland, which in turn pushes up Brisbane property prices.

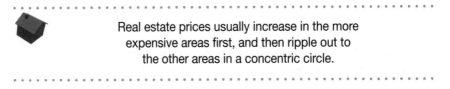

Real estate prices usually increase in the more expensive areas first, and then ripple out to the other areas in a concentric circle.

Be careful about upgrading your home from the outer ring to the inner ring during the latter stages of the property cycle because you could miss the boom due to the ripple effect. You might buy into higher prices, but miss out when you sell because it has not arrived yet. Conversely, you might be able to double dip if you buy into the outer ring in the latter part of a boom. The best approach is to keep your old property if possible, to build your property portfolio and save on transaction costs (see 'Building a property portfolio' in chapter 5).

### Keep your properties when you move

One of my colleagues had the misfortune of moving around too much. He lived in Castle Hill before the M2 motorway opened, but worked in the Sydney CBD and decided to move to a location closer to transport. So he sold up and bought in Campbelltown in the mid-1990s because it was cheap and had an express train service to the CBD. Unfortunately, he missed most of the growth in the Hills district that followed the opening of the M2 motorway. After living in Campbelltown for a few years, he realised that it was too far away from his workplace. So he moved again, this time to a townhouse in Hurstville, where the boom was already well under way. Unfortunately, the same thing happened again, and he missed out on the growth in the south west that followed the opening of the M5 motorway. If only he had kept the properties each time he moved.

## Specific factors

So far we have discussed general factors that drive the price, and hence the capital growth, of all properties. Specific factors that affect the price of a particular property include land size, shape and slope, building size, the number of rooms, age, condition, and parking facilities. These factors can be reduced to just two: the land and the building. This is how valuers determine the value of a property.

There is a widely held belief that you should buy the *worst house* in the *best street*, not the *best house* in the *worst street*, because there is more scope for capital growth when the prices of the properties in the street rise. In addition, there is more scope for adding value to the worst houses, whereas the capital growth opportunities of the best houses have already been exhausted.

But this adage only has merit if the worst house on the street is underpriced relative to the other houses. In my experience, it is usually the opposite situation. The prices of older properties in need of repair, plus the cost to bring them to the same standard as the better houses, tend to be more than the prices of better houses. This is because there is a lot of demand for older properties that can be renovated, which pushes up their price, and there is usually less competition for the better houses because they cost more than the median price.

I personally prefer to buy the better houses in the street because I sometimes find that the better houses are overcapitalised; that is, the owners spent more on the houses than they can recoup from the sale price. The market value of these properties is less than their intrinsic value (see 'Timing the market' in chapter 6). On the other hand, I have never found the worst properties to be overcapitalised. So do not buy properties based just on anecdotal evidence, but assess each one on a case-by-case basis.

## Transaction costs

Real estate transaction costs are substantial, especially in contrast to shares, and are one of the main disadvantages of investing in real estate. A round trip can cost almost 10 per cent of the property value. That is, you are losing 10 per cent of the property's value just by entering and leaving the market. If your equity contribution is 20 per cent, then this can be equivalent to 50 per cent of your equity. Buying costs include the following (with indicative New South Wales costs):

▸ Contract stamp duty ($18 000 for a $500 000 property). The stamp duty payable in each state can be found through the respective Office of State Revenue.

▸ Loan fees, which include application fees ($0 to $800), valuation fees ($0 to $300) and a mortgage insurance premium if your loan-to-valuation ratio is greater than 80 per cent ($0 to thousands of dollars).

▸ Mortgage stamp duty and registration fees (nearly $2000 for a $500 000 mortgage). These are being phased out in New South Wales (owner-occupied housing loans from 1 September 2007 and investment housing loans from 1 July 2008).

▸ Building inspection ($250 to $600) and pest inspection fee ($150 to $300), and strata inspection fee for apartments ($150 to $300).

▸ Conveyancing fee ($1000).

Selling costs include the following:

▸ Agent's sales commission (2 to 3 per cent of the property sales price plus advertising costs).

▸ Legal costs to prepare the contract of sale.

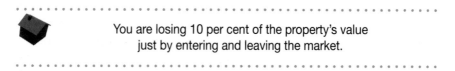

You are losing 10 per cent of the property's value
just by entering and leaving the market.

In addition, search costs are a big hidden cost. For example, some people spend every weekend for six to twelve months inspecting properties before they find the right one. Selling a property is also time consuming and inconvenient. It takes much more time than buying and selling shares.

## Rental income

The rent from real estate is not directly comparable to the interest from bonds and cash or the dividends from shares because, unlike the other asset classes, real estate requires significant holding costs that reduce the gross rent. Therefore, the more appropriate income measure to use is the *net* rent.

## Gross rent

The gross rent (or just rent for short) is what the tenant pays the landlord to occupy the property. Figures 4.3 and 4.4 show the rents on median three-bedroom houses and two-bedroom apartments in each state. Over the long term, rents have increased more steadily than property prices, although there was a sharp rise in the mining capital cities from 2005 to 2008 due to the commodities boom, and all over Australia in 2008 due to the increase in interest rates from the subprime market collapse. Over the long term, rent increases are constrained by the increase in average wages. If rents grow much more than this, some tenants will not be able to afford to rent. They might move back home with their parents or share their tenancy, which reduces the demand for rental properties and hence rents.

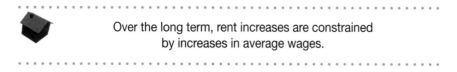

Over the long term, rent increases are constrained
by increases in average wages.

Over the last 25 years, the rent on median three-bedroom houses has increased by around 3.5 to 6.0 per cent per annum in Australia (Sydney and Melbourne are at the lower end, and the smaller capital cities are at the upper end).[15] This is slightly above the inflation rate of 4.3 per cent,[16] thus rents have increased slightly in real dollars. However, median house prices have risen at around twice this rate at 8.0 to 9.5 per cent per annum,[17] causing the gross rental yield to fall to historical lows.

The supply of rental properties also affects rents. When vacancy rates are low, such as after a downturn in the property market and new construction grinds to a halt, landlords can raise rents as tenants compete for a shortage of rental accommodation. Similarly, an increase in the number of owner-occupiers in an area will also drive up rents as the number of available rental properties falls. In contrast, an excess supply of rental properties restrains rental yields in the short term. For example, after the completion of a block of high-rise apartments, rents around the area will be weak for many months as investors compete to rent out their apartments. A similar situation occurs market-wide at the top of a property boom as a glut of new developments come onto the market and push up vacancy rates and moderate rents.

Interest rates are also a strong determinant of rents. Higher interest rates push rents up, as investors increase rents to service the higher interest cost of their loans. Rents can increase dramatically when there is a shortage of rental properties, in combination with higher interest rates. For example, following the interest rate rises over 2007 and 2008, rents rose strongly in every capital city.

Expressing the gross rent as a percentage of the price of the property gives the gross rental yield:

Gross rental yield = Total rent ÷ Price

Due to vacancy periods this is usually less than: Rent per week × 52 ÷ Price. As a rule of thumb, when calculating the gross rental yield, multiply the rent per week by 50 to allow for two weeks' vacancy each year. When the rent per week is similar to the price in thousands, this equates to approximately a 5 per cent yield. For example, a $200 000 house generating $200 in rent per week has a yield of 5.2 per cent ($200 \times 52 \div 200,000$).

Make sure you review the rent on your investment property at least every year, and increase it in line with market rates. If you do not, when rents take off it will be difficult to pass on all of the increase at once.

Make sure you review the rent on your investment property at least every year.

Figure 4.9 shows that gross rental yields have fallen across Australia over the last two decades, in line with the reduction in interest rates, which fell by almost two-thirds over the 1990s. Despite a 50 per cent increase in interest rates over the five years to 2008, with the exception of Sydney, the gross rental yields fell further in the other capital cities due to the strong increase in property prices (although this is starting to reverse now). The small capital cities traditionally paid a high rental yield. However, with the run up in property prices over the last few years, some of them are returning similar rental yields to Sydney and Melbourne. Sydney's rental yields have risen almost in line with interest rates over the last five years, driven by rising rents and stagnant property prices.

The level of rents constrains the increase in house prices. If house prices run too far ahead of rents, such as in the early 2000s, then it would make more sense to rent a property than buy it because it would be cheaper to pay the rent than fund the property (interest and holding costs). This reduces the demand for houses, so prices move sideways for a number of years until rents catch up. On the other hand, when house prices have been in the doldrums for many years a sharp increase in rents is a stimulus for prices because buying starts to become an attractive option again.

## Figure 4.9: gross rental yields[18]

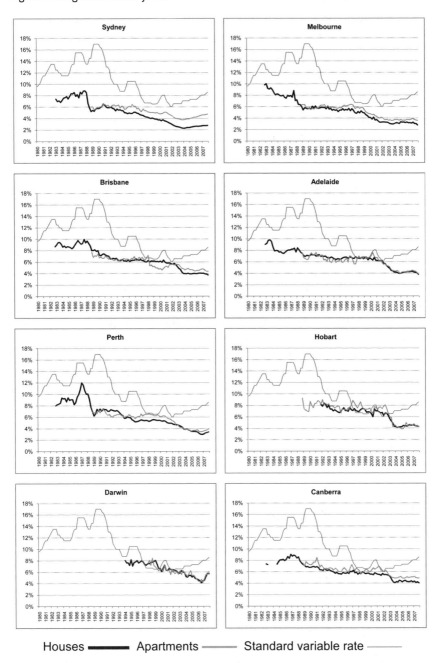

## Absolute vs relative rental yields

Some authors claim to have a secret formula that determines the maximum price you should pay for a property. The secret formula usually turns out to be a calculation that gives an *absolute* rental yield of at least 10 per cent. These include that the rent per week is twice the property price in hundreds of thousands or the property price is not more than one hundred times the monthly rent. For example, if the rent per week is $200 and the property price is $100000, this gives a rental yield of 10.4 per cent ($200 \times 52 \div 100000$); and if the monthly rent is $1000, and the price is $100000 (no more than one hundred times the monthly rent), this gives a rental yield of 12 per cent ($1000 \times 12 \div 100000$).

Blindly following this rule of thumb can be hazardous to your wealth for two reasons. Firstly, you overpay when interest rates are high. For example, in the late 1980s when interest rates almost reached 20 per cent, a 10 per cent rental yield would send you broke very quickly. Secondly, you miss out on good investments when interest rates are low. For example, in 2001–02 interest rates dropped to around 6 per cent. This would have pushed prices up so that the best rental yields in the market might have been only 8 per cent. If you had stayed out of the market then you would have missed out on some good buying opportunities.

If you want to assess whether the property market is overpriced or underpriced, just looking at the rental yield in isolation is not sufficient. Instead, you need to compare the *relative rental yield*—calculated as Rental yield ÷ Average home loan rate—against historical values. You can use the standard variable rate as a proxy for the average home loan rate; however, you should bear in mind that no one nowadays pays the standard variable rate on their property loans.

Compare the *relative rental yield* against historical values to assess whether the property market is overpriced or underpriced.

Figure 4.10 shows that even though the absolute rental yield for median three-bedroom houses in Sydney dropped to 4 per cent in 1998, the relative rental yield hovered around the peaks of the last two decades. That is, the absolute rental yield in 1998 was consistent with the absolute rental yield of 5.5 per cent in 1994 and 9 per cent in 1988. Furthermore, while absolute rental yields were at historical lows between 2 and 3 per cent from 2003 to 2007, the relative rental yield was no lower than in 1989, when absolute rental yields were around 5.5 per cent.

Figure 4.10: Sydney median house absolute vs relative rental yield[19]

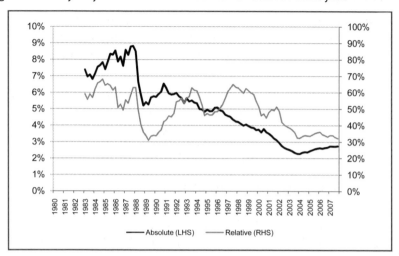

When the relative rental yield is low, property markets are overpriced, and you are better off renting than buying because the rent is relatively cheaper than the interest on the mortgage and the cost of equity. Conversely, when the relative rental yield is high, property markets are underpriced, and you are better off buying. Generally, if you buy when the relative r.ental yield is high you will be buying in the Buying Zone (see 'Timing the market' in chapter 6) because the high relative rental yield encourages renters and property investors to enter the property market, which will drive prices up.

## Rental guarantees

Sometimes developers offer rental guarantees to attract investors to new developments. Usually, these rental guarantees are for yields significantly higher than market yields. The main problem with this arrangement is that the rental guarantee masks a lack of rental demand. Remember there are no free lunches. At best, the developer marks up the price of the properties to pay for the rental guarantees, so you end up paying yourself the higher rent in a roundabout way. At worst, you overpay for the property (the extra rent is less than the price mark-up) and at the expiry of the rental guarantee the value of the property falls by more than the price mark-up due to a lack of demand. Always ask yourself: if this is such a good investment, why do the developers need to provide a guarantee? Good investments do not need a rental guarantee.

Good investments do not need a rental guarantee.

## Holding costs

The cost of investing in real estate is significant and is one of its main disadvantages. This is why it is important to distinguish between gross and net rents, and to do this you need to know the holding costs.

The main holding costs are:

▸ The property manager's fee of 5 to 8 per cent of the gross rent plus one week's rent for finding a new tenant. The management fee covers finding and checking potential tenants, rental collection, quarterly/half-yearly inspections and organising tradespeople to take care of maintenance problems.

▸ Council and water rates, which depend on the location of the property.

▸ Maintenance expenses, which depend on the age and condition of the building. This can be a significant cost for older buildings.

▸ Insurance. Building insurance with liability cover is a minimum requirement. For apartments, this is included in the strata levy. You can also take out landlords' insurance to protect against damage to the property by tenants, loss of rent if the tenant does not pay, and other costs. A good agent will help you avoid this problem by doing thorough reference checks on tenants.

▸ If you own a number of properties then you could be liable for land tax as well.

▸ The above costs are cash costs that you have to pay out of your pocket immediately. There is also the non-cash cost of depreciation of the building and fixtures and fittings. Although it is not a cash cost, it needs to be taken into account, because it will eventually have to be paid for. As an indication, the Australian Taxation Office allows investors to depreciate 2.5 per cent of the building, and higher rates for fixtures and fittings.

▸ Owners of units have to pay a strata levy that covers the management, administration, repair and maintenance of the common property. The fees vary with the age of the building and the extent of the common property facilities such as lifts, gyms and swimming pools.

## Net rent

The gross rent is what the tenant pays you. It is not what you get to put in your pocket after paying the interest on the mortgage. You still have holding costs to take care of. The net rent is the gross rent less holding costs. The annual holding cost can be up to 30 per cent or more of the gross rent. That is, the net rent can be as low as 70 per cent or less of the gross rent. This is the reason why banks only take 70 to 80 per cent of the rental income of an investment property into account in calculating the serviceability of the loan. Table 4.3 shows the net yield calculation for two of my properties.

Table 4.3: calculating net rental yields

| Example 1 | | Example 2 | |
|---|---|---|---|
| Gross rent | 10367 | Gross rent | 21539 |
| Management fee | −862 | Management fee | −1315 |
| Rates | −1530 | Rates | −1432 |
| Maintenance expenses | −264 | Maintenance expenses | −30 |
| Insurance | −150 | Insurance | −250 |
| Net rent | 7562 | Net rent | 18512 |
| | | | |
| Net rent ÷ Gross rent | 73% | Net rent ÷ Gross rent | 86% |

# Growth vs income

With all investments, there is an inverse relationship between capital growth and income yield, and real estate is no exception. That is, the higher the capital growth, the lower the rental yield that can be expected from the property, and vice versa, so that the total yield is similar between different types of properties. It is not possible, for example, for properties to have high capital growth *and* high rental yield over the long term because the demand for these properties would push their prices up, which in turn pushes capital growth and rental yields down, turning these properties into moderate capital growth and moderate rental yield properties.

For example, houses in the outer suburbs pay high rental yields but have low growth prospects. In contrast, houses in the inner city are in high demand and have strong capital growth, but pay low rental yields. Houses have higher growth rates than apartments due to the higher land content, but rental yields are lower. In turn, vacant land has a higher growth rate than houses, but generates no income.

High-capital-growth properties provide higher after-tax returns than similarly priced high-rental-yield properties (see 'The effect of tax' in chapter 9). However, to reap the capital growth over the long term, you have to be able to service the loan in the short term. A high-rental-yield/low-capital-growth property is much easier to service than a low-rental-yield/high-capital-growth property. You should strike a balance that fits your individual situation. For example, high-income professionals might be able to support a portfolio of high-growth houses and apartments in the inner ring. In contrast, if you are building a property portfolio on a moderate income, you might have to spread your properties along the growth–income continuum. So your portfolio might also include some houses in the outer suburbs or apartments that pay a high rental yield to assist with serviceability.

> High-capital-growth properties provide higher after-tax returns than similarly priced high-rental-yield properties. However, to reap the capital growth over the long term, you have to be able to service the property in the short term.

The serviceability advantage of high-rental-yield properties should not be underestimated because it:

▶ lets you get into the property market sooner, and take advantage of the power of compounding

▶ allows you to buy more properties and have a bigger asset base working for you

▶ helps you to hold the properties for the long term.

The disadvantage with high-rental-yield properties is that they incur more tax since income tax is paid earlier and at double the rate of capital gains held for more than 12 months. Another drawback of high-rental-yield properties is that it is tempting for you to spend the income rather than reinvesting it in more properties. This is an important consideration because the benefits of compounding are exponential over the long term. High-capital-growth properties do not have this problem since you cannot spend unrealised capital gains unless you draw down the equity.

Some people mistakenly think that a major disadvantage of high-capital-growth properties is their inability to provide sufficient income, such as in retirement, because unlike shares real estate is lumpy and you cannot just sell one bedroom if you need some more income. However, there is an alternative to selling the whole property. You can use debt strategies that convert the capital into income through home equity loans and reverse mortgages (see 'Other uses of equity' in chapter 7). While this process is more complex than the high income generated by high-rental-yield properties, the income is tax-free because it is a loan, unlike rental income.

# Buying vs renting

To buy or to rent, that is the question. With rental yields so low compared to interest rates, renting seems a very attractive alternative to buying a home. However, if you can take out a standard loan, I suggest you aim for the buying option for three reasons. No, not because rent money is 'dead money'. Rent is a lot cheaper than interest and other property ownership costs, and if you invest the difference plus the equity into a sensibly geared share fund you can probably achieve at least similar returns to real estate over the long term. Therefore, you are probably better off renting rather than buying, *provided* you invest the difference.

> You are probably better off renting rather than buying, *provided* you invest the difference. However, I suggest that you aim for the buying option.

However, most people just spend the difference. One of the advantages of real estate is that it is a form of forced saving. If you do not own a property in retirement, you need a larger nest egg than someone that does. The average rent on an apartment is $300 to $400 a week, so a renter would need an extra $15 000 to $20 000 a year in income, or $200 000 to $300 000 in capital (using a 7 per cent capitalisation rate), compared to someone who has paid off a home. Most people need a nest egg of around $500 000 in retirement to generate a comfortable income of $35 000. So someone who does not own their own home would need to accumulate an extra $200 000 to $300 000, or 50 per cent more, to cover the rent. It is very hard for most people to save and invest this difference, and this is why it is often best to aim to buy.

A home can provide additional funds in retirement. In fact, many people (partially) fund their retirement by downsizing from their suburban houses to smaller and cheaper accommodation. An alternative is to use a home equity loan or reverse mortgage to tap into the equity without having to sell your home and incur transaction costs. You can also generate additional income by taking in boarders after the kids have moved out.

Your home is exempt from the asset test for the pension, irrespective of its value. This is a significant advantage compared to non-homeowners. Non-homeowners can own more assets than homeowners outside of their home and still qualify for the full pension, but it is only a fraction of the value of most homes.

If servicing a property is too much of a burden, you should consider buying an investment property and renting. In effect, the Tax Office is helping you service the property. The cost is that you lose the capital gains tax exemption on a primary residence. However, if you never sell the property this is not a problem. This arrangement also gives you the flexibility to live where you want.

If you cannot get a standard loan because of income documentation or credit problems you are probably better off renting. The extra interest of non-standard loans makes renting a much more attractive option. You could try to put all of the savings into superannuation, which provides a very tax effective environment, and perhaps use some of the proceeds to buy a home in retirement to maximise your pension benefits.

If you decide to, or have to, go down the rental route, consider a long-term lease. Not only does this give you more stability, it also gives the landlord more financial certainty. In return, you might be able to negotiate a discount on the rent. Another consideration is cost versus proximity. Many singles choose to rent close to the CBD for lifestyle reasons such as proximity to cafes and restaurants, even though rental costs are much higher compared to other suburbs. However, when you take transport costs and travel times into account (double for a couple), it might make more sense to rent a rundown old unit in the inner city than a large new house/townhouse in the outer suburbs.

# 5 Spread

To become financially independent, you need to build a portfolio of investments that generates enough income to replace your salary. As you build your portfolio, it is important that you spread or diversify your investments across and within different asset classes such as real estate, shares, bonds and cash. This is the principle of not putting all of your eggs in the one basket. That way, if one asset class or investment underperforms, it might be balanced out by the strong performance of another asset class or investment. For example, in 2008, while the real estate market across Australia was weak, cash was earning its highest returns in over a decade. Investors that were only invested in real estate would have struggled in 2008 compared to those that also had some cash savings. When you spread your investments, you increase the security of your portfolio while maintaining the expected yield, or increase the expected yield while maintaining the security of your portfolio.

> When you spread your investments, you increase the security of your portfolio while maintaining the same expected yield.

In theory, to achieve spread with real estate buy uncorrelated properties that do not all move in the same way all the time. That is, buy properties from markets that are out of phase, such as those in different states and even overseas. However, in practice it is difficult to achieve spread with real estate because it requires such a big outlay. Moreover, with prices so high nowadays, many people cannot afford to buy even one property, let alone a portfolio of properties. However, after you buy your first property, you can build a property portfolio by not selling your home each time you move and using the increase in equity in your existing properties as a deposit for your next property.

> To achieve spread with real estate, buy properties
> from markets that are out of phase.

There are two main risks with building a property portfolio. Firstly, there is the risk of overextending yourself, especially near the top of the market after you have had some success during the uptrend and start getting greedy. You can reduce this risk and improve the security of your portfolio by only buying one property at a time. The second risk is that you could be ripped off because you do not have a good grasp of local prices and conditions. Buyers from Sydney in particular, who are used to paying high prices, need to be especially careful that they do not rush into bargains in other states and get scammed by two-tier marketers. Your best defence is to familiarise yourself with local prices. Speak to a number of different local agents to get a feel for prices in the area. Where available, it might be possible to use Defence Housing Australia (DHA) properties as a price guide. If you decide to proceed, get an independent valuation as a final check.

## Out-of-phase markets

Real estate markets tend to move in similar cycles, but at different points in time. If one market runs too far ahead of another, property prices in the hot market become less affordable, causing people to migrate to the cheaper markets, which in turn pushes up property prices there. For example, interstate migration from Sydney to Brisbane increased after Sydney property prices skyrocketed in 2000 to 2003, pushing up Brisbane property prices as Sydney property prices peaked and fell.

Figure 5.1 shows property prices from two markets in two different situations. In the first, the two markets are in phase and correlated: both are rising and moving sideways at the same time. In the second, the two markets are out of phase and uncorrelated: while one is rising the other one is moving sideways. An example of out-of-phase markets are Perth and Sydney over 2004 to 2007. Perth house prices doubled while Sydney house prices declined by around 10 per cent.

Figure 5.1: markets in phase and out of phase

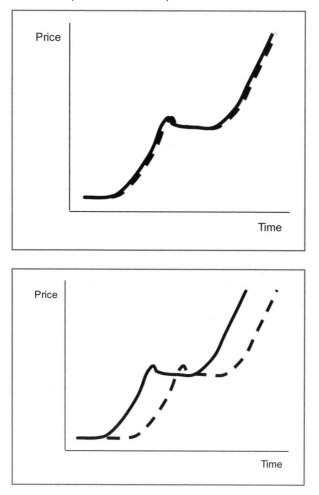

Within a market are submarkets that can also be out of phase. For example, in 2007 house prices in many of Sydney's inner ring suburbs (the eastern suburbs, inner west and North Shore) rose by more than 10 per cent, while houses in the outer suburbs remained stagnant.

## Buy in other states

Some real estate investors have a system where they focus all of their investing activity in a small area that they know very well, such as in a particular regional area or around where they live. They reason that this gives them a good feel for market prices and increases their chances of buying a property below market value. The main drawback of this strategy is the lack of spread; all of your eggs are in one basket. If that area loses a key employer, you face high vacancies and falling prices.

On the other hand, when you spread your investments around the country you reduce the chance of the whole property portfolio underperforming. You will never have all your money in the worst performing market, such as Sydney in 2004 to 2007. However, you will also never have all your money in the best performing market (Perth in 2004 to 2007).

In addition, when you spread your property investments across different states, you reduce your land tax bill, since land tax is calculated on the total land value (excluding principal residence) of your property holdings in a particular state (see 'Land tax' in chapter 9).

## Buying overseas

When you buy properties overseas, you achieve an additional level of spread. The country's economic cycle will probably be out of phase with Australia's and, therefore, its property market will probably be out of phase with Australia's. However, the exchange rate introduces an additional level of complexity and risk. While it provides additional spread to your assets (some will be in Australian dollars, others will be in the foreign currency), you can get into financial strife if you do not follow the matching principle, which states that assets and liabilities should be matched as closely as possible. In this case, you should match the currency of the assets and liabilities. That is, the loan that funds the property should be in the same currency as the foreign property. Similarly, you should only fund local properties with a local loan, even if foreign interest rates are less than half of Australian interest rates.

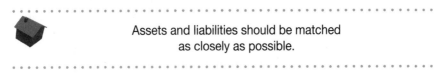

Assets and liabilities should be matched
as closely as possible.

This will be much clearer with an example (see figure 5.2). Say you bought a $100 000 (all monetary amounts in Australian dollars) property in the US when the Australian dollar was only equal to half of the US dollar. However, you funded it with an $80 000 mortgage in Australian dollars and a $20 000 deposit. If the Australian dollar doubles against the US dollar and reaches parity, but nothing else changes, the loan outstanding would remain the same at $80 000, but the value of the property would halve in Australian dollars, falling to $50 000. The value of your equity would fall by the reduction in the value of the property in Australian dollars. In this case, it results in negative equity of $30 000.

To make matters worse, your interest cost would remain the same, but the rental income would fall by half.

Figure 5.2: unmatched foreign real estate

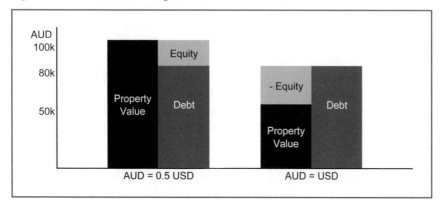

Obviously, if the Australian dollar depreciated against the US dollar the value of the property and your equity would rise while the loan outstanding would remain the same. Similarly, the rental income would rise while the interest cost remained the same. However, your first investment goal should be security — to avoid losing money. In addition, your original objective of investing overseas was to spread your property investments, not to speculate on the currency. Therefore, you should match the currency of the property and the loan. In this case, the loan would be denominated in US dollars to be in the same currency as the property.

This is still not a perfect hedge because the equity component of the property is unhedged. In this example, if the loan was denominated in US dollars, when the Australian dollar doubled against the US dollar the value of the property would fall to $50 000 and the value of the loan would fall to $40 000, leaving you with $10 000 in equity. This is better than an unmatched scenario, but you would still be out of pocket by $10 000.

Most investors will not have the sophistication to hedge the equity component. They should just leave it unhedged to take advantage of the additional spread provided by another currency. This situation is acceptable, as long as you understand the risks.

Finally, if you do decide to buy property overseas you should conduct thorough research as you would normally do in Australia, instead of relying on the word of an investment seminar spruiker. Many unsuspecting Australian investors have been duped by two-tier marketing scams. You should also stick to the developed countries. While there is more scope for capital growth in the developing countries, there is also much greater economic and political risk.

## Building a property portfolio

If you already own a property, whether it is your own home or an investment property, then you are well on your way to achieving financial independence. However, most people stop after their first property. This is a pity because one property is usually insufficient to provide for your retirement because you still need a place to live. If you decide to focus on real estate to fund your retirement, you will need to build a portfolio of properties. For example, a retired couple that owns a portfolio of just two completely paid off median-priced properties in Sydney could generate additional income of around half of average weekly earnings to supplement their (part) pension. They would live in one and rent out the other. They could also supplement their income by drawing down the equity on the properties (see 'Other uses of equity' in chapter 7).

People who already own property have a significant advantage over first-timers for two reasons. Firstly, they already have experience in buying real estate, and will be less fazed by their next purchase. Secondly, they might have built up enough equity in their first property to use to piggyback into another property, without having to outlay any money (see 'Piggybacking' in chapter 7). The cost of servicing a second property is also much easier because not only does the tenant assist with the rent, but the Tax Office also chips in with deductions for expenses and depreciation. Therefore, if you already own a property it might be much easier to buy another one than you think.

If you already own a property it might be much easier to buy another one than you think.

## Don't sell when you move

When most people move house, they sell their home and buy a similar one, and in the process spend around 10 per cent of the purchase price on transaction costs. Selling a primary residence does not attract capital gains tax. However, if it was an investment property that had doubled in price, then depending on your marginal tax rate it might cost you another 20 per cent of the purchase price in capital gains tax. (Say you bought a property for $500 000 and it doubled in price to $1 000 000. The capital gain is $500 000. It will take the property more than 12 months to double in price so you will only be taxed on half of the capital gain. If you were on the highest marginal tax rate your capital gains tax would be $500 000 × 0.5 × 46.5 per cent = $116 250, which is over 20 per cent of $500 000.)

If instead you try to keep your old home as an investment property, you only need to find another 10 per cent equity compared to the selling alternative (see table 5.1). There might already be some excess equity in the old home, in which case you might be able to afford to buy the new property with no money down. However, you will probably have to outlay some money each week to service the investment property over the next few years. Therefore, one of the easiest ways to build a property portfolio is to keep your old home as an investment property when you move house. Since you are generating income from the property, you will be able to deduct all expenses associated with the property, including the interest expense on the mortgage (see 'Principal residence vs investment property' in chapter 9).

Table 5.1: equity required for keeping vs selling

|  | Keeping | Selling principal residence | Selling investment property |
| --- | --- | --- | --- |
| Equity | 20% (for new property) | 10% (transaction costs) | 30%* (transaction costs + CGT) |

* Depends on capital gains.

One of the easiest ways to build a property portfolio is to keep your old home as an investment property when moving house.

## Use the increase in equity in your property portfolio

Building a property portfolio by keeping your old home when you move is haphazard. You will have a much better chance of achieving financial independence if you take matters into your own hands and systematically build a property portfolio instead of waiting for when you move house. One way to build a share portfolio, called dollar cost averaging, is to set aside a fixed amount regularly to buy more shares. Dollar cost averaging is not feasible with real estate due to its lumpy nature. Instead, you have to wait until the equity in your existing properties increases enough to buy another property for your portfolio (see 'Piggybacking' in chapter 7).

However, you should only do so when the property market is in the Buying Zone (see 'Timing the market' in chapter 6). The optimal property-buying pattern might look something like table 5.2, depending on the property cycle. It does not involve buying a property a year, as advocated by most real estate investment seminars, but one a year (or one every second year, or whatever you can afford) for a few years, then nothing for a few years, and then repeating the cycle again. The advantage of buying in the Buying Zone is that, apart from building a margin of safety into your price, the value of your property portfolio will increase steadily during the Buying Zone. This allows you to buy more properties by tapping into the increase in equity. If there is insufficient equity, just wait until the next Buying Zone.

Table 5.2: optimal property buying pattern for Sydney

| Year | 1996 | 1997 | 1998 | 1999 | 2000 | 2001 | 2002 | 2003 | 2004 | 2005 | 2006 | 2007 |
|------|------|------|------|------|------|------|------|------|------|------|------|------|
| Buy  | 1    | 1    | 1    | 1    | 1    | 0    | 0    | 0    | 0    | 0    | 0    | 1    |
| Sell | 0    | 0    | 0    | 0    | 0    | 0    | 0    | 0    | 0    | 0    | 0    | 0    |

**One a year for a few years,
then nothing for a few years ...**

I bought a bunch of houses in Sydney between 1996 and 2000, when market values were less than intrinsic values, by funding half of the purchases from my income and the other half by piggybacking on the increase in equity of the existing properties. I did not have any out-of-pocket costs as all of the properties were negatively geared with positive cash flow. This was possible because rents were rising despite interest rates almost halving from their mid-1990s levels (see figures 4.3 and 4.9). However, after 2000 prices had taken off and it was very hard to find any value in the market. So I focused on the other states and the stock market. Value emerged again in some parts of the Sydney market in 2007 and I started buying again.

You should only add more properties to your portfolio when the property market is in the Buying Zone.

## Focus on values, not numbers

You should keep score of your property portfolio by its net value and not the number of properties you own. For example, a block of ten $50 000 flats in a regional area is only equivalent in value to one median Sydney three-bedroom house in 2008. The advantage of cheap properties is that they pay a higher rental yield, which allows you to buy and service more properties. However, this comes at the cost of lower capital growth, and hence lower after-tax returns (see 'The effect of tax' in chapter 9). In contrast, expensive properties in high-demand locations have higher capital growth and pay a lower rental yield. They are only affordable for those on high incomes or who have a large deposit. In addition, it is easier to manage a few properties than many, but it can take much longer to rent out an expensive property.

### It's portfolio size that counts

Steven bought his home on the water in Sydney's northern beaches for $700 000 in 1995 and estimates that the value of his property has increased to $3 000 000 ten years later.

Mary 'controls' about 100 properties in the major regional areas with a partner that have a ballpark value of $6 000 000.

It appears that Mary has good spread in her property portfolio. However, most of her properties are high rental yield/low capital growth. She could improve her spread by diversifying away from the regional areas and along the income–growth continuum. There is a lot of scope for improving the spread in Steven's portfolio. However, he has chosen the ideal location near the water, which will ensure strong long-term capital growth. His real estate investment philosophy is to put all of his eggs in the one basket and watch it like a hawk. He achieves spread with other asset classes.

## Only buy one at a time

Unless you are an experienced property investor who has been through at least one property cycle, it is usually best to only buy one property at a time in case you get into financial difficulty. Think of this as spreading the timing of your purchases. Novice investors usually enter the property market at the top of the cycle when it is making headlines. They see some paper gains and try to make up for lost time by overextending themselves, thinking that the uptrend will last forever. When interest rates rise and the market turns, these investors are unable to service their loans and the lenders foreclose on the properties. In the fire sale that ensues, they can end up losing their home as well.

Riskier still is the use of excessive leverage to buy more than one property at a time. The later stages of a property bull market are flooded with get-rich-quick seminars teaching novices how to make a lot of money in real estate in a short space of time, with little effort. Based on strong past capital gains, the investors are guided, lemming-like, into buying two or three off-the-plan apartments using deposit bonds. They do not bother to check whether they are paying a fair price or if they qualify for finance, thinking that they can flip the properties for a quick profit if necessary.

However, when settlement time arrives the market conditions have reversed. The area they bought in is saturated with new apartments; prices fall 20 to 30 per cent below what they paid and vacancy rates reach double digits. Not only is finance harder to obtain, but for some the nightmare is compounded by their personal circumstances taking a turn for the worse: they lose their job. Instead of financial independence, they face the prospect of losing their home and bankruptcy.

Remember your *first goal is not to lose money*, and the second is to make money. Take the time to build your property portfolio securely over a number of cycles.

Take the time to build your property portfolio securely over a number of cycles.

## Two-tier marketing

Two-tier marketing is a scam where out-of-area investors are sold property at inflated prices to what locals pay. It rose to prominence in the 1990s when thousands of Gold Coast properties were sold to Sydney and Melbourne investors each year. Two-tier marketing is most effective when local prices are significantly cheaper than where target buyers live. For example, to Sydney property investors—where the median house price is over $500 000—a $300 000 Queensland property appears to be a bargain. However, it might only be worth $250 000 or less.

Another example of two-tier marketing can be found in Buffalo, New York. At its peak, Buffalo had a population of nearly 600 000. It has since declined to less than 300 000, resulting in an excess supply of properties. Many of the properties are in disrepair, and at one stage some traded for less than $4000. They have been re-sold many times by scammers who work with associates to artificially inflate the value of the properties to sell to unsuspecting interstate and foreign buyers for many times their purchase price.[1]

Two-tier marketing typically operates as follows:

▸ The scammers invite you to an investment seminar that describes how 95 per cent of people will retire in poverty ('dead or dead broke'). Some seminars nowadays are quite disingenuous. They are presented as a one- or two-day free educational seminar that would normally cost thousands of dollars, and then almost as an afterthought (supposedly) there is an opportunity for seminar attendees to take advantage of the specialised services of the seminar promoters to source real estate.

▸ They feed you misinformation. They explain why you cannot rely on superannuation for your retirement and highlight the dangers of investing in shares (how you can lose your shirt in a market crash). They then extol the benefits of investing in real estate and that with negative gearing you only need a few dollars each week to service an investment property. They also imply that it is a strategy for smart people because you are using someone else's money to get rich.

▸ They then offer you a personal consultation to see whether you qualify for the next stage and to answer any questions. The ideal targets have a lot of equity in their home.

▸ Qualified clients are offered discounted flights and accommodation to inspect properties.

▸ When you get there, a financial adviser runs a computer model to show you that a $200 000 (or some other value) investment property only costs a few dollars a week after tax to service, and doubles in value in seven to ten years. You only need to buy one a year for a few years and in no time you will be financially independent.

▸ The salespeople show potential buyers a few properties and pressure them to buy on the spot by telling them there is so much interest that if they do not act right away they will not get a second chance.

▸ For the buyer's convenience, the salesperson recommends a solicitor and financier, all located in the same building, and the sale is finalised before the buyer flies home.

Some of the techniques scammers use to entice the gullible include:

▸ Only a select number of people qualify for the special offer. Presenting the sale this way entices you to sell yourself. It is also very logical; you cannot rip someone off if they do not have any money or equity.

▸ Providing free or cheap flights, transport and accommodation to inspect distant properties. Beware of inducements: remind yourself that there are no free lunches in life and that someone has to pay for these.

▸ Optimistic forecasts (which should be a clear warning sign). Forecasts of capital growth rising steadily at 10 per cent per annum are unrealistic. In the past, when inflation was much higher, property prices rose at 8.5 per cent per annum over the whole cycle. If you had bought near the top of the cycle, your capital growth would have been less than 8.5 per cent per annum. Similarly, if you had bought a unit with a high rental yield the capital growth would have been less than 8.5 per cent per annum. In addition, past returns do not guarantee future returns. Inflation is likely to be lower in the future, and therefore capital growth will probably be lower, at around 5 to 6 per cent per annum. Also, do not forget that the net rental yield is significantly less than the gross rental yield after you allow for holding costs. It is closer to 3 to 4 per cent than 5+ per cent.

▸ One-stop-shop services, to prevent you from finding out the local price, including financial planning, sales and marketing, valuation, financing and conveyancing. Most, if not all, of these service providers are in on the scam and will not provide independent advice. If you ask for their opinion, they will probably recommend the investment.

▸ Pressure to sign on the spot. Do not be pressured to sign anything without doing your own research and independent checks (see chapter 12, 'Research'), such as with local agents who can show you comparative sales. There is nothing more stupid than shopping all day to save a few hundred dollars on a big-screen TV but buying an investment property without doing any research. If you are worried about missing out on a great deal, reassure yourself that bargains never fall into the laps of novices who don't do any research.

 There is nothing more stupid than shopping all day to save a few hundred dollars on a big-screen TV but buying an investment property without doing any research.

Investors duped by two-tier marketing pay significantly above market value (up to 30 per cent or more), which wipes out their future yields and more. Some cannot afford to hold on to the property and have to sell at a big loss, and might lose their homes in the process. If they hold onto the property for more than one cycle, they might be able to recoup some of the losses. Unfortunately, many investors who can do not hold on to the property because they were misled about the steady growth in prices and rents. In reality, the property market never works this way. The market could move sideways for many years before rising sharply for a few years.

The key to avoid being scammed by two-tier marketing is to familiarise yourself with local prices and always get at least a second *independent* quote for everything. Find out the median price for the area to recalibrate your frame of reference, especially if you live in an area where property prices are high. Then get comparable sales statistics from different local agents. For example, 'How much are two-bedroom apartments selling for in that new development down the road? How does this compare to the price of established two-bedroom apartments?' If after doing thorough research you are still interested in purchasing a property, get an *independent* valuation of the property and make sure you never use any of the service providers recommended by the salesperson, including the mortgage broker/lender.

Always get at least a second *independent* quote.

If you use a rigorous buying process you will never get into a situation where you are pressured to buy anything. For example, if you apply the 80/20 Principle (see 'The 80/20 Principle' in chapter 12), you would ask the salesperson for the indicative price over the phone. When you compare it to recent sales, it should be obvious that the asking price is similar to some of the sales (out-of-area sales) but significantly higher than the rest of the sales (local sales). If they refuse to give you a price over the phone, this should be a clear warning sign not to get on the plane.

## Defence Housing Australia

Defence Housing Australia (DHA) is a government business enterprise that offers investors properties with leases for three to twelve years, with options for a further three years (see <www.dha.gov.au>). In effect, DHA is guaranteeing zero vacancy; they still pay you the rent even if the property is not tenanted. Note that DHA does not guarantee the level of rents, which are set according to market rents. In addition to the guaranteed rental period, DHA pays for all maintenance as well as repainting and recarpeting at the end of the lease period, depending on the term of lease. In return, they charge a 15 per cent fee, double the usual property management fee of 7 per cent.

New investors are attracted to DHA properties because they like the certainty of the arrangement (and because DHA is a government business enterprise, and the properties are usually only a few years young). What they might not realise is that they pay a premium for this peace of mind. Prices can be up to 10 per cent higher than comparable properties and are set on a take-it-or-leave-it basis so there is no scope for negotiation. You should be reasoning this way: if there is rental demand for the property, there is no need to pay a premium for the no vacancy guarantee. If demand is weak, and you need the guarantee, then you should not be investing in the property in the first place. Before you buy a DHA property, you should check the prices, rents and vacancy rates of comparable properties with local agents.

One benefit of DHA properties is that they provide a ceiling on the price that you should be prepared to pay for similar properties in the area. If the asking price for a comparable property is close to a DHA property, chances are the property is overpriced. This is especially useful if you are not familiar with local prices.

### Branching out

I was originally very apprehensive about investing outside my home state to achieve the necessary spread. Since I have only ever lived in one state, thoughts of overpaying for an interstate property via two-tier marketing or having my property sit vacant for months crossed my mind. I considered DHA properties, but after doing some research for my first interstate property I realised that I could buy a comparable property for nearly 8 per cent less, or a slightly older property that paid a similar rent for around 12 per cent less. By analysing the cost–benefit of a DHA property objectively, I was able to allay my fears.

# 6 Time

If property prices increased steadily over time, making money in real estate would be just a matter of spending time in the market. You could buy at any time, as long as the yield was greater than the interest cost of the loan. You would not trade, or flip, the property because the significant transaction costs and capital gains tax on investment properties reduces your after-tax return (see 'The effect of tax' in chapter 9). However, the property market is not as straightforward as this. In real life, property prices move in cycles, driven by the greed and fear of buyers and sellers. So making money in real estate requires spending time in the market *and* timing the market.

Timing the market means not buying real estate at just any time, but only when the real estate market is having a sale. This occurs in the Buying Zone, when market values are less than intrinsic values. That way you build a *margin of safety* into your purchase price, in case future yields are less than expected. You can determine the Buying Zone using graphical analysis, fundamental analysis or technical analysis.

## Time in the market

Time is the key determinant of whether you make any money in real estate. Real estate is a long-term investment because of the high transaction costs involved. If you are not sure you can hold a property for the long term, you should not even consider investing in real estate because you can easily lose tens of thousands of dollars if you have to sell a property quickly in the short term. The way to steer clear of this is to avoid buying near the top of the market and be conservative with your forecasts. How would you cope with a 20 to 50 per cent increase in interest rates? What if you were out of work for six months? What if the property did not earn rent for three months and you had to find $5000 to fix a problem?

The longer your time in the market, the more your yield will benefit from the power of compounding. Most people are dumbfounded by the power of compounding over the long term. For example, median house prices in Australia only increased by 8.8 per cent per annum over the 45 years from 1960 to 2004.[1] This does not seem much, until you convert it into dollars at the end of the period: a 45-time increase in house prices. A median house worth $10000 in 1960 increased in value to $450000 in 2004. Although $450000 in 2004 dollars is worth much less than $450000 in 1960 dollars, it is still significant. It is not realistic to extrapolate this historical performance into the future by suggesting that a $500000 house in 2007 could be worth $22500000 in 2051, since future returns are likely to be lower due to lower future inflation. This is because central banks around the world nowadays are much more proactive in using interest rates to manage inflation.

Rents also grow over time. A rental yield of 5 per cent in 1960 gives a rent of nearly $10 per week. At a similar rental yield in 2004, it becomes nearly $450 per week. The loan outstanding, however, stays the same (if you do not pay off any of the balance), and while the interest payable fluctuates over time, it does so around a long-term average value. Suppose you bought a median $10000 house in 1960 with a 20 per cent deposit of $2000 and borrowed the remaining $8000 from the bank. The standard variable rate fluctuated between 5 per cent and 17 per cent over this period,[2] but averaged around 9 per cent. This means that the weekly interest bill fluctuated between $8 and $26, and averaged $14. While the interest bill would be a heavy burden compared to the rent in the initial years, it became insignificant compared to the rent in 2004.

Table 6.1 summarises the long-term benefit of investing in real estate. This is what investing in real estate is all about.

Table 6.1: the long-term benefit of investing in real estate

|  | 1960 | 2004 |
|---|---|---|
| House price | $10000 | $450000 |
| Loan* (20% LVR) | $8000 | $8000 |
| Weekly rent** (5% yield) | $10 | $450 |
| Weekly interest bill (average 9% p.a.) | $14 | $14 |

\* Assuming the loan is interest only; that is, you do not pay off any of the balance outstanding. Otherwise, the interest bill would be even lower.

\*\* For simplicity, I have not included any outgoings apart from interest, which could reduce the gross rent by 20 to 30 per cent.

## Flipping

Flipping (trading) real estate is only for dummies. You have to be very gullible to believe seminar promoters who suggest that you can find bargain properties at a 10 to 20 per cent discount to market value and then flip them for a quick profit. Even desperate sellers are not prepared to discount by that much. Moreover, there are plenty of buyers willing to accept a lower discount, so you will face stiff competition. This also assumes that you can buy significantly below market and then turn around and sell at market. In the unlikely event that you manage to make a profit after covering significant transaction costs, you still have to pay capital gains tax on your profits. If you hold on to the property instead, not only will you defer capital gains tax, but you also get a 50 per cent discount if you sell it after 12 months (see 'Capital gains tax' in chapter 9).

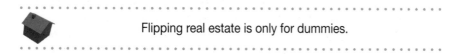

Flipping real estate is only for dummies.

In Australia, the turnover rate for real estate is around 7 per cent per annum. That is, around 7 per cent of the housing stock is bought and sold each year. It is very hard to get rich turning over real estate regularly. If you need to relocate, consider the possibility of retaining your old home as an investment property and buying a new one to live in. The rent on the old property will help cover the interest cost. In the process, you could save transaction costs of nearly 10 per cent of the value of the property, which is 50 per cent of the equity for a property funded with 20 per cent equity and 80 per cent debt.

One of the reasons why many people do not make money in real estate is that they only buy when everyone else is buying. Then as prices plateau and move sideways for many years, they grow impatient and sell out in frustration, just before the next uptrend. Unlike the stock market, where you can check prices every day, you might not see any tangible benefit of investing in real estate until five years after you buy because real estate prices do not increase in a steady trend, but in spurts. Patience is critical to successful real estate investing.

Real estate prices do not increase in a steady trend, but in spurts. Patience is critical to successful real estate investing.

Even if you bought at the wrong time, do not panic because prices will rise again. Do not get frustrated if other capital cities or suburbs take off, and try to chase them, because your area will eventually catch up. Real estate cycles take between seven and ten years, so you should not invest in real estate unless you have at least this kind of time horizon and sufficient income to service the property for as long as necessary. One risk is that if you sell a property you will spend the proceeds instead of buying other investments. On the other hand, if you hold on to the property you have to service the loan, which is a good way of disciplining yourself to save and invest.

### Time heals buying mistakes

In 1998 I bought a three-and-a-half year old four-bedroom house in a large new development in Brisbane, at a 21 per cent discount to the original cost of the land and building. I did not get a bargain price, as this was the market price at the time. The property had been on the market for a few months at this price, and if I had put the property back on the market I would have got what I paid for it. The property sold at such a large discount to its cost price for two reasons.

Firstly, the property was overcapitalised. It included high-quality fixtures and fittings and a good location that was only of value to homeowners. Since investors could not get any additional rent for these extra features, they were not prepared to put any value on them. Secondly, since the development was very large, there was a constant stream of land and brand new properties coming on to the market. Older properties (three or four years old) sold at a discount of 10 to 15 per cent of brand-new properties. I decided to adopt a contrarian strategy and buy an older property*, reasoning that in a few years the brand-new properties would be 'old' too. Once the development ran out of land, the value of all properties would appreciate and the 'old' property discount would narrow.

That is exactly what happened. Seven years later, the value of my property had increased by 150 per cent. While I did not get a bargain on price when I bought, I did get a bargain on the extras, which now support a higher property value and rent.

If you look back at Brisbane house prices in figure 4.3, you will see that the original investor sold at the worst time possible — just before the huge run-up in prices. If she had been more patient and kept the property, she would have doubled her cost price in 10 years. If she had 20 per cent equity in the property, she would have made a 500 per cent return on her equity in 10 years, instead of a 100 per cent loss on her equity in three and a half years (not including transaction costs).

This example highlights the importance of both time and timing with real estate. If you buy at the wrong time, try to keep the property at least for another cycle if you want to make any money. It also shows clearly that magnification works both ways.

\* Note that in this example, the 'older' property was still quite new compared to most of the other properties on the market.

## The real estate cycle

Instead of increasing steadily, real estate prices fluctuate around a long-term trend (the intrinsic value) in cycles that last seven to ten years. Figure 6.1 shows Sydney's median house prices over the last 28 years. The arrows indicate the start of each cycle. Sydney house prices are the most volatile in Australia. The prices in other capital cities do not fluctuate as much; the peaks and troughs are not as extreme as Sydney's.

Figure 6.1: Sydney median house price cycles[3]

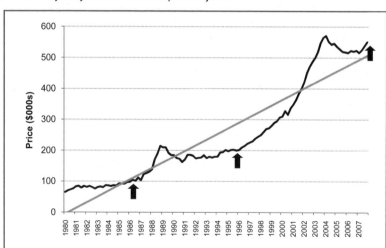

The cycles are driven by a number of factors, the most important being the economic cycle, interest rates and the public's emotional cycle of greed and fear. Real estate cycles have four stages (see figure 6.2). The name of each stage describes the actions of professional or experienced investors during the cycle (accumulation/distribution) or describes the action of prices (uptrend/downtrend).

Figure 6.2: the four stages of the real estate cycle

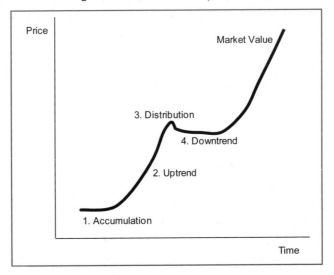

The first stage, the bottom of the cycle, is known as the *accumulation* stage. The excess supply of properties from the last boom results in high vacancy rates which slows down construction and drives property prices sideways for a number years while demand absorbs the excess supply. The market is gripped with fear as the last novice investors sell out in desperation. In contrast, experienced investors start to buy again. They see the tremendous value in the market and take advantage of the 10 to 20 per cent 'sale'. Buying during this stage involves the lowest risk (highest security).

> The time to get interested is when no one else is.
> You can't buy what is popular and do well.
>
> *Warren Buffett*

Over time, increased demand from population growth causes vacancy rates to fall. The market starts to pick up from its lows. The second stage, known as the *uptrend*, begins. Experienced investors buy more as the uptrend is confirmed and this pushes up property prices and attracts new construction with higher profits. It usually takes two to three years before supply can respond to the increase in demand, resulting in a sharp rise in property prices over a number years.

After a few years, the novices start to notice the uptrend. When the property market makes headlines, greed overcomes them and they jump on board the trend and push it up even higher. They have seen how much money was made in the uptrend over the last few years, and expect to make a killing. They attend property investment seminars and scramble for overpriced developments. However, the experienced investors realise that the trend has already gone on for a number of years and is becoming overpriced. They start selling to the novices as prices level off in the third stage, known as the *distribution* stage. Buying during this stage involves the highest risk (lowest security).

Eventually supply exceeds demand and vacancy rates rise, causing prices to fall. This is the fourth stage, known as the *downtrend*. The cycle usually takes seven to ten years, and then repeats itself.

The novices are relying on the 'bigger fool' theory, that someone will be willing to pay a higher, even more ridiculous price than what they paid, to make a profit. However, markets do not work this way, and buying at the top of the market is a sure way to lose money.

> **Buying at the top of the market is a sure way to lose money**
>
> A one-bedroom Cabramatta (Sydney) unit bought in November 2003 for $262 500 was sold at a mortgagee repossession auction in September 2006 for $95 000 (a 64 per cent loss). A four-bedroom Meadow Heights (Melbourne) house bought in July 2005 for $455 000 was sold in November 2006 for $345 000 (a 25 per cent loss).

## Timing the market

While time in the market is critical to creating long-term wealth, timing the market is also very important, especially when prices move in distinguishable cycles. If you look back at figure 6.1, you can see that house prices *overshoot* the long-term trend by up to 20 per cent on the upside and the downside of each cycle. If you take a long-term buy-and-hold approach with real estate, it makes sense to try to buy when market prices are below the long-term trend. This is the *value approach* used by investors such as Warren Buffett in the stock market.

If you manage to do this, you can *add* up to 20 per cent once-off to your long-term returns. Similarly, if you buy in the peaks you can *reduce* your long-term returns by up to 20 per cent. The difference between buying at the right time and the wrong time can be up to 40 per cent of the intrinsic value of the property. With most properties leveraged by up to five times, the difference in return on equity could be up to 200 per cent, which is significant. So now when someone tells you that the best time to buy real estate is yesterday (that is, any time in the past), just ignore them.

Figure 6.3 shows property prices over a cycle. The *market value* is the price ascribed by the market, and is volatile because it is driven by the greed and fear of buyers and sellers. Superimposed on the market value is the *intrinsic value*, the long-term value at any point in time because it measures the net present value of future cash flows. The intrinsic value is much more stable than the market value. Note how the market value overshoots the intrinsic value on the upside during the top of the cycle (driven by greed) and on the downside at the bottom of the cycle (driven by fear).

Figure 6.3: market value vs intrinsic value

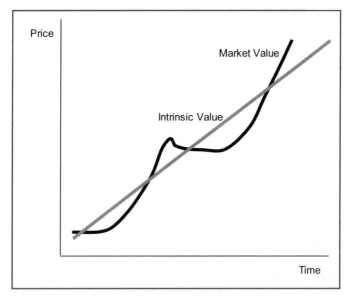

If we define the Buying Zone as when market value is less than intrinsic value, our goal is to buy only in the Buying Zone (see figure 6.4). Note that when I talk about timing the market I do not mean timing it to the day, like in the stock market. The Buying Zone extends over a few years, so timing the market for real estate means buying in the right couple of years.

The problem is that the market does not ring a bell during the Buying Zone. However, there are three ways to identify the Buying Zone: graphically, using fundamental analysis and using technical analysis. Fundamental and technical analyses are common methods of picking shares in the stock market. They also have similar applications in the real estate market, with slight modifications. You should use all three methods as a crosscheck, and the more convergence you get, the stronger the entry signal.

> The Buying Zone occurs when market value is less than intrinsic value.

Figure 6.4: only buy in the Buying Zone when market value < intrinsic value

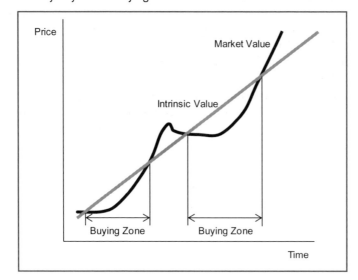

## Graphical analysis

The Buying Zone occurs during the accumulation stage and early uptrend of the real estate cycle. The accumulation stage usually starts three to four years after the last peak and the early uptrend occurs during the first three to four years after prices start to rise. Therefore, the Buying Zone is from three to four years after the last peak to three to four years after prices start rising again. The problem with graphical analysis is that only Sydney and to a lesser extent Melbourne house prices are volatile enough to show clear cycles. However, the advantage of graphical analysis is that you can use it to determine the Buying Zone at the suburb level and finetune your buying decision.

The Buying Zone occurs during the accumulation stage and early uptrend of the real estate cycle, from three to four years after the last peak to three to four years after prices start rising again.

## Fundamental analysis

Fundamental analysis compares the price of real estate (market value) to its intrinsic value based on cash flow. The best time to buy occurs when the property market is having a 'sale', with prices discounted by up to 20 per cent from the intrinsic value. At this time, the cash flow is greatest relative to price. In the case of real estate, the cash flow is the rental income. However, just looking at the gross rental yield in isolation is not sufficient because it does not take into account the cost of funding the property. The relative rental yield does take into account the cost of funding and is calculated as the gross rental yield divided by the standard variable rate. (The standard variable interest rate has been a good proxy for the cost of funds. However, over the last few years the average cost of funds has fallen well below the standard variable interest rate.)

Fundamental analysis compares the price of real estate to its intrinsic value based on cash flow.

Figure 6.5 shows the price of a median three-bedroom house against the median relative rental yield over the last 28 years in Sydney (I have used a four-quarter moving average of the rental yield to smooth out the spikes). The relative rental yield has fluctuated between 35 per cent and 70 per cent. That is, gross rents have fluctuated between 35 per cent and 70 per cent of the standard variable rate. The best value buying opportunities in Sydney were in 1984 to 1986, 1992 to 1994 and 1997 to 1999 when the relative rental yield was 60 per cent or more (shown by the arrows). So the Buying Zone occurs when the relative rental yield is 60 per cent or more. This is not just restricted to Sydney, but also applies to the other capital cities. If you look at the price graph, you will see that these periods correspond to the accumulation stage and early uptrend of the property cycle. That is, they broadly correspond to the Buying Zone determined by graphical analysis.

The Buying Zone occurs when the relative rental yield for the market is 60 per cent or more.

Figure 6.5: Sydney median house price vs relative rental yield[4]

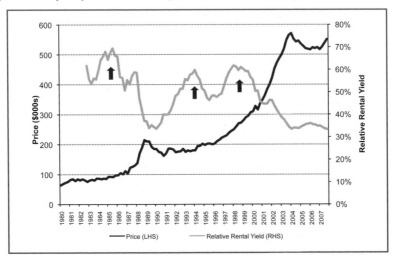

Buying when the relative rental yield for the market is high (60 per cent or more) ensures that you do not buy near the peaks of the property cycle. The reason the buying criterion is 60 per cent, and not 40 per cent, say, is that when the relative rental yield for the market drops below 60 per cent investing in the property market starts to become unattractive. To see why this is the case, I need to introduce the concept of economic value added (EVA). EVA measures profit after allowing for the cost of capital. Say you had $100 000 and you decide to borrow another $400 000 at 7 per cent per annum to buy a $500 000 property. If the property makes $5000 (capital growth and net rent), most people would think that they made a profit of $5000. However, if your cost of capital was 7 per cent, your EVA is –$2000 ($5000 – $7000). The net return from the property was insufficient to cover your cost of capital. If you had put the $100 000 in an online savings account you would have earned almost 7 per cent on it or $7000.

EVA measures profit after allowing for the cost of capital.

For a property:

EVA = Capital growth + Net rent – Interest cost – Cost of capital

= Capital growth + Net rent – (Interest rate × Debt) – (Cost of capital rate × Equity)

If the cost of capital rate is equal to the interest rate, then:

EVA = Capital growth + Net rent – Interest rate × (Debt + Equity)

= Capital growth + Net rent – Interest rate × Property value

If we define EVA per cent as EVA ÷ Property value, and divide both sides by the property value, then:

EVA per cent = Capital growth rate + Net rental yield – Interest rate

We saw before that the net rental yield is only around 70 per cent of the gross rental yield because an investment property incurs significant holding costs. In addition, we saw that future capital growth will probably be around 5 to 6 per cent per annum. However, 1 per cent of this is due to the capital injection by owners, so the net capital growth will probably be around 5 per cent per annum. If we use the standard variable rate to represent the interest rate, we get:

EVA per cent = 5 per cent + (70 per cent × Gross rental yield) – Standard variable rate

Over the last 10 years the standard variable rate has fluctuated around 7 per cent per annum.

If the relative rental yield for the market was 60 per cent (Gross rental yield = 60 per cent × Standard variable rate), we get:

EVA per cent = 5 per cent + 70 per cent × (60 per cent × Standard variable rate) – Standard variable rate

= 5 per cent – 58 per cent × Standard variable rate

= 5 per cent – 58 per cent × 7 per cent

= 1 per cent

With most properties leveraged by up to five times, the 1 per cent EVA is equivalent to a return on equity of 5 per cent per annum (5 × 1 per cent). This is in addition to the cost of capital of 7 per cent per annum (equal to the standard variable rate), giving a total return on equity of 12 per cent per annum. This is a satisfactory return.

If the relative rental yield for the market was only 40 per cent (Gross rental yield = 40 per cent × Standard variable rate), we get:

EVA per cent = 5 per cent + 70 per cent × (40 per cent ×
                  Standard variable rate) – Standard variable rate

              = 5 per cent – 72 per cent × Standard variable rate

              = 5 per cent – 72 per cent × 7 per cent

              = 0 per cent per annum

This means that the total return on equity is only equal to the cost of capital of 7 per cent per annum (equal to the standard variable rate). This is an unsatisfactory return. If the return on equity is only equal to the standard variable rate, you would not bother to invest in real estate because it entails taking on additional risk for no additional return. You would be better off putting the money in an online savings account to earn close to the standard variable rate or investing in other asset classes such as shares.

You might think there is not much difference between a relative rental yield of 60 per cent and 40 per cent for the property market. For a standard variable rate of 7 per cent, the difference is only around 1.5 per cent per annum. However, all other things being equal, when the property market only pays a relative rental yield of 40 per cent, it is *50 per cent overpriced* compared to when it pays a relative rental yield of 60 per cent.[5]

When the property market only pays a relative rental yield of 40 per cent, it is 50 per cent overpriced compared to when it pays a relative rental yield of 60 per cent.

Note that this analysis uses the long-term returns for the property market and long-term interest rates. The actual returns can vary significantly in the short term. In addition, the returns for a particular property can vary significantly from the long-term returns of the property market (see 'Specific factors' in chapter 4).

There is some conservatism in my analysis. Firstly, virtually no one pays the standard variable rate any more. In addition, there are tax benefits that improve your returns. You can treat this conservatism as a margin of safety or you can start buying when the relative rental yield for the market is less than 60 per cent (but not significantly less). However, if future long-term capital growth is less than 5 per cent per annum or long-term interest rates are more than 7 per cent per annum, your returns will suffer.

**A contrarian right from the start**

Some of my friends think that I am lucky to have started in real estate at the bottom of the cycle during the Buying Zone in the 1990s. In fact, the key to my success has been my *value approach* to assessing investments. One evening in a ski lodge in the mid 1990s one of my fellow skiers complained dejectedly about the many years of poor returns from her investment property in Adelaide. I did not know much about real estate then, so I listened intently. I reasoned that if real estate had performed so poorly for so long, it was due for a pick up. I had made some good returns in the stock market, so — after doing some research — I decided to diversify into real estate. This is how I started investing in real estate.

## Technical analysis

Technical analysis looks at the impact of the interaction of supply and demand for real estate on prices. The best measure of this is the vacancy rate. Figure 6.6 shows the price of a median three-bedroom house against the vacancy rate over the last 28 years in Sydney. (I have used a four-quarter moving average of the vacancy rate to smooth out the spikes.) When supply exceeds demand, vacancy rates are high, which restrains prices. When supply is tight, vacancy rates fall, which pushes prices up.

> Technical analysis looks at the impact of the interaction of supply and demand for real estate on prices.

The best time to buy, according to technical analysis, is when vacancy rates are at their lows, as indicated by the arrows in figure 6.6. The best buying opportunities in Sydney were in 1985 to 1988, 1995 to 1998 and 2007 to 2008. If you look at the price graph, you will see that these periods correspond to the accumulation stage and early uptrend of the property cycle. They broadly correspond to the Buying Zone determined by graphical analysis and fundamental analysis. The reason for this is that when vacancy rates are at their lows (the technical analysis signal), landlords can charge a high relative rental yield (the fundamental analysis signal) because of the high demand for rental properties relative to supply.

Figure 6.6: Sydney median house price vs vacancy rate[6]

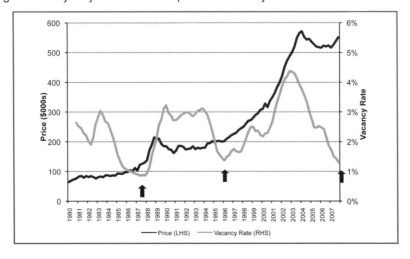

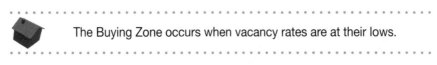

The Buying Zone occurs when vacancy rates are at their lows.

Interestingly, in 2007 to 2008 the relative rental yield was at its lows over the last 28 years (see figure 6.5), despite vacancy rates being at their lows (see figure 6.6). This is the first major divergence in fundamental and technical signals over the last 28 years. This is mainly due to the industrialisation of China, a once-off event. The growth in the Chinese economy drove the commodities boom, which in turn underpinned the strong growth in the Australian economy since 2003. This resulted in strong wages growth, which—combined with rising oil prices, also mainly caused by the industrialisation of China—led to rising inflation. This forced the Reserve Bank to raise interest rates by 50 per cent, which pushed the relative rental yield down to its lows. However, growth and inflation are slowing, and as interest rates fall the relative rental yield will rise again and fundamental and technical signals will converge.

In summary, the Buying Zone occurs when market value is less than intrinsic value. This can be determined as the accumulation stage and early uptrend of the real estate cycle, from three to four years after the last peak to three to four years after prices start rising again, or when the relative rental yield for the market is 60 per cent or more or when vacancy rates are at their lows. I recommend that you use more than one signal as a crosscheck.

# 7 Equity

Real estate is usually financed by a combination of two different sources of funds. The first is *equity*, the money that comes out of your own pocket. Equity starts off as the value of your deposit. The second is *debt*, which is money that you borrow from other people. The key difference between equity and debt is that the amount of outstanding debt is fixed over time if it is not repaid, while the equity value grows over time in line with the growth in the property's value (see figure 7.1). Equity is the *residual* value of the property. Figure 7.2 shows that equity can increase even faster by paying off the debt over time. However, if the property value falls over time the equity value falls by the same amount (see figure 7.3). Negative equity occurs when the property value falls below the value of the debt. This means that if you sell the property you will not raise enough cash to repay the loan. It is common for the buyers who purchase at the top of the cycle to have negative equity when prices fall.

Real estate is usually financed by a combination of two different sources of funds. The first is *equity*, the money that comes out of your own pocket. Equity starts off as the value of your deposit. The second is *debt*, which is money that you borrow from other people.

Figure 7.1: increasing equity with increasing property value

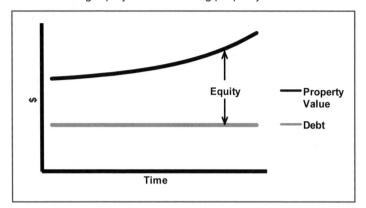

Figure 7.2: increasing equity with increasing property value and reducing debt

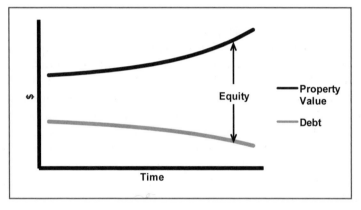

Figure 7.3: decreasing equity with decreasing property value

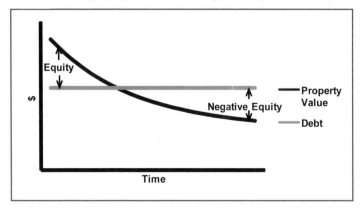

Saving up a deposit is the first step in becoming a property owner. Buyers usually want to put as little equity into a property as possible to get into the market earlier and to magnify their returns. However, lenders want buyers to put as much equity into a property as possible to increase their security. The less equity a buyer puts into a property, the greater the likelihood of a lender incurring a loss if they have to foreclose on a property and sell it to recover the loan. Therefore, lenders charge a higher interest rate and require buyers to buy mortgage insurance when the level of equity is low (usually less than 10 or 20 per cent). Too little equity also reduces the security for the buyer because they have to service a higher interest cost arising from the larger amount borrowed and the higher interest rate charged.

> Too little equity reduces the security
> for the buyer and the lender.

Lenders typically require 20 per cent equity for a standard loan. It could take a long time to save for a deposit of 20 per cent of a property's value, but it is a safe strategy. Generally the only time you should consider a smaller deposit is during the Buying Zone of the property cycle. In this situation you might be better off getting into the property market before it takes off. However, you should only investigate this option if you have a secure income and emergency funds. On the other hand, if the property market has run strongly for a number of years, you can take your time to save the full 20 per cent deposit. Getting into the property market at this point in time is risky, and it is even riskier if you have less than 20 per cent deposit.

Once you have bought your first property, you can use the increase in equity to piggyback into other properties. Although this strategy does not require you to physically put any money down, it is not really a 'no money down' strategy because you have to put your equity down, and that is as good as putting down cash. However, it is more advantageous than selling your existing property and putting down the cash as a deposit because you do not incur any transaction costs (or capital gains tax for an investment property). Novices without much money relish the prospect of getting into the property market with no money down. However, you should bear in mind that there are no free lunches, and that these strategies are either risky or not financially viable.

Like cash, equity has other uses, but it has the advantage of being more tax-efficient. If it is drawn down as income to live on, it is tax-free because it is accessed as a loan, unlike other sources of income. If it is used for investing, you can use the whole amount, unlike say a deposit, which comes from after-tax savings. The disadvantage is that you cannot access the 20 per cent of the property's value that has to remain as a buffer for the lender.

# Deposits

There are a number of ways to find the funds for a deposit on a property. The methods that involve hard work over time are usually the most secure, while the 'advanced' or 'secret' methods promoted by some real estate investment seminars that require little effort and no money down are the riskiest.

Let's have a look:

▶ Saving for the deposit takes a long time, but you have proven that you can live frugally and save money, and it will be much easier to service the mortgage than any of the other ways.

▶ Piggybacking (see below). If you already own a property with some spare equity, you can piggyback on this equity into a new property without having to outlay any money. The lender, in effect, lends you the deposit on the new property secured on the available equity in your existing property.

▶ Parents can give their children a hand in buying their first property by letting them piggyback on the equity in their home. You might view this arrangement as lending the kids their inheritance. However, you should be aware that if you do this you are guaranteeing their loan with your home as security. The risk is if your children are unable to make the repayments on the loan, the lender forecloses on the property and sells it at a loss, and then comes after *your* home.

▶ It might take one person a long time to save enough for a deposit, but you can speed things up if you pool your resources with family and/or friends. You have to agree on a number of issues beforehand, such as how to deal with someone who loses a job and cannot pay his or her share of the mortgage; otherwise, it can get messy down the track.

▶ You can use equity financing, also known as equity sharing. A financial institution or individual contributes the equity for a disproportionate share of profits when the property is sold. For example, they lend you the 20 per cent equity and you pay the 'interest' on this loan with 40 per cent or 50 per cent of the capital gains when the property is sold. It is hard enough to make money from real estate under a normal financing arrangement, let alone one that costs a large chunk of the capital gains. Therefore, I do not encourage this approach.

# Piggybacking

The biggest obstacle to buying an investment property is finding the money for the deposit. You can overcome this problem by using the available equity in your home (or your parents' home if you do not own one) to buy another property, and then after a few years use the increase in equity in both properties to buy a third property. You repeat the process again and again to build your property portfolio.

You repeat the piggyback process again and again to build your property portfolio.

For example, let's say your home is valued at $500 000 and you still owe $200 000 on the mortgage (see figure 7.4). The equity in your home is $300 000 ($500 000 – $200 000). You could sell your home to turn this equity into cash to buy another property, but you would incur transaction costs (and capital gains tax if it was an investment property). A better solution is to borrow against the equity. You will not be able to use all of the equity in your home for the new property; however, you will not incur the transaction costs. More importantly, you get to keep your home, and therefore have a bigger asset base (two properties as opposed to one) to build your wealth.

Continuing with the example, most lenders require 20 per cent equity for each property. Thus, of the $300 000 equity, $100 000 (20 per cent of $500 000) needs to be left behind for your home. The available equity is therefore $200 000 ($300 000 – $100 000). A quick way to calculate the available equity is:

Available equity = 80 per cent × Property value – Debt

The $200 000 available equity can be used to buy another $500 000 property. You would borrow $100 000 against the available equity as a 20 per cent 'deposit' for the other property, and a further $25 000 to cover stamp duty and purchase costs. (This leaves $75 000, which you could take as a line of credit to update the new property or to buy some shares, or you could save it for the next purchase.) Overall, you are borrowing $125 000 secured against the available equity in your home and a further $400 000 secured against the new property. Thus, without outlaying any of your money you are able to buy a second property by piggybacking on the available equity in your home.

Figure 7.4: piggybacking on the equity in your home

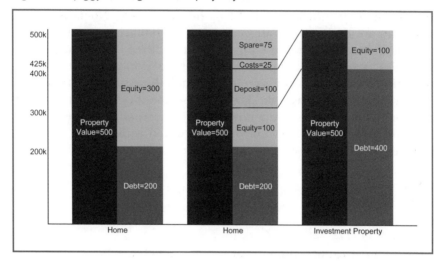

Some people are scared of debt and will try to pay off their home first before buying any further properties. The interest is not tax deductible and therefore the pre-tax return is almost double the interest rate for people on the highest marginal tax rate (see 'Comparing pre-tax returns' in chapter 9). However, this delays your entry into the investment property market at today's prices. Depending on the stage of the property cycle, it might be more advantageous to buy another property using the available equity in your home rather than paying off the mortgage.

### Build your portfolio with the piggyback process

The total debt on my property portfolio purchased in the last Buying Zone is more than the total purchase price of the properties. However, the value of the properties has appreciated over time and the LVR is only around 50 per cent. Note that the LVR measures the total value of the loan to the total *current* value of the properties. In particular, the debt on the first few properties is significantly higher than the purchase price as I have regularly drawn down the increase in equity to purchase more properties and shares.

# Say no to 'no money down'

Real estate investment seminars and spruikers sometimes teach 'advanced' strategies to get into the property market that require no deposit (that is, no money or equity). Novices bite at these strategies because they do not have any funds or experience. No-money-down strategies are dodgy. They are very risky, not financially viable or only feasible in the imagination of novices—or all three. If no-money-down strategies were sound, experienced investors would consistently use them. But they do not. The people who teach these strategies to novices usually have a hidden agenda. The more people they can get to buy the developments they are marketing, the more commission they receive from the developers. They are only concerned with making the sale; whether you make any money out of it is your problem.

> No-money-down strategies are dodgy.
> There are no free lunches in life.

Some of the no-money-down strategies promoted include:

▸ 100 per cent finance. Some financial institutions will lend the whole purchase price (and even acquisition costs) of an owner-occupied property to buyers with strong cash flow. However, mortgage insurance of up to 3 per cent of the value of the property is required. Even if you have a stable income, this kind of arrangement is risky because you do not have a demonstrated saving habit. Furthermore, it is imprudent to overextend yourself financially. How will you cope if you lose your job, or if interest rates rise by 50 per cent as they did in 2007 to 2008? Furthermore, the financial institutions usually charge a higher interest rate to cover them for the higher risk, which reduces your yield and makes the investment less viable.

▸ Clayton's deposit. You might be able to borrow the deposit through personal loans or credit cards. The comments for 100 per cent finance apply here. Note that this is an even riskier strategy because the interest rates are significantly higher.

▸ Second mortgage. The seller lends you the deposit by taking out a second mortgage on the property. This kind of arrangement is very rare in Australia, and the sellers who might entertain it will want something in return for their troubles, such as a mark-up on the sales price and interest rate on the second mortgage. These mark-ups reduce your yield and make the investment less viable.

- Wraps and lease options (see 'Vendor financing' in chapter 8). Wraps and lease options vendors sell properties at above market value and charge above market interest rates/rents. These mark-ups reduce your yield and make the investment unviable.

- Buy below market value and get the property revalued to its market value and you have created a deposit out of thin air. For example, you buy a property for $80 000 and then get it revalued to $100 000 market value and create a $20 000 deposit out of nothing. It is virtually impossible to buy significantly below market value, and it is even more unlikely for novices without any money to do so. In any case, the lender will only lend to the lower of the purchase price or valuation. So even in the unlikely event that you manage to buy a property for, say, 20 per cent below market value, the lender will only use the purchase price as their valuation. If you refinance the property later you will be able to get it revalued to its market value, however this requires a deposit in the first place.

- Buy two off-the-plan properties, flip one at settlement for a profit, and use the proceeds as the deposit for the property you keep. You will still need to come up with the funds for two deposit bonds, although these are significantly less than the deposit. This is a very risky strategy. Even if you could buy two deposit bonds simultaneously (deposit bond issuers dissuade investors from doing this for their own protection), what will you do at settlement if prices fall instead of rise? In addition, you will incur transaction costs and possibly capital gains tax that will eat into your yield.

I mentioned before that your first consideration should be the security of your investment, and only then should you think about making money. Risky strategies might get you a foothold in the property market if everything goes right, but if they do not work you could end up bankrupt (and lose your home, if you own one). There are so many other investment strategies, with or without property, where you can make money with much more security that you should never even consider risky property strategies.

Always approach an investment with a view to investing right across the cycle. Everything might look rosy because the market is going up, but will you be able to hang on to the property if its price falls by 10 or 20 per cent, interest rates rise by 20 to 50 per cent and vacancy rates double or triple? Also, do not be so naive to think that you can on-sell the property quickly for a profit, because every other seminar attendee will be looking to do the same thing, and this will automatically drive prices down.

---

### What will you do if prices fall instead?

In 2001, an investor in her early 50s spent $6000 on two deposit bonds to buy two off-the-plan apartments in Sydney's inner city to fund her retirement. Eighteen months later, she tried to sell the apartments before settlement but found that they were valued at more than $70 000 less than what she had paid. The sale fell through and she did not have the money to complete the settlement. As a result, she now owes the deposit bond company more than $70 000.

---

It is difficult enough to make money from real estate under normal conditions. Strategies where you have to pay above the standard interest rate and/or market value are unviable. They eat into your yield and therefore do not satisfy the second condition of making money. They also do not satisfy the first condition, because the chance of loss is much greater when you pay an inflated price. There is no point investing in the property market if you will lose money, or not make any money.

The corollary is that if you do not have a suitable deposit you are probably better off not investing in the property market. To do so is risky or not financially viable. Remember that real estate is not the only investment available to provide for your retirement. Shares are just as attractive, and they do not require as large an initial outlay as real estate.

> If you do not have a suitable deposit you are probably better off not investing in the property market.

## Other uses of equity

We have already seen an example of using the available equity in a property to piggyback into another property. Other uses of equity include:

▶ Supporting an investment property until it becomes cash flow positive (that is, equity buys you time). For example, if you recently bought an investment property and are unexpectedly laid off, you might not have to sell it if you have a lot of available equity in your home. You can draw down some of the equity to fund the interest and holding costs until the property becomes self-sustaining (cash flow positive).

▸ Buying other investments such as shares. Instead of piggybacking into another property, you can piggyback into other investments. After a strong run in the real estate market, this is the approach I use to rebalance my portfolio.

▸ Supplementing your income when you retire. You do not have to change your lifestyle in retirement and you do not have to sell any property if you supplement your income by drawing down some of the available equity as needed using a home equity line of credit. The best thing about this income is that it is tax-free. The interest on the line of credit is capitalised, which reduces the available equity. Some lenders will even cover any negative equity when the loan is repaid. The downside of this strategy is that there will be less for the kids to inherit, but that is their problem. A variation of this strategy is withdrawing a tax-free lump sum to cover an emergency such as an operation.

▸ Consolidating and refinancing other debt. If you cannot make any progress in paying off the outstanding balance on high-interest credit cards and personal loans, you are better off drawing down some of the available equity in your home to pay off these loans. In effect, you are replacing a number of high-interest loans with one lower interest loan.

▸ Purchasing consumer goods and services such as big-screen TVs and holidays. This is not recommended until you reach your financial goals as it reduces your asset base. If you *have* reached your financial goals you should enjoy the fruits of your labour.

The main risk of drawing down the available equity is that you overextend yourself. In effect, you are just borrowing more money against the available equity. If circumstances change, you might not be able to service the extra interest and you could end up losing the property.

# 8 Magnification

Magnification, also known as gearing and leverage, is the use of other people's money. I have called it magnification because it can magnify your returns manyfold. However, magnification works both ways: it will multiply both profits and losses. If you use magnification sensibly you can reduce the time it takes to achieve your financial goals because it allows you to invest more and therefore achieve a greater yield than you could with just your own money. Another advantage of magnification is that the interest cost is tax deductible (see chapter 9).

Magnification will only work if you can earn a higher yield than the interest cost of your borrowings. This is usually the case in the long term, because over the long term the average yield (capital growth and net rent) on real estate exceeds interest rates (see figure 22.1 for a comparison of Sydney median house yields against the standard variable interest rate). However, real estate prices move in cycles, and in the short to medium term magnification could result in a loss, such as when prices move sideways. Therefore, you should only use magnification if you are prepared to invest for the long term and have the funds to support the outgoings of the property in the short to medium term.

> Magnification will only work if you can earn a higher yield than the interest cost of your borrowings.

Magnification is *the* main advantage of real estate. You can borrow more secured on real estate than shares or any other investment. However, too much magnification is risky and reduces the security of your investment. In fact, the greatest risk in real estate is overextending yourself. If you cannot make the repayments, perhaps because you lose your job or there is a sharp rise in interest rates, the lender will foreclose on your property. If the value of the property falls below the value of the debt, and you do not have any other assets, you will end up bankrupt.

> Magnification reduces the security of your investment —
> you cannot go bankrupt if you do not have any debt.

Getting into the property market usually requires some form of debt. However, in my experience novice investors tend to get carried away with debt and gear to the hilt to speed up their financial independence. Experienced investors, on the other hand, treat debt with respect and use it conservatively. To reduce the risk of bankruptcy, make sure you leave a generous buffer between your assets and debt, and only borrow as much as you can comfortably service. Remember, you cannot go bankrupt if you do not have any debt.

> I pointed across the street to a man holding a
> cup and with a seeing eye dog.
> I asked, 'Do you know who that is?'
> Marla said to me: 'Yes, Donald. He's a beggar.
> Isn't it too bad? He looks so sad!'
> I said, 'You're right. He's a beggar, but he's
> worth about $900 million more than me.'
>
> *Donald Trump,* The Art of the Comeback

Just as it is risky to borrow too much, it is also risky not to borrow at all. If you define risk as not being able to achieve your financial goals, then not borrowing to buy real estate could be risky in the long term because it precludes you from participating in a strong growth asset for a long time. How long would it take you to save half a million dollars to buy a median house in Sydney?

> Just as it is risky to borrow too much,
> it is also risky not to borrow at all.

---

**Not all debt is bad**

I had a high-school friend who grew up thinking that *all* kinds of debt were bad. It took him and other members of his family nearly 20 years to save enough money to buy a house on a busy main road. It was all they could afford with just their own savings. Unfortunately, by the time this happened, the property market had already risen threefold. If they had been more receptive to magnification they could have gotten into the property market a lot earlier and enjoyed the capital growth.

---

How much you can borrow depends on your personal credit rating, the security for the loan and your ability to service the loan, and is measured by the loan-to-valuation ratio (LVR). I use a variation of the LVR, called the magnification ratio, to measure how much I have leveraged my equity. Your choice of loan, including the interest rate and lending criteria, depends on your employment and credit situation. Most readers will qualify for standard loans that charge the lowest interest rates. There are also non-conforming loans that cater for people who cannot document their income or have poor credit histories. A third option is financing provided by the seller.

You should choose the lowest interest rate loan and ignore the expensive bells and whistles to maximise your yield. Use a principal and interest loan for your principal residence and an interest-only loan for investment properties to conserve your cash. Every six to twelve months you should check that the interest rate on your loan is still competitive, otherwise do a cost–benefit analysis to see if it is worthwhile refinancing your loan. Lastly, you need to be able to distinguish between the different types of gearing—from negative gearing to positive cash flow—to understand how much money you need to service a property.

# Magnification ratio

With real estate you need to clarify what your return is relative to because, unlike other investments, it is usually partly funded by yourself and partly by debt. The property value is funded by equity (your contribution) and debt (your liability). Therefore, you can measure your return relative to the value of the property (the return on property value) or relative to the equity you contributed (the return on equity). The magnification ratio measures how many times debt is used to leverage up your equity and links the return on equity with the return on property value.

If we define the magnification ratio as Property value ÷ Equity, then:

Return on equity  =  Return on property value ×
Magnification ratio

Assume that you bought a property for $100 000 at the start of the year with $20 000 of your own money and $80 000 borrowed from the bank, and it pays a net rent of $5000, and increases in value to $110 000 at the end of the year.

The return on property value (ROPV) is 15 per cent ([5 + (110 − 100)] ÷ 100).

The return on equity (ROE) is 75 per cent ([5 + (110 − 100)] ÷ 20).

Alternatively, the magnification ratio is 5 (100 ÷ 20), giving an ROE of 75 per cent (15 per cent × 5). What this means is that by outlaying only $20 000 you made $15 000, or a 75 per cent return on your outlay (equity) because you leveraged it up five times. If you had paid cash for the property instead, the return on your outlay (equity) would be equal to the return on property value or only 15 per cent because your magnification ratio was only 1.

Note that magnification works both ways. If the property's value falls to $90 000 at the end of the year your return on property value is −5 per cent ([5 + (90 − 100)] ÷ 100), and your return on equity is magnified five times to −25 per cent ([5 + (90 − 100)] ÷ 20).

# How much can you borrow?

Before you apply for a loan, you should get a copy of your credit record at <www.mycreditfile.com.au> to check for and correct any inaccurate information. You can get a free copy if you are willing to wait up to 10 working days; otherwise there is a nominal charge. Your credit record is your personal credit rating. It contains information such as your applications for credit over the last five years and payment defaults. When you apply for a loan, the lender will look at your credit record to assess your credit risk. Each time you sign a privacy document you are giving the lender your permission to check your credit record. You should only apply for credit when you absolutely need to, and not every time you get a pre-approval offer because too many applications for credit in a short space of time could indicate that you are in financial trouble.

Provided you have a good credit rating, the amount of money you can borrow depends on two factors: security and serviceability. Security refers to the ability to repay the loan principal, while serviceability refers to the ability to meet the interest payments. To ensure sufficient security the lender secures the loan against the property and lends less than the value of the property. The LVR measures the ratio of the loan to the value of the property securing the loan. The value of the property is determined by the lender's valuer, and is usually equal to the purchase price.

LVR = Loan ÷ Property value

The LVR depends on the price you paid for the property and the size of your deposit, and hence how much you need to borrow. If you manage to buy a property for a good price you can afford a smaller loan. If you borrow at more than 80 per cent LVR, the lender will usually require you to take out lenders' mortgage insurance to protect them against default. The cost of lenders' mortgage insurance can be up to 3 per cent of the value of the loan, depending on how much you borrow. However, sometimes the banks will reduce this ratio based on market conditions. For example, when there was an oversupply of inner city apartments, the banks reduced LVRs for some of these properties to 60 per cent.

The LVR is not just restricted to one property, but can be calculated on a *portfolio* of properties. Suppose you bought a property for $100 000, putting down $20 000 yourself and borrowing $80 000 from the bank, to give an LVR of 80 per cent. Three years later, the value of the property increases to $130 000. The LVR is now 62 per cent, assuming it is an interest-only loan and you did not repay any of the principal. You can use the increase in equity to buy another property without outlaying any money. The bank will lend you another $120 000, if you can service the debt, to buy another property for $120 000, because the LVR on these two properties is 80 per cent: (80 000 + 120 000) ÷ (130 000 + 120 000). The increase in value of the first property allows you to borrow an additional $24 000 (80 per cent × 130 000 − 80 000). This amount effectively becomes the deposit on the new property. The value of the new property that this deposit can support is $120 000 (24 000 ÷ 20 per cent).

You should avoid *cross-collateralising* your loans—that is, using two or more properties as security for a loan—where possible. Ideally, all of your loans should be stand-alone, with one property securing each loan. The main disadvantage of cross-collateralisation is that it is unwieldy; you cannot just move one loan to another lender. In addition, you have less control over your assets when something goes wrong. If you default on a cross-collateralised loan (secured on two investment properties and your home, say) and there is insufficient security, the lender could sell any or all of the properties securing the loan to recover the money. For example, the lender might sell your home because it has the most equity, whereas if you had your way you might sell the two investment properties. If you have to cross-collateralise to piggyback on the available equity in an existing property, when you refinance make sure you refinance into separate loans if you have sufficient equity.

Your ability to service a loan is measured by the debt service ratio (DSR), which needs to be less than 1.0, and is calculated as follows:

DSR $=$ Loan repayment $\div$ 'Serviceable' income

$=$ Loan repayment $\div$ (30 per cent $\times$ Gross salary + 70 per cent $\times$ Gross rental income)

Lenders want sufficient 'serviceable' income to cover loan repayments. The rest of the income is for you to pay tax and live on. The lender also does not take into account all of the gross rent because some is needed to cover the holding costs of an investment property. Note that the percentages vary from lender to lender. The typical amounts are 30 to 35 per cent of gross salary and 70 to 80 per cent of gross rental income. Of these two criteria (LVR and DSR), it is usually the DSR that limits how much you can borrow, since with mortgage insurance lenders are prepared to lend at over 100 per cent LVR. This is where high-rental-yield, low-capital-growth properties have the advantage of improving your serviceability.

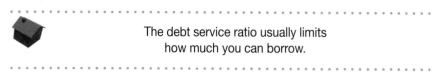

The debt service ratio usually limits
how much you can borrow.

# Types of loans

There are two main types of loans, which depend on your employment and credit situation. Standard loans are typically provided by the banks to borrowers in permanent full-time employment (around 60 per cent of the working population). Standard loans charge the lowest interest rates. Borrowers in casual or part-time employment unable to show a consistent income or those with a poor credit history can apply for non-standard loans (also known as non-conforming loans) that charge a higher interest and/or lend less. There is a less common third type of financing, called vendor financing, where the vendor sells you the property *and* provides the financing. You should usually avoid this third option because of the unfavourable terms, lack of transparency and credit risk.

## Standard loans

Loans can be *variable interest* or *fixed interest*. The interest rate on a variable interest rate loan changes during the life of the loan, usually in line with the Reserve Bank's cash rate. The recent subprime market collapse pushed up the cost of wholesale funding, forcing lenders to pass on some of this cost to borrowers. As a result, variable interest rates increased beyond the usual increase in the Reserve Bank's cash rate. However, this situation is unlikely to persist beyond the next few years.

The *term* of a loan is the maximum time you have to repay the loan. For variable interest loans, the term is usually 25 or 30 years. A longer term spreads the repayments over a longer period and so they are lower, but you end up paying more interest over the term of the loan. The interest rate on a fixed interest rate loan is fixed for the term of the loan, typically one to five years in Australia. It reverts to a variable interest rate loan at the end of the term or you can fix it for another term. Australian fixed-interest terms are short compared to other countries such as the United States where 30-year fixed-rate mortgages are the norm.

Lenders are now required by law to calculate a *comparison rate*—also known as an *annualised average percentage rate (AAPR)*—when advertising their interest rates. The comparison rate calculates an equivalent fee-free interest rate that allows consistent comparison between different loan products with different interest rate structures and fees. It takes into account factors such as honeymoon rates, upfront costs such as loan application fees and ongoing fees such as monthly account-keeping fees. The comparison rate calculations are based on standard assumptions about the size, term and conditions of the loan, and are therefore appropriate for most people.

The *standard variable rate* is the banks' reference rate that applies to fully featured loans. It has fluctuated around a wide range over the long term; between 5 per cent and 17 per cent over the last 45 years (see figure 4.7) and 6 per cent and 9.6 per cent over the last 10 years (see figure 8.1). However, nowadays virtually no one pays the standard variable rate. According to the Reserve Bank, the average interest rate is around 0.5 to 0.7 per cent less than the standard variable rate due to the competition between lenders.

*Professional packages* offer discounts of 0.5 to 0.75 per cent on the standard variable rate to 'professionals' for fully featured products. However, if the lender wants your business, anyone earning a reasonable salary is likely to qualify just by asking for it. If professional packages are not possible for you, consider *basic variable rates* that are similar to professional package rates but apply to no-frills loans with only basic features. Sometimes you might be better off with a basic variable loan than a professional package.

Fixed-interest loans have the advantage of certainty in budgeting, while variable-interest loans offer flexibility. It is not easy to forecast future increases in interest rates and profit by fixing interest rates. Even experts such as the banks get it wrong, and in any case the fixed rates already price in anticipated increases in interest rates. The disadvantage of fixed-rate loans is that you might not be able to make extra repayments, and if interest rates fall it could cost tens of thousands of dollars to pay out the loan early.

When fixed rates are above variable rates (such as in June 1994—see figure 8.1), the market expects variable rates to rise (which they did). When fixed rates are below variable rates (such as in December 1995), the market expects variable rates to fall (which they did). However, the market does not have a crystal ball, and things do not always turn out as expected. For example, in June 2003 fixed rates were below variable rates in expectation of a slow-down in the Australian economy and a fall in interest rates. However, the economy maintained its momentum, driven by the commodities boom which put pressure on wages. Inflation was further fuelled by rising food (due to the drought) and oil prices. As a result, the Reserve Bank raised interest rates 12 times between May 2002 to March 2008. In the five years between June 2003 and June 2008, the standard variable rate rose by 50 per cent. Some of this was driven by the subprime market collapse, and was in addition to the increase in the Reserve Bank's cash rate.

Figure 8.1: standard variable rate vs three-year fixed rate[1]

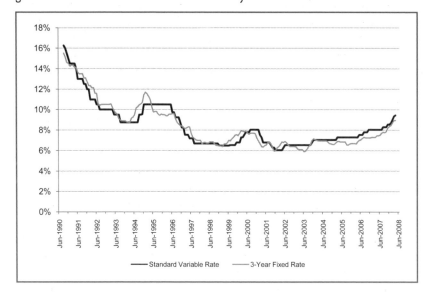

Most people tend to switch to fixed rates after interest rates have risen a few times. However, by then fixed rates are near their peak, in anticipation of a fall in variable rates. If you prefer the certainty of fixed rates, the best time to switch is when fixed rates are at their lows.

That way, even if variable rates fall, they are unlikely to fall much further than the fixed rates. However, there is a good chance that variable rates will hover around or rise above the level of fixed rates.

Some lenders try to entice first home owners with *honeymoon rates*. These are attractive introductory rates, 1 to 2 per cent below the standard variable rate, that last for six to twelve months before reverting to their normal level. The lenders impose hefty *deferred establishment fees* (exit fees) to avoid hit-and-run borrowers. The true cost of the loan is given by the comparison rate (the AAPR). I do not suggest you use honeymoon rates as they tend to be more costly than other loans over time.

A *home equity loan* is secured on the available equity in a property. Most lenders will only accept a first mortgage. There are two types of home equity loans. The first allows borrowers to borrow a lump sum, while the second is a *line of credit* that lets borrowers draw down the loan as required, up to a limit. Interest is only payable on the outstanding balance and is automatically added to the outstanding balance when it is below the limit. It is a good idea to set up a line of credit for emergencies or to take advantage of unexpected opportunities.

Retirement is a time to be enjoyed. If you are short of cash in retirement, spend the kids' inheritance. *Reverse mortgages* are similar to home equity loans that allow asset rich but income poor homeowners to borrow against the equity in their home. They work in the opposite way to a home loan. The balance outstanding increases as interest is added to the principal (instead of reducing from repayments under a home loan). The principal and interest is only due when the borrower dies or moves out of the home. The interest charge is higher than the standard variable rate and LVRs are usually restricted to around 50 per cent to ensure that the lender has enough equity to cover the interest. However, because it is a loan, the income is tax-free.

A *bridging loan* is a short-term loan used to finance the purchase of a property while the owner waits for the sale or settlement of an existing property. The interest rate charged is higher than for normal loans. The principal is payable after settlement of the existing property, subject to a maximum term, such as 12 months.

Loans can be *principal and interest* or *interest only*. With a principal and interest loan, you repay part of the principal with each interest payment. Initially the bulk of the repayment is interest; over time, as the loan balance reduces, the principal component increases. The outstanding balance is reduced to zero by the end of the term of the loan. With an interest-only loan, there is no repayment of the principal for a specified number of years (usually five years), after which the loan reverts to a principal and interest loan.

*Deposit bonds* allow buyers to purchase an investment property without having to pay a deposit when contracts are exchanged. The buyer pays the bond's issuer a fee to guarantee that the deposit will be paid at settlement. Whereas a typical deposit requires tens of thousands of dollars, a deposit bond might cost only a few hundred dollars. If the buyer does not proceed with the purchase, the seller calls on the bond issuer for the deposit, who in turn will try to recover the amount from the buyer. Deposit bonds are usually used to speculate on off-the-plan property by providing investors with very high leverage during the construction stage.

## Non-standard loans

Non-standard loans (also known as non-conforming loans) cater to borrowers unable to arrange standard loans due to insufficient income documentation because they are casual workers or self-employed, or they have a poor credit history. They are tailored to the individual circumstances of the borrower, unlike standard loans, which are off the shelf. Non-standard loans usually charge 2 per cent or more above the standard variable rate and incur additional fees.

*Low documentation loans* cater to borrowers with insufficient documentation of regular income, such as the self-employed. The lending criteria is less strict, sometimes only requiring a signed statement of income from an accountant, but borrowers pay a higher interest rate on a lower LVR loan (around 65 per cent versus 80 per cent for standard loans).

*High LVR loans* allow buyers without a deposit to enter the property market. Loans can be over 105 per cent of a property's purchase price to cover transaction costs. These loans attract a higher interest charge and are subject to some restrictions. The demand for these loans usually occurs near the top of the cycle. However, this is exactly the wrong time to be using these loans because buying at the top of the cycle entails the highest risk and the low or negative returns over the following years do not justify the higher risk or interest charge.

If you borrow more than 80 per cent of the value of a property, most lenders will require *lenders' mortgage insurance (LMI)*. The once-off premium costs around 1 to 3 per cent of the value of the loan, and increases with increasing LVR. For example, on a $300 000 loan the premium is between $3000 and $9000. Note that lenders' mortgage insurance only protects the lender, and not you. If you default (fail to make a payment) and the lender forecloses on the property and sells it for less than the outstanding loan amount, the mortgage insurer covers the lender for any shortfall. However, the mortgage insurer will pursue you to repay the debt.

If you are just starting out and need lenders' mortgage insurance you are probably borrowing too much. You should avoid mortgage insurance, because while it allows you to buy a property without having a full deposit, it increases the purchase price without providing you with any protection for the increase in risk. That is, mortgage insurance reduces the yield, without improving the security of your investment. You should stick to 80 per cent LVR loans to avoid overextending yourself, especially if you have not proven that you can save a standard deposit. You will look like a genius if you put very little money down and the property doubles in value in three years, but how will you cope with a 50 per cent rise in interest rates and a 20 per cent slump in prices and you are geared to the hilt?

## Vendor financing

Vendor financing refers to non-traditional financing techniques that originated in the United States, and involves some form of financing provided by the vendor. Vendor financing was initially promoted on the *buy* side to help investors without much money purchase and finance a property with as little of their own money as possible. This usually involved paying above market values to get the seller to carry back a second mortgage or some other arrangement with the terms. Vendor financing is now promoted on the *sell* side, using wraps and lease options to help investors generate positive cash flow. Their targets are unsophisticated buyers who dream of owning their own home but cannot purchase and finance a property under conventional means.

When a vendor *carries/takes back a second mortgage*, they are effectively lending the buyer part of their equity. So instead of receiving cash for this part of the equity, the seller receives it in instalments. The usual promoted advantage for the seller is that it makes the deal more attractive for the buyer, which results in a higher price or a faster sale. However, this is not a common strategy because most lenders will not allow secondary financing. Furthermore, it is risky for the seller because the strategy allows the buyer to buy the property at above their traditional financing limits. In addition, the arrangement becomes messy if the buyer becomes delinquent in the repayments.

A *wrap* (also referred to as *vendor financing* in Australia) is a form of financing provided by the property seller instead of the traditional lenders. The wrapper buys a property using a standard loan and re-sells it under an instalment sales contract by providing the buyer with a loan. The wrapper retains ownership of the property until his or her loan is repaid. It is called a wrap because the wrapper's loan to the buyer 'wraps around' his or her standard loan. The interest rate on the wrap is usually 2 per cent or more higher than the standard variable rate. In addition, the selling price is usually 20 per cent or more higher than the wrapper's purchase price to allow for future capital gains. The wrapper usually requires a small deposit, which they sometimes conveniently make equal to the First Home Owner Grant. Wrappers need to ensure that they do not contravene privacy laws (for credit checks) and consumer credit laws.

A *lease option/rent-to-buy* arrangement allows potential buyers without a deposit to lease a property with the option to buy it. The option buyer pays the seller a premium at the start of the lease for the right, but not obligation, to buy the property on agreed terms by a later date. The premium is usually applied to (that is, reduces) the purchase price of the property, also known as the exercise price, if the option is exercised; otherwise, it is forfeited to the seller. The purchase price is usually 20 per cent or more higher than the seller's purchase price to allow for future capital gains. The rent is also higher than market rents. If the option is exercised, part of the rent may be applied to the purchase price. In addition, the tenant pays all holding costs such as rates and maintenance costs. The cost (rent plus holding costs) to the tenant as a percentage of the market value of the property is usually higher than conventional interest rates.

Table 8.1 compares the different types of financing options for purchasing a $100 000 property.

Table 8.1: traditional vs vendor financing

|  | Traditional financing | | Vendor financing | | |
|  | Standard | Non-standard | 2nd mortgage | Wrap | Lease option |
|---|---|---|---|---|---|
| Deposit | 20 000 | 30 000 | 5 000 | 10 000 | 0 |
| 2nd mortgage | – | – | 20 000* | – | – |
| Debt | 80 000 | 70 000 | 80 000 | 110 000 | 0 |
| Purchase price | 100 000 | 100 000 | 105 000 | 120 000 | 120 000 |
| Option fee | – | – | – | – | 3 000** |
| Market value | 100 000 | 100 000 | 100 000 | 100 000 | 100 000 |
| Interest rate | 7% | 9% | 7% | 9.5% | 12%** |

\* The interest on the second mortgage is usually higher than conventional interest rates.

\*\* The option fee is usually applied to the purchase price if exercised.
'Interest rate' is the rental yield paid to the seller plus holding costs.

The table also shows how wraps and lease options work: an investor buys and finances a property under standard loan terms (from column 2) and resells it to unsophisticated buyers under wrap/lease option terms (to column 5 and 6) to cover transaction costs and make a profit. The parameters are indicative only and vary from deal to deal. As you can see, there are no free lunches with vendor financing. Moreover, some lunches are more expensive than others. The wrapper/lease option seller charges a *higher price* and a *higher interest rate/rent* for the *same* property in return for accepting a lower deposit and providing financing that you might not be able to get elsewhere.

> The wrapper/lease option seller charges a *higher price* and a *higher interest rate/rent* for the *same* property in return for accepting a lower deposit and providing financing.

Wrap and lease option sellers target the buyers that traditional lenders reject, despite the high default/turnover rate (including where the tenant moves on under a lease option and does not exercise the option to buy), because unlike traditional lenders they are rewarded when default/turnover occurs. Fortunately, the increased availability of non-conforming loans has made selling wraps and lease options more difficult. In addition, higher property prices and higher interest rates have pushed wraps and lease options out of reach of many unsophisticated buyers.

If you are a first home buyer having trouble saving enough for a full deposit and cannot obtain finance from the banks or mortgage originators, it is very tempting to turn to vendor financing (wraps and lease options) to pay for your home in instalments. After all, it is how you probably pay for your car and other big ticket items. However, vendor financing a property is a very expensive commitment because the terms are very unfavourable, and if you fall behind in your repayments you could lose the property and the instalments you have already paid. If the traditional lenders do not think that you can service a standard loan, it is very risky to commit to the much more onerous requirements of a wrap or lease option.

If you cannot obtain a standard loan you are usually better off renting and investing in shares and other investments, because at least there you pay the same as everyone else. The 2 per cent extra interest charged on non-standard loans can mean the difference between an average return and a poor return or even a loss. The 2 per cent extra interest and the 20 per cent price mark-up charged by vendor financing can mean the difference between a poor return or a loss and losing the property and the instalments you have already made. (Note that the

2 per cent extra interest and 20 per cent price mark-up are indicative only; they can be a lot higher.) To make matters worse, if you need to turn to non-standard loans or vendor financing, you will probably not be able take full advantage of the tax deductions, which makes it even harder to service the loan for an investment property.

If you cannot obtain a standard loan, you are usually better off renting and investing in shares and other investments.

Another problem is that vendor financing lacks the transparency of traditional financing due to the bundling of the sale of the property and the provision of finance in one package. Unfortunately, most buyers —especially the unsophisticated buyers targeted by wrappers and lease option sellers—do not have the expertise to unbundle the two components and price them separately to see the true costs, which are much more onerous than traditional financing.

Finally, vendor financing has much more credit risk than traditional financing, which reduces the security of your investment. The problem arises from the seller retaining the title of the property. If for some reason they are unable to make the repayments on their standard loan, their lender will take possession of the property, and you will lose the possibility of owning the property, regardless of the instalments you have already made.

# Choosing a loan

Magnification is a long-term wealth-creation strategy, not a tax-minimisation strategy. Therefore, you should try to minimise your loan cost. Saving one percentage point on a $400 000 loan saves $4000 in interest *each year*. Most people do not think about their interest cost when property prices are rising and everyone is a winner. However, if you focus on getting the lowest cost loan from the start, you will be able to achieve your financial goals much quicker. This might mean giving up some fancy features, which only save you a few dollars in the short term but cost thousands in extra interest over the long term.

## Sources of funds

You can borrow money for residential property from two primary sources of funds:

▸ Traditional lenders, such as banks (ANZ, Commonwealth Bank, NAB, Westpac and so on), building societies and credit unions that source approximately half of their funds from their deposit base and half from wholesale funding in the domestic and global capital markets. When the funding arrangements expire, they roll them over (refinance).

▶ Non-traditional lenders, such as mortgage originators (Aussie Home Loans, Wizard, and so on) that source all of their funds from the wholesale funding markets.

The entry of the non-traditional lenders has led to increased competition in the mortgage market, resulting in lower borrowing cost and loan products with more features. Both traditional lenders and non-traditional lenders can deal either directly with borrowers or through mortgage brokers who offer home loan products from a number of lenders, including traditional and non-traditional lenders. Although mortgage brokers can help borrowers compare interest rates and loan features from a number of different lenders, they are remunerated through upfront commissions (0.5 to 0.7 per cent of the loan value) and annual trailing commissions (0.15 to 0.25 per cent of the loan value) by the lender, and so might not recommend the best loan product if it pays no commission.

## Lowest interest rate

The best loan is usually the cheapest loan—the one with the lowest comparison rate. The comparison rate is an equivalent fee-free interest rate which allows consistent comparison between different loan products with different interest rate structures and fees. The easiest way to find the cheapest loan is to run your eye down a comparison table of home loans in the newspapers and on the internet (see the resources section at the back of this book). Check a number of different sources to make sure you have a good coverage of lenders. Start with the lender with the lowest comparison rate and see if the loan is suitable for your needs (for example, it might only be available to first home buyers, or the maximum loan is only $250000). If not, move on to the next cheapest one.

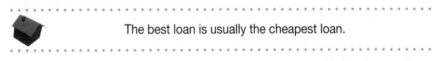

The best loan is usually the cheapest loan.

An alternative approach is to find out the standard variable rates of the Big 4 banks (see the resources section for more detail). Table 8.2 shows that the banks' standard variable rates at 8 August 2008 were around 9.61 per cent. Next, ask the banks for their *best* rates. Note that virtually no one nowadays pays the standard variable rate, with discounts ranging from 0.5 to 0.7 per cent or more. Finally, compare these best bank rates with the rates for other lenders and ask them if they can beat them. For example, Lender 1 had a variable rate of 8.82 per cent, which was a 0.79 per cent discount from the standard variable rate, and Lender 2 had a variable rate of 8.61 per cent, which was a whopping 1.00 per cent discount from the standard variable rate. Make sure you check that the lenders are not about to increase their rates from the quoted ones. For example, Lender 2 decided to hold their rates steady after all the other lenders increased their rates by 0.21 per cent.

Table 8.2: standard variable rates (8 August 2008)

| Lender | Standard variable rate |
|---|---|
| ANZ | 9.62% |
| Commonwealth Bank | 9.58% |
| NAB | 9.61% |
| Westpac | 9.61% |
| Lender 1: Std var. – 0.79% | 8.82% |
| Lender 2: Std var. – 1.00% | 8.61% |

Mortgage brokers will not usually have the cheapest loans because the interest rate needs to cover their commission. They might tell you that the lender pays for their commission, but the lender has to recoup it from somewhere. Furthermore, the amount of commission that different lenders pay them could bias their recommendations. If you are considering a mortgage broker, make sure you get them to disclose all of the upfront and ongoing trailing commissions they will earn from your loan first. Ask for this information both in percentage and dollar terms.

Some of the cheapest loans are rebadged direct loans from the banks. The banks can keep the interest rates on these loans low because they do not have to pay a commission to mortgage brokers or the costs of a branch. Examples include Homepath from the Commonwealth Bank and one direct from ANZ. Other cheap lenders sometimes source the funds from the banks and rebadge the loans, but use the banks' back-end infrastructure.

Some of the cheapest loans are rebadged
direct loans from the banks.

## Ignore the bells and whistles

Generally, extra features such as a mortgage offset account or a line of credit are not worth the extra interest cost over the basic interest rate. If you are unsure, calculate the cost compared to the benefit for yourself. For example, a mortgage offset account is a savings account linked to your loan account. The balance in the savings account is offset against the balance owing on the mortgage. So instead of earning a negligible interest rate, the savings account is in effect earning interest at the mortgage rate.

If you have a mortgage of $100000 at 7 per cent per annum and a spare $1000 in the mortgage offset account, the interest payable is only on $99000. This is a saving of $70 (7 per cent on $1000), since you would earn negligible interest on the $1000 if it was deposited in a bank transaction account. However, if the cost of having the mortgage offset account is an extra 0.25 per cent per annum, the total interest cost on the loan would be $7177.50 (7.25 per cent × $99000), compared with $7000 on a basic loan without the mortgage offset feature (7.0 per cent × $100000). You would be paying an extra $177.50 for the privilege of saving $70 in interest. Nowadays, the prevalence of online savings accounts paying high interest rates makes mortgage offset accounts even less viable. The use of a mortgage offset account can also have some tax benefits, but these are small compared to the higher interest cost.

## The features you really need

There are only a few features that you really need in a loan. If your situation is tight and you cannot manage if interest rates rise sharply, it is best to fix your loan for the first few years. Over time, as your income rises (salary and rent for an investment property), you have more of a buffer and can leave the rates variable. Otherwise, stick to variable interest rate loans. Some borrowers hedge their bets with a *split loan* that is part fixed and part variable. But if this involves paying a higher interest rate and additional fees, you are probably better off sticking with either a variable or fixed rate loan.

Use a principal and interest loan for your principal residence so you can pay off the loan as quickly as possible because the interest is not deductible. You can always tap into the available equity later on if you need it to piggyback into another property. For investment properties, use interest-only loans to maximise your tax deduction and conserve your cash flow to buy more properties.

## Fees

Fees are part of the cost of a loan. They can be incorporated into the interest rate or costed separately. The key is to negotiate the fees upfront before pre-approval, when you have more leverage because you can walk away. Ask for a discount and justify it with anything. For example, you deserve a discount because you are a professional or you have other business with the lender or you are taking out a large loan or a second loan with the lender. Remember, if you do not ask you will definitely not get a discount.

Fees include:

▸ Application or establishment fee of around $500 to $750 (can be waived).

▸ Legal fees, either included in the application fee or itemised separately (around $350).

▸ Valuation fee of around $250 (can be waived). Make sure you negotiate for a copy of the valuation report beforehand, especially if you have to pay for it.

▸ Ongoing account-keeping fee of $5 to $10 per month (can be waived).

▸ Discharge fee of around $300.

▸ Deferred establishment fee or exit fee that reduces on a sliding scale in the first five years (for example: 1 per cent of the loan value in the first three years, 0.5 per cent in the fourth year and 0.25 per cent in the fifth year).

▸ Mortgage stamp duty and registration fees, which are government charges.

▸ Small miscellaneous fees such as settlement fee, cheque fees, dishonour fees, progress payment fee and cancellation fee.

# Refinancing

Most of the people who refinance their loan only do so when interest rates rise. However, you should survey the market every six to twelve months to make sure that your loan is still competitive. In addition, you should refinance if your circumstances improve. For example, if you have secured a permanent job it will probably be worthwhile to refinance from a non-conforming loan to a standard loan.

If the interest rate on your loan is no longer competitive, the first step is to speak to your current lender and ask for a reduction in your interest rate. If this is not possible, ask whether you can switch to a lower rate product for no cost. You should always investigate this option first, because it is the cheapest. The lender will probably waive the exit fees and application fees, although there might be a switching fee.

If your current lender cannot accommodate you, do a cost–benefit analysis of whether it is worthwhile switching to a lower cost lender. The key factors to take into account are the deferred establishment costs (exit fees) of your current loan and the application fees of the new loan, and the interest rate differential. Most deferred establishment fees are staggered over the initial years, so when you are nearing the end of this term the comparison reduces to a comparison of the interest rate differential over the application fees. You can then work out how long it takes to break even and profit from switching. If you only have a small loan, it could take a while before you enjoy any of the benefits of refinancing.

### A small difference in interest can make a big difference

For seven years, I had one of the best loans around. It nearly always had the lowest interest rate — excluding first homeowners' loans, which I did not qualify for and are only for small amounts — and no fees of any kind except for a small settlement discharge fee. As an added bonus, it was fully featured, allowing me to borrow more without incurring any fees as my properties increased in value. The lender subsequently introduced a range of new fees, but did not grandfather them (apply them to existing borrowers).

One day another lender offered a rate 0.25 per cent cheaper than mine. After doing my due diligence on the lender, I decided to refinance some of my loans. The cost–benefit analysis I did was as follows.

**Cost**
Establishment fee: 0.15 per cent first year*
Exit fee: loan repaid in first three years: 1 per cent; fourth year: 0.5 per cent; fifth year: 0.25 per cent.

**Benefit**
New rate: 0.25 per cent cheaper each year.

Everything else was the same between the lenders.

Clearly, I would be worse off if I repaid my loans within the next four years. However, I was not planning to sell any of my properties any time soon, so I ended up saving 0.1 per cent in the first year and 0.25 per cent thereafter. For example, on a $400 000 loan this is a saving of $1000 each year.

* This consisted of the legal and valuation fees of the new lender and the settlement discharge fee of the old lender. Take the total fees and divide by the loan principal.

Note: I had many loans, and made sure to discharge them on the same day to incur the settlement discharge fee only once. However, make sure that you also spread your lenders, not because they might go bankrupt — you do not care because *they* are lending *you* money — but to spread your borrowing costs. That way, if the funding cost of a particular lender increases more than other lenders, and they pass on the increase to you, you will not face that increase across all of your loans.

# Paying off your debts

The quickest way to pay off debts is to start with the non–tax-deductible debt first and tackle the highest interest loans first. (Obviously, you will pay off your debts quicker if you have the lowest interest loan in the first place.) Paying off a loan generally only makes sense with your home loan because it is not tax deductible. Risk-averse buyers might try to pay off their home loan first before investing in anything else. This is generally not an optimal strategy. You might be better off using the funds to buy an investment property when the property market is in the Buying Zone. That way you have a larger investment base working for you, and you will be able to achieve your financial goals much faster.

> The quickest way to pay off your debts is to start with the non-tax-deductible debt first and tackle the highest interest loans first.

As you become more comfortable with the use of good debt, you will realise that there is no need to pay off the principal on any of the loans. This is because, over time, the balance outstanding remains the same, while the value of the property increases steadily over the long term. So while the loan-to-valuation ratio might be around 80 per cent now, in 20 years' time it might drop to 20 per cent after the property doubles in price twice, and then 5 per cent, and so on.

# Types of gearing

It can get very confusing when people talk about positive and negative gearing, let alone positive and negative cash flow. The easiest way to understand these terms is to look at a real estate investor's profit and loss and cash flow statements (see table 8.3). From the profit and loss statement, the gross rent (1) is the investor's 'revenue'. From this, holding costs (2) such as the property manager's commission, water and council rates, maintenance expenses and insurance premiums are deducted to give the net rent (3). Holding costs are *cash* expenses. From the net rent, interest (4) is subtracted to give the pre-tax cash flow (5). All of the items up to here involve the receipt or payment of cash.

Table 8.3: profit and loss and cash flow statements of a real estate investor

| Profit and loss | Cash flow | Funding source |
|---|---|---|
| 1 Gross rent | 1 Gross rent | Tenant |
| 2 Holding costs | 2 Holding costs | |
| 3 Net rent | 3 Net rent | |
| 4 Interest | 4 Interest | |
| 5 Pre-tax cash flow | 5 Pre-tax cash flow | |
| 6 Depreciation | 8 Tax credit/debit | Tax Office |
| 7 Pre-tax profit/loss | 9 After-tax cash flow | Investor |
| 8 Tax credit/debit | 10 After-tax cash flow p.w. | |

Depreciation (6) is a *non-cash* expense that is deducted from the pre-tax cash flow to give the pre-tax profit/loss (7) and hence the amount of tax payable. The pre-tax profit/loss is the investor's profit or loss, before considering tax, from the investment property. If it is a profit (positive), this is known as positive gearing. That is, positive gearing occurs when the rent covers *all* expenses and interest. If it is a loss (negative), this is known as negative gearing. That is, negative gearing occurs when the rent does not cover *all* expenses and interest.

> Positive gearing occurs when the rent covers *all*
> the expenses and interest and you make a profit.
> Negative gearing occurs when the rent does not cover
> *all* expenses and interest and you make a loss.

If you are positively geared, your pre-tax profit/loss is positive and you have to pay tax on it, which becomes a tax debit (8). If you are negatively geared, your pre-tax profit/loss is negative. You can deduct this loss against other sources of income to reduce your overall tax payable. This is your tax credit (8).

The cash flow statement is similar to the profit and loss statement but only takes cash items into account. The after-tax cash flow (9) is equal to the pre-tax cash flow (5) plus the tax credit/debit (8). If you are negatively geared and the after-tax cash flow is positive, you are negatively geared with positive cash flow, otherwise you are negatively geared with negative cash flow.

Thus, negative gearing with a positive cash flow occurs when the rent plus tax credit exceeds all *cash* expenses and interest. Negative gearing with a negative cash flow occurs when the rent plus tax credit does not cover all *cash* expenses and interest. If you are positively geared then you will always have positive cash flow. Figure 8.2 summarises the different types of gearing.

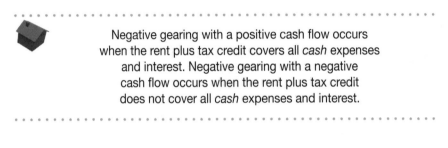

Negative gearing with a positive cash flow occurs when the rent plus tax credit covers all *cash* expenses and interest. Negative gearing with a negative cash flow occurs when the rent plus tax credit does not cover all *cash* expenses and interest.

Figure 8.2: types of gearing

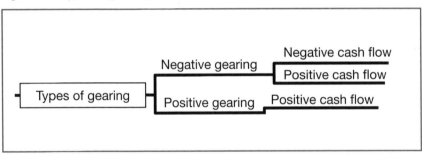

The point of all these different types of gearing and cash flow is:

▶ When you reach a positive cash flow situation (irrespective of the type of gearing), the property puts money in your pocket. If the cash flow is negative, you have to pay money from your pocket to support the property.

▶ If the gearing is positive, you have to pay tax on the profit from the property. If the gearing is negative, you get a tax refund from the loss on the property (if you have other income to offset the loss).

- An intermediate situation is negative gearing with positive cash flow. You make a loss and get a refund, but the property puts money in your pocket. The tax refund turns the negative cash flow into positive cash flow.

- Investment properties typically start out as negative gearing with negative cash flow. Over time, as the rent increases they become negative gearing with positive cash flow. As the rent increases even more, they become positive gearing with positive cash flow. While the property is negatively geared, the Tax Office helps you service the property with a tax refund on the loss if you have other income to offset the loss. When the property becomes positively geared, you have to pay tax on the property.

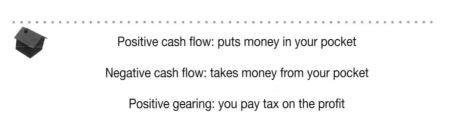

Positive cash flow: puts money in your pocket

Negative cash flow: takes money from your pocket

Positive gearing: you pay tax on the profit

Negative gearing: you get a tax refund on the loss

Negative gearing with negative cash flow ⇨
negative gearing with positive cash flow ⇨ positive gearing

## Positive cash flow

There are four ways to achieve a positive-cash-flow property:

- Put down a large deposit on the property so that the interest cost is small compared to the rent.

- Buy a property significantly below market value so that the interest cost is small compared to the rent.

- Find a property that pays a high rental yield.

- Buy a property in the Buying Zone when market value is less than intrinsic value.

The first point is not relevant because we need to compare properties with the same LVR, say 80 per cent, for the comparison to be meaningful. The second one is as rare as hen's teeth. In fact, I have never managed to buy one. Therefore, positive-cash-flow properties reduce to being high-rental-yield properties or properties bought during the Buying Zone. Even then, it is difficult to find positive-cash-flow properties.

From a funding perspective, positive gearing is better than negative gearing with a positive cash flow, which in turn is better than negative gearing with a negative cash flow. However, positive-cash-flow properties do not necessarily produce better overall returns than negatively geared properties because of the inverse relationship between capital growth and rental yield. Positive-cash-flow properties pay a higher rental yield than negatively geared properties, but have lower capital growth, while high-capital-growth properties have higher capital growth but a lower rental yield. However, the after-tax returns on negatively geared properties are higher than positive-cash-flow properties, all other things being equal (see 'The effect of tax' in chapter 9).

> From a funding perspective, positive cash flow is better than negative cash flow. However, the after-tax returns on negatively geared properties are higher than positive-cash-flow properties, all other things being equal.

Positive-cash-flow properties are rare because it does not make sense for tenants to pay more to rent than to service the mortgage on a property. In normal economic conditions, positive-cash-flow properties sometimes occur in:

▸ regional and rural areas with a declining population and hence low growth

▸ areas where rental demand is stronger than buying demand, such as mining towns that have a high workforce turnover

▸ the outer suburbs.

The properties in many regional and rural areas are priced on a high rental yield to compensate for the lack of growth from a declining population base. Despite the high rental yield, demand from locals is weak because they have only seen static or falling prices. During a real estate boom, investors from the city attracted by the high rental yield drive up prices and turn the positive cash flow properties into negatively geared ones. Out-of-area demand can be fleeting and masks the true local demand. If you buy on the back of out-of-area demand you are speculating based on the greater fool theory. That is, you are relying on even sillier buyers coming in after you to provide your return.

Areas with strong rental demand, such as mining towns, are dependent on a cyclical industry. When commodity prices are strong, everything is rosy, but when the cycle turns and commodity prices fall, there will be large lay offs, causing rents and property prices to plummet, and vacancy rates to soar. Most novices tend to buy these types of properties at top-of-the-cycle prices, which means that they will lose money over the long term. There are additional, specific risks that can affect property prices, such as the mine running out of reserves earlier than expected.

Properties in the outer suburbs of a city also pay a high rental yield to compensate for low growth. This stems from the relative low demand for these properties and high supply, since land is more readily available than in the inner suburbs. They are less risky than properties in regional and rural areas and mining towns, and so the rental yield on offer is lower. These properties are a secure way of entering the property market since the property is self-funding, and therefore any capital gains are a bonus. However, demand from investors has made these properties very scarce, and most now start out as negative gearing with negative cash flow.

Positive-cash-flow properties are self-funding,
and therefore any capital gains are a bonus.

## Negative gearing with negative cash flow

A much more common situation is negatively geared properties with negative cash flow. You make a loss initially, which you use to reduce income from other sources. The losses provide tax credits that lessen your cash flow burden. You fund the deficit out of your own pocket until rents rise enough for the property to be positive cash flow and then positively geared. When a property becomes positive cash flow, it becomes self-funding on a cash basis. That is, the rent is sufficient to cover the interest and all cash expenses. The excess cash flow can then be used to pay down the loan principal or buy more investments.

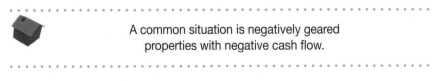

A common situation is negatively geared
properties with negative cash flow.

A property only becomes truly self-funding when it becomes positively geared. Then the rent is sufficient to cover the interest and all expenses, including depreciation (see 'Non-cash expenses' in chapter 9), since it is a cost that you will have to service one day. Note that you have to compare apples with apples with depreciation expenses as well. For example, a 40-year-old house with no depreciation expense left would be more positively geared than a newer house with a much bigger depreciation expense, all other things being equal. However, this does not make it more attractive financially than the newer house.

Negative gearing only works if two conditions are met:

▸ The future capital gains must be greater than the income loss for you to come out ahead in the end.

▸ You must have other sources of income or cash reserves to fund the negative cash flow until the property becomes self-funding. Otherwise, you might have to sell the property before you can reap the capital gains to offset your income loss.

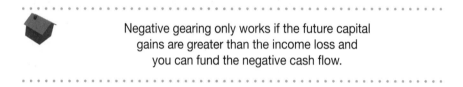

Negative gearing only works if the future capital gains are greater than the income loss and you can fund the negative cash flow.

# Servicing a property

Servicing the loan on a property and the holding costs can be tough when interest rates are high. However, the assistance of the tenant and the Tax Office makes it more manageable. The most important consideration is whether you can cover the after-tax cash flow.

## After-tax cash flow

Most investment properties start off as negatively geared with negative cash flow. This means that initially you have to contribute to the funding of the cash costs of the property. From table 8.3, dividing the after-tax cash flow (9) by 52 gives the after-tax cash flow per week (10), which is your weekly out-of-pocket cost of owning a negatively geared, negative-cash-flow investment property. The cash flow statement shows the three parties that service the cash costs of an investment property: the tenant pays the gross rent (1), the Tax Office contributes the tax credit (8), and you cover any residual amount; the after-tax cash flow (9).

Table 8.4 (overleaf) shows the profit and loss and cash flow statements of one of my properties in the first year of purchase (yes, I keep good records). My marginal tax rate was 47 per cent (plus the 1.5 per cent Medicare levy) over this time. In the first year, the property was negatively geared with positive cash flow. There is a large depreciation allowance because the property was new. This resulted in a large pre-tax loss of –$5151.24. However, I was able to use this loss to reduce the tax on my other income, giving me a tax credit of $2498.35. The tax credit is a tax refund that increased my pre-tax cash flow from –$1537.31 to an after-tax cash flow of $961.04, or $18.48 per week. That is, each week the property puts $18.48 in my pocket in addition to any unrealised capital gains. Note that I did not have to wait until the end of the financial year for the tax credit because I applied for an income tax variation (see 'Principal residence vs investment property' in chapter 9).

Table 8.4: profit and loss and cash flow statements: year 1

| Profit and loss | | Cash flow | |
|---|---|---|---|
| Gross rent | 8270.00 | Gross rent | 8270.00 |
| Holding costs | –2130.45 | Holding costs | –2130.45 |
| Net rent | 6139.55 | Net rent | 6139.55 |
| Interest | –7676.86 | Interest | –7676.86 |
| Pre-tax cash flow | –1537.31 | Pre-tax cash flow | –1537.31 |
| Depreciation | –3613.93 | Tax credit/debit | 2498.35 |
| Pre-tax profit/loss | –5151.24 | After-tax cash flow | 961.04 |
| Tax credit/debit | 2498.35 | After-tax cash flow p.w. | 18.48 |

Seven years later, the gross rent almost doubled (see table 8.5), and the value of the property increased by almost 150 per cent. The disparity in the growth rate of the property's value and the gross rent could be due to three factors: firstly, the property is overpriced; secondly, the rent increases have not caught up with the rise in property prices; and thirdly, the rental yield was high to start with. In reality, all three factors contributed to the disparity. Rents had been rising strongly, while prices had started to level off after a strong run. In addition, the suburb had transformed from a low demand–high yield suburb to a high demand–high growth suburb.

The combination of the increase in the gross rent with the reduction in the depreciation allowance turned a large pre-tax loss into a small pre-tax profit. Therefore, I now had to pay the Tax Office $116.04 in extra tax for the profit on the investment property. The tax debit reduces the pre-tax cash flow from $2777.81 to an after-tax cash flow of $2661.77, or $51.19 per week. Now each week the property puts $51.19 in my pocket in addition to any unrealised capital gains. Note that the interest expense has also risen, but this was due to interest rates rising from the lows of the cycle. In future, I expect interest rates to fluctuate around this seven-year range, while the gross rent will continue to rise.

Table 8.5: profit and loss and cash flow statements: year 8

| Profit and loss | | Cash flow | |
|---|---|---|---|
| Gross rent | 15080.00 | Gross rent | 15080.00 |
| Holding costs | –3839.12 | Holding costs | –3839.12 |
| Net rent | 11240.88 | Net rent | 11240.88 |
| Interest | –8463.07 | Interest | –8463.07 |
| Pre-tax cash flow | 2777.81 | Pre-tax cash flow | 2777.81 |
| Depreciation | –2538.55 | Tax credit/debit | –116.04 |
| Pre-tax profit/loss | 239.26 | After-tax cash flow | 2661.77 |
| Tax credit/debit | –116.04 | After-tax cash flow p.w. | 51.19 |

# Easier in the Buying Zone

Initially you could contribute anywhere from $20 to $100 per week to service your property. Over time, as the rent increases your contributions will become less and less, until one day the property pays you cash. The initial amount you have to contribute depends on the stage in the cycle that you purchased the property.

Servicing a property is much easier when you buy in the Buying Zone. If you buy in the Buying Zone, you might only have to contribute a few dollars per week or the property might even be negatively geared with positive cash flow. On the other hand, if you buy near the top of the cycle during the distribution stage you might have to pay hundreds of dollars each week to support the property. The reason for this is that while the *rent* increases relatively steadily over the cycle in line with the *intrinsic value* of the property (see figures 4.3 and 4.4; the sharp rise in rents in the mining capital cities from 2005 to 2008 due to the commodities boom is an anomaly), the *mortgage* and hence the *interest cost* you have to pay varies with the price of the property and hence moves in line with *market values* (see figure 8.3, overleaf).

Thus, you could be buying at 20 per cent below intrinsic value during the Buying Zone and hence borrowing 20 per cent less and paying 20 per cent less in interest. Or you could be overpaying by 20 per cent above intrinsic value at the top of the cycle, and hence borrowing 20 per cent more and paying 20 per cent more in interest. The price differential of up to 40 per cent of intrinsic value means that you might have to borrow 40 per cent more at the top of the cycle compared to the Buying Zone, and hence your interest cost will be 40 per cent more. However, the rent is the same (relative to intrinsic value), regardless of how much you borrow. Therefore, you could be out of pocket for $100 per week, instead of, say, $20 per week in the Buying Zone.

Figure 8.3: rent vs interest cost

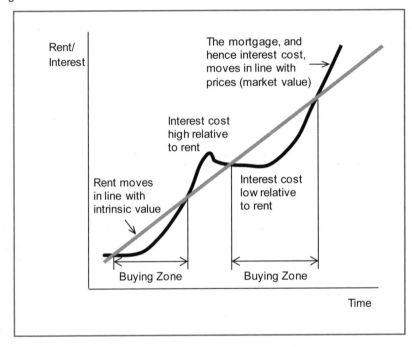

So not only does timing your purchase determine the extent of potential capital gains, it also determines how much money you have to contribute each week to service the mortgage on property.

# 9 Tax

Tax is our financial contribution to society. It is usually levied as a percentage of income, property value or value added, and is used by the government to pay for public projects and services such as roads, schools, national defence and welfare. It seems paradoxical, but paying tax is good. It means that you are on your way to achieving your financial goals. You should pitch in and pay your fair share of tax, but only what you have to, because tax is a cost that reduces your yield. Income and capital gains tax and GST are federal taxes (see <www.ato.gov.au> for more detail), while stamp duty and land tax are state taxes (see your state or territory Office of Revenue website in the resources section for further detail).

Paying tax is good — it means that you are on your way to achieving your financial goals.

## Income tax

Income tax is levied on taxable income, which is calculated as assessable income less all allowable deductions. Deductions consist of expenses incurred in the production of assessable income that are not of a capital nature. Generally, income is taxed only when it is received and expenses are allowed only when they are incurred.

Taxable income = Assessable income − Deductions

Gross tax = Tax rate × Taxable income

Tax payable = Gross tax − Offsets + Medicare levy

The tax rate levied depends on the level of your taxable income. Table 9.1 shows the current marginal tax rates—the tax rate levied on an additional dollar of income. The first $6000 you earn is tax-free. A 15 per cent marginal tax rate is levied on each dollar you earn between $6001 and $34000. The tax payable on incomes between $34001 and $80000 is $4200 (15 per cent of $28000) plus 30 per cent of each dollar earned between $34001 and $80000, and so on. In addition, a Medicare levy of 1.5 per cent is payable depending on the level of your income. Individuals and families on higher incomes who do not have appropriate private hospital cover have to pay the Medicare levy surcharge (1 per cent of taxable income), in addition to the Medicare levy. Tax offsets such as imputation credits reduce the amount of tax payable.

Table 9.1: marginal tax rates 2008–09

| Taxable income ($) | Tax ($) | Percentage on excess |
|---|---|---|
| 1–6000 | 0 | 15% |
| 6001–34000 | 4200 | 30% |
| 34001–80000 | 18000 | 40% |
| 80001–180000 | 58000 | 45% |

## Principal residence vs investment property

Your principal residence (the home you live in) does not generate any income, therefore the expenses incurred are not tax deductible. Investment properties, on the other hand, generate rental income, which is taxable, and therefore the costs incurred are tax deductible. If there is a net loss this can be used to reduce the tax payable on your other income. You can apply to the Tax Office for an income tax variation withholding (ITVW, formerly known as a 221D) to reduce your income tax withheld by your employer instead of waiting for a refund at the end of the year. Where your other income is insufficient to absorb the loss, it is carried forward to the next tax year.

The Tax Office provides a comprehensive document (*Rental Properties 2007* at the time of writing; see the resources section) each year to help property investors complete their tax return, including detail on how to treat hundreds of expense items. These costs can be categorised into cash and non-cash expenses.

## Cash expenses

The main cash expenses of investment properties include:

▶ Stamp duty on the property and other buying and selling costs, which are capital costs and are not deductible. When the property is sold they are added to the cost base of the property to reduce capital gains tax.

▶ Interest on the loan, which is deductible. For a principal and interest loan, only the interest component of the loan repayment is deductible. Note that when you build an investment property, the interest cost incurred during construction is capitalised. That is, it is added to the cost base of the property to reduce future capital gains tax, but is not deductible. You can prepay up to 12 months' interest in advance and claim a tax deduction in the current financial year.

▶ Borrowing costs. The loan application fee, valuation fee and loan stamp duty are deductible by spreading equally over the first five years of a loan, or the term of the loan if shorter.

▶ Loan discharge costs, which are deductible.

▶ The property manager's fees, which are deductible.

▶ Council and water rates, which are deductible.

▶ Insurance costs, which are deductible.

▶ The cost of travelling to inspect your investment property, which is deductible.

▶ Land tax on investment properties, which is deductible.

▶ Repair and maintenance costs, which are deductible. Maintenance involves the restoration of an item to its previous condition, and the replacement of part of an item rather than the whole item.

## Non-cash expenses

The non-cash expenses include the depreciation of:

▶ the building and capital works

► the fixtures (items fixed to the property such as kitchen cabinets and bathroom vanities) and fittings (items attached to the property such as light fittings and blinds).

From 16 September 1987, the construction cost of the building and structural improvements are depreciated at 2.5 per cent per annum over 40 years. When the property is sold, the depreciation allowance is (partially) clawed back through capital gains tax by reducing the cost base.

The cost of fixtures and fittings is depreciated according to their effective life either using the prime cost or diminishing value methods. If you are unable to precisely determine the costs, a quantity surveyor, whose fee is deductible, can provide you with a depreciation schedule for each item.

The prime cost method depreciates a fixed amount over the effective life of the item each year, while the diminishing value method depreciates a constant proportion of the remaining value each year. The diminishing value method usually starts with a higher depreciation value than the prime cost method but progressively reduces over time. Depreciation rates typically vary between 5 and 20 per cent. Your tax agent will choose the method that provides the greatest tax benefits in the initial years.

Investment properties incur capital gains tax like any other investment. Your principal residence, on the other hand, is exempt from capital gains tax. You can rent out your principal residence for up to six years, and provided that you do not claim another property as your principal residence during this time it is still considered your principal residence and is exempt from capital gains tax. In addition, if the property makes a loss you can offset this against other income like any other investment property. If you rent out the property for more than six years in a row, capital gains tax is payable on the proportion of the capital gain after the six years.

If you have difficulties servicing your principal residence, perhaps after a sharp rise in interest rates, one alternative to selling the property is to rent it out for a few years and rent a cheaper place for yourself. The extra rent and tax refund can be used to help service the mortgage. This option also saves on transaction costs, and if you rent the property out for less than six years you still retain the capital gains tax exemption. Similarly, if you have a deposit saved for a home but do not think that you can service the property, consider buying an investment property and renting for a while so that you get a tax refund to help you service the property. The downside is that there is no exemption for capital gains during the time that the property is rented out.

**I rent yours and you rent mine**

One of my colleagues adopted this strategy, with a twist. He and his brother could not afford to buy two properties after the strong rise in Sydney property prices in 2003, so they bought an older house together, demolished it and built a duplex. The twist was that they decided to rent each other's half, rather than living in their own, which allowed them to deduct the interest, depreciation and other expenses. The drawback of this strategy is that they forego the capital gains tax exemption on their principal residence if they ever decide to sell.

# Capital gains tax

A capital gain is the profit on selling an investment for more than its cost base. Unlike income, which is taxed as it is accrued, capital gains are only taxed when realised. An exception is your own home (your principal residence) and assets acquired before 20 September 1985, which are exempt from capital gains tax. Note that capital gains tax is triggered on exchange of contracts, not settlement. So if you exchanged contracts for an investment property on 30 June 2008 and settled on 11 August 2008, the capital gains are included in your 2008 financial year tax return.

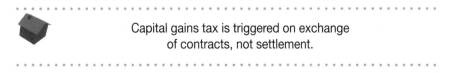

Capital gains tax is triggered on exchange
of contracts, not settlement.

Capital gains tax used to be levied on the *real* capital gains. That is, you were allowed to index the cost base of your investment to take inflation into account. On 21 September 1999, a simpler capital gains tax system was introduced with transitional arrangements. As long as you hold an investment for 12 months, you are only taxed at your marginal tax rate on half of the capital gains. Therefore, time is an important consideration for capital gains tax. If you are on the top marginal tax rate, when you sell can result in a difference of approximately 25 per cent of the capital gains (approximately 50 per cent × 50 per cent). For example, if you are on the top marginal tax rate and have an unrealised capital gain on an investment property bought 10 months ago, you should hold on to the property for at least another two months unless you think that its value will drop by 25 per cent or more of the gain. You should also consider the impact of transaction costs before deciding to sell.

In addition, there is a (partial) clawback of the building and capital works depreciation deductions when you sell because you have to reduce your cost base by those amounts. It is only a partial claw back because if you hold the property for more than 12 months the claw back is only at half your marginal tax rate, even though you deducted the expenditure at your marginal tax rate. You also benefit from the time value of money since the claw back occurs after the deduction, and only when you sell.

The best way to minimise capital gains tax is to hold on to your investments for as long as possible. Not only is the effective capital gains tax rate lower after 12 months, if you do not sell the investment you do not incur capital gains tax. Alternatively, since it is taxed at your marginal tax rate, try to defer selling to a year where your income is low, such as when you retire or go on maternity/paternity leave. Even then, do not realise all of the investments at once if possible, but stagger them over a number of years to minimise capital gains tax.

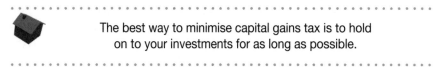

The best way to minimise capital gains tax is to hold on to your investments for as long as possible.

For example, an investor on the top marginal tax rate of 45 per cent (plus the 1.5 per cent Medicare levy) invests in a negatively geared property and makes a loss of $10 000 a year. He can deduct this loss against other income to get a tax refund of $4650, giving an after-tax loss of $5350. This is offset by the increase in the property's value that results in an unrealised capital gain of $10 000. On a pre-tax basis, there is no change in the investor's net worth (−$10 000 + $10 000 = 0). However, on an after-tax basis, there are three possibilities:

▸ The investor sells the property within 12 months. He has to pay capital gains tax of $4650 on the full capital gains of $10 000, giving an after-tax profit of $5350. On an after-tax basis there is no change in the investor's net worth (−$5350 + $5350 = 0).

▸ The investor sells the property after 12 months. He only has to pay capital gains tax on half of the capital gain of $10 000 ($2325 = 46.5 per cent × $5000), giving an after-tax profit of $7675. On an after-tax basis, the investor's net worth increases by $2325 (−$5350 + $7675 = $2325). This is possible because he can deduct the full loss at his marginal tax rate, but capital gains tax is only levied on half of the capital gains at his marginal tax rate because he held the investment property for more than 12 months.

▸ The investor does not sell the property. Therefore, he does not have to pay any capital gains tax. On an after-tax basis, the investor's net worth increases by \$4650 (–\$5350 + \$10 000 = \$4650). In reality, the investor is even better off under this scenario than the other two because he does not incur any transaction costs, which are significant for real estate.

Capital gains are more tax-efficient than income. Therefore, you can reduce the amount of tax payable by minimising your income and maximising your capital gains because of the different tax treatment. Companies in the United States try to do this by paying out a low dividend yield, because US dividends are taxed under the classical (double-taxation) system. You can copy this approach by gearing into high-growth investments that pay a low income yield, such as high-growth real estate. Note that this strategy is not restricted to high-growth real estate; it also applies to high-growth stocks, for example.

> You can reduce the amount of tax payable by minimising your income and maximising your capital gains because of the different tax treatment.

In the initial years you will make an income loss, which is deductible at your marginal tax rate, and is known as negative gearing (see 'Types of gearing' in chapter 8). However, the key to this strategy is not the negative gearing but taking advantage of the different tax treatment between income and capital gains. Negative gearing just helps you service the loan in the initial years. Over time, the rental income will increase and the property will become cash flow positive. The strategy will still be beneficial because the bulk of the property's return will still come from capital growth instead of rental income. The risk with this strategy is that too many investors adopt it, bidding prices up so that the future capital gains are insufficient to offset the income loss.

> The key to this strategy is not the negative gearing, but taking advantage of the different tax treatment between income and capital gains.

# The effect of tax

Tax reduces your yield, and more importantly it reduces the effectiveness of compounding. I showed before how increasing the rate of return on your investment increases your proceeds exponentially (see 'The power of compounding' in chapter 4). Similarly, reducing the rate of return on your investment reduces your proceeds exponentially. As a result, you have to invest for longer to achieve the same level of returns. Thus, tax robs you of time.

For example (see figure 9.1), assume that you invested $500000 (the value of a median three-bedroom house in Sydney) today and it increases in value by 10 per cent per annum. At 10 per cent per annum, the value of your investment doubles approximately every seven years (see 'The Rule of 72' in chapter 4), increasing to $1000000 in year 7 and $2000000 in year 14. At the end of 30 years, it is worth $8700000. However, if your return of 10 per cent per annum is taxed at the highest marginal tax rate of 45 per cent (plus the 1.5 per cent Medicare levy), you are left with an after-tax return of only 5.4 per cent per annum. At 5.4 per cent per annum, the value of your investment doubles every 13 years, increasing to $1000000 in year 13 and $2000000 in year 27. At the end of 30 years, it is worth $2400000. If you needed to turn the $500000 into $1000000 to retire, for example, then tax has effectively robbed you of six years (year 13 – year 7).

Figure 9.1: the effect of tax (highest marginal tax rate)

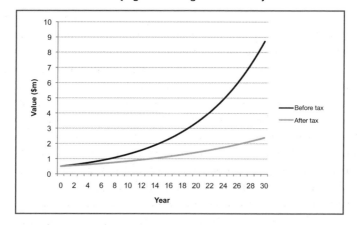

The effect of tax on investment properties is not as clear-cut as the previous example. Firstly, the returns from real estate comprise the rental income and capital growth of the property. The rental income is taxed each year at your marginal tax rate while the capital growth is only taxed when you sell the property, and only at effectively half of your marginal tax rate if you hold it for more than 12 months. In addition, there are holding costs and interest costs to deduct against the rental income and other income.

However, the same principle still applies. The most effective way to minimise the effect of tax on your returns is to focus on high-capital-growth properties over high-rental-yield properties, provided both are priced to provide the same yield. This is because most of their returns are in the form of capital growth, which is only taxed when you sell. If you never sell you do not incur any capital gains tax. Even if you eventually sell, as long as you hold for more than 12 months the capital gains will only be taxed at effectively half of your marginal tax rate. On the other hand, the returns from high-rental-yield properties are mainly in the form of rental income, which is taxed at your full marginal tax rate every year.

### The Warren Buffett way

Warren Buffett's phenomenal returns of over 20 per cent per annum in the stock market over 50 years are mainly due to his strategy of buying and holding *high-growth* stocks and rarely selling them, so he incurs very little tax.

You can copy Buffett's strategy by buying high-capital-growth properties instead of high-rental-yield properties, and never selling them.

For example, let's suppose Investor A buys a $500 000 one-bedroom apartment near Bondi Beach, while Investor B buys five $100 000 three-bedroom houses in one of the regional areas and both investors are on the highest marginal tax rate. Assume that both properties are priced to provide a 10 per cent per annum yield. However, the Bondi apartment pays a 2 per cent rental yield with 8 per cent coming from capital growth, while the houses in the regional area pay a 10 per cent rental yield, with no capital growth expected due to the declining population. If neither investor sells over the next 30 years, the before-tax return of both investors will be close to the before-tax graph in figure 9.1. However, the after-tax return of Investor A will be close to the before-tax graph as well, because she only pays tax on a small rental yield, while the after-tax return of Investor B will be close to the after-tax graph, since all of his return is in the form of rental income, and is taxed. Most types of properties fall between these two extremes, so their after-tax returns will fall somewhere between the two graphs.

Obviously if all investors target high-growth properties and push their prices above fair value, while the prices of high-rental-yield properties fall below fair value due to a lack of demand, then you might be better off focusing on high-rental-yield properties. For example, suppose every investor piles into high-growth properties, pushing the price of the Bondi apartment to $1 000 000 so that its yield is now only 5 per cent per annum. At the same time, the lack of interest in the three-bedroom houses in the regional area results in their prices falling to $50 000 each, so that their yield is now 20 per cent per annum. The three-bedroom houses in the regional area are now much more attractive than the Bondi apartment on a before- *and* after-tax basis.

## Comparing pre-tax returns

The income yields on different types of investments can only be compared validly when it is done on the same basis. Different types of investments have different tax treatment on their income yields, although they all have the same capital gains tax treatment (with a few exceptions, such as your principal residence is capital-gains-tax free). Franked dividends are after tax (at the corporate rate), while rents and interest income are pre-tax. To compare different types of income yields, it is easiest to add back any tax paid to compare them on a pre-tax basis. For shares, the pre-tax income yield is the dividend paid plus the imputation credit, called the grossed-up dividend yield.

The interest on the mortgage on your principal residence is not tax deductible, hence the equivalent pre-tax return is higher than most people realise because they are paying the interest off from their after-tax income. The equivalent pre-tax return is:

Interest rate ÷ (1 – Marginal tax rate)

For people on the top marginal tax rate, the pre-tax yield from paying off their mortgage is roughly two times the interest rate. Figure 9.2 shows the equivalent pre-tax return on paying off the 7 per cent interest on a mortgage for different marginal tax rates.

Figure 9.2: equivalent pre-tax return on a 7 per cent mortgage

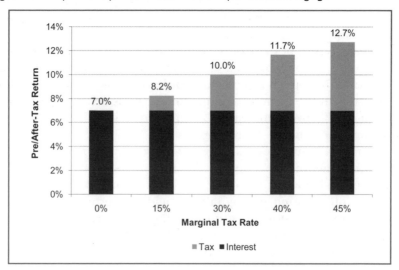

## Pay off non-deductible debt

The interest on non-deductible debt has to be paid out of your after-tax income, which on a pre-tax basis is effectively double the rate for people on the highest marginal tax rate. Consumer debts, such as credit cards, charge up to 17 per cent or more, which on a pre-tax basis can be over 30 per cent. Paying off consumable debt can be one of the best investments that you ever make because it provides a very high equivalent pre-tax return with zero risk. You should pay off the debt with the highest interest rate first, which typically is credit card debt. Obviously, you should avoid consumable debt in the first place.

An extension to this principle is to pay off the principal of the mortgage on your principal residence first, before paying off the principal on the mortgage of any investment properties, as the interest on your principal residence is not tax deductible. The easiest way to do this is to use interest-only loans for all investment properties and a principal and interest loan for your principal residence. Use any spare money to accelerate the repayment of the principal on your principal residence.

The only exception to paying off the mortgage on your principal residence is if the property market is in the Buying Zone and you can afford to buy another property. Then you are better off conserving your cash flow to service the new investment property until it becomes self-sustaining. This way, you will have a larger asset base working for you and you will be able to achieve your financial goals quicker.

## GST

The sale of existing residential property or land is not subject to GST, the 10 per cent goods and services tax. GST only applies to the cost of new residential property purchased directly from a developer. It is also included in the price for the construction of a new property. The services associated with the purchase or sale of a property, such as the agent's commission, attract GST. Similarly, while rents are GST-free, the services associated with property management, such as the property manager's commission, attract GST.

## Stamp duty

Stamp duty is a state tax levied on the transfer of property. The contract of sale is rubber-stamped to show that the buyer has paid the stamp duty. The amount of stamp duty varies by state and whether the property is the principal residence or an investment property. Table 9.2 (overleaf) shows the stamp duty payable on a $300 000 and a $500 000 investment property in each state at 31 July 2008.

First home buyers in some states are entitled to a reduction in stamp duty. For example, in New South Wales no stamp duty is payable on properties up to $500 000. Furthermore, in Victoria, and only Victoria, stamp duty is calculated on the proportion of construction completed when the property is purchased. This can result in tens of thousands of dollars in savings in stamp duty for off-the-plan purchases.

Table 9.2: stamp duty by state/territory (31 July 2008)

| Purchase price | $300 000 | $500 000 |
| --- | --- | --- |
| New South Wales | $8 990 | $17 990 |
| Victoria | $13 070 | $25 070 |
| Queensland | $8 925 | $15 925 |
| Western Australia | $8 835 | $17 765 |
| South Australia | $11 330 | $21 330 |
| Tasmania | $9 550 | $17 550 |
| Northern Territory | $10 414 | $23 929 |
| Australian Capital Territory | $9 500 | $20 500 |

# Land tax

Land tax is a state tax levied on the total land value held by an individual in that state (except in the Northern Territory) that exceeds a threshold (except in the ACT). For example, in New South Wales the land tax rate for 2008 is 1.6 per cent (plus $100) on the combined value of all taxable land in excess of the $359 000 threshold. The threshold and tax rate varies for each state and territory (see your Office of State Revenue website in the resources section for more detail). The land value of your principal place of residence is usually exempt up to a certain value. Land tax affects houses much more than townhouses and apartments due to the higher land content.

Although land tax is a cost of being in the real estate business, most people underestimate its significance. In states such as New South Wales, where the value of a house is skewed towards the land value, land tax can reduce your yield by 1 per cent per annum. Compared to net rental yields of 2 to 4 per cent per annum, this is a significant cost. The best way to minimise your land tax bill is to spread your property portfolio around the country to take advantage of the tax-free threshold in each state.

For example, assume that the tax-free thresholds of State A and State B are $200 000 and $300 000 respectively. If you own two investment properties with land value of $250 000 each in State A, you are liable for land tax on the $300 000 land value over the tax-free threshold ($250 000 + $250 000 – $200 000). But if one of the properties was in State A and the other in State B, you would only be liable for land tax on the $50 000 land value over the tax-free threshold in State A ($250 000 – $200 000). You would incur no land tax in State B since the land value is below that state's tax-free threshold.

Unlike stamp duty, which is a one-off charge when you purchase the property, land tax must be paid every year that you own the property. As a result, land tax is a tax-deductible expense, while stamp duty (on investment properties) is added to your cost base. Furthermore, land tax is only payable on the land value, whereas stamp duty is payable on the total property value.

# 10 Bringing it together

**SYSTEM T™** is an investment framework where you can use the individual components to build your real estate portfolio. However, your results will be much more effective when you use all the components together. The following formula is a simplistic representation of how **SYSTEM T™** works to build your property portfolio.

If you start with **E** dollars in equity and you gear it up **m** times and invest it in real estate for **T** years, and the average net yield on your property portfolio is **y** per cent per annum and your tax rate is **t** per cent per annum and your chance of success is **s**, then your expected proceeds will be:

Proceeds = $s \times m \times E \times [1 + y \times (1 - t)]^T$ – Total interest cost

**E** is your initial equity, money that either you saved up or was 'loaned' to you by your parents who let you piggyback on their home.

**m** is the magnification ratio, or how much you gear up your equity (**m** = Property value ÷ **E**). For example, if you put down a deposit of $100 000 and borrow another $400 000 to buy a $500 000 property, your **m** is 5.

**y** is the average net yield on your property portfolio (capital growth plus net rental yield). Buying in the Buying Zone will boost your yield, while buying at the top of the market will reduce your yield or even turn it negative. In addition, doing the boring things such as minimising your holding costs and interest costs will boost your yield and reduce your total interest cost respectively, which boosts your proceeds.

**t** is your average effective tax rate each year, which reduces your after-tax yield. It depends on your marginal tax rate, but more importantly whether you incur any tax or not. For example, if you just buy and hold high-capital-growth properties your **t** will be very low. On the other hand, if your strategy is to flip high-rental-yield properties your **t** will be high, for the same marginal tax rate.

**T** is the number of years you invest your equity in the property market. The earlier you start and longer you invest, the more you benefit from the power of compounding.

**s** measures the security of your property portfolio as a probability between 0 and 1. Multiplying the other components by **s** gives you the expected proceeds. That is, the higher the security, the better your chances of achieving the full proceeds.

Finally, spread enters into the equation by increasing the security of your portfolio while maintaining the same expected yield. So think of **s** as standing for both security and spread.

Total interest cost is the total interest you incur on the debt in your property portfolio over **T** years.

Like most things in life, too much of the **SYSTEM T**™ components can be bad for you because they involve trade-offs. Remember, there are no free lunches. For example, you might be wondering, 'Couldn't I shortcut the investment process by increasing my magnification ratio from the usual 5 to 20, or infinity, by taking out a high LVR loan?' No, because borrowing too much reduces the security of your investment to an unacceptable level. If interest rates rise by 50 per cent (which they did in 2007–08) or you lose your job and are unable to service the property, you will lose the property. So increasing magnification comes at the cost of reducing security.

In summary:

▸ Increasing security reduces yield. For example, some people are too scared to invest in the real estate market (or the stock market), and instead leave their savings in term deposits. They have more security in the short term, but this comes at the cost of reducing their yield. In addition, this might lead to lower security over the long term because they are unable to meet their financial goals.

▸ Increasing yield reduces security. For example, you might consider speculating on real estate in developing countries to improve your yield. If all goes well you might achieve yields of 50 per cent per annum for many years. However, if things do not turn out as expected you could lose everything. So increasing yield comes at the cost of reducing security. Increasing yield also increases tax by increasing income tax and capital gains tax when you sell.

▸ Increasing spread increases security for a given yield, or increases yield for a given level of security.

▶ Increasing time increases security because it smooths out the volatility in property prices and interest rates, and increases yield because you have more time for compounding to work for you. Time also reduces tax because you only have to pay capital gains tax on half of the gains if you hold the investment for more than 12 months.

▶ Increasing equity reduces magnification because you do not have to borrow as much. It increases security because you can better weather the volatility in property prices and interest rates, but reduces yield because your return on equity will be lower since you are holding more equity. Increasing equity also reduces time because it takes longer to save for a bigger deposit.

▶ Increasing magnification increases yield because you can have more properties working for you. However, this comes at the cost of reducing security. Increasing magnification also reduces income tax because the interest expense is deductible.

▶ Increasing tax reduces your after-tax yield. For example, if you sell an investment property you incur capital gains tax, which reduces your after-tax yield.

# Part III:
# The buying process

The hardest part about getting into real estate is the buying process. If you do not know what you are doing it can take a long time. When I conducted an informal survey of family and friends, I found that it took them from 'over two months' to 'over a year' of looking before they purchased. Moreover, they all use a buying process that is very different to mine. They spend all of their time inspecting properties, whereas I spend the bulk of my time at my desk on research.

If the property market is in the Buying Zone you can start the buying process. The buying process starts with pre-approval of your loan so that you do not waste your time looking at properties that you cannot afford. Next, spend most of your time researching when, where, and what property you should buy and how much you should pay for it. Only then should you conduct your inspections. After you inspect each property, try to determine a valuation for it based on the sum of the land and building value. That way, you will be much more informed in your negotiations with the seller or bidding at auction.

When your offer is accepted under a private treaty sale, you have to decide whether you want to exchange contracts right away to take the property off the market or wait until you are satisfied with your building and pest inspections and obtain final approval of your loan before proceeding. Each state and territory provides a property buying guide with specific detail for that state or territory that complements the buying process I describe here (see the resources section for more detail).

I include in the appendix a comprehensive example of one of my recent property purchases to demonstrate each of the main steps in the buying process.

# 11 Pre-approval

You should resist the urge to inspect properties before you get pre-approval for a loan because you could be wasting your time looking at properties that you cannot afford. A pre-approval, also known as an approval in principle or a conditional approval, occurs when a lender is satisfied with your preliminary financial information (income, assets and liabilities), and determines that you qualify for a loan. A pre-approval does not guarantee that the lender will lend you the money. After pre-approval, the lender asks for more detailed information, such as past tax returns, to verify the preliminary information and underwrite your credit risk.

Even when this is satisfactory, the loan will still be subject to valuation. Never commit to buying a property until the loan approval is *unconditional*. Most of the time the valuation will be satisfactory, as the price represents fair market value. The price becomes the new market value. However, sometimes the valuation will indicate that the price is excessive. The lender may choose to reject the loan application because the property value does not sufficiently secure the loan. If you have not committed to the property you can just walk away with a small loss (usually the 0.25 per cent deposit to the seller and possibly building and pest inspection costs and conveyancing costs). Do not use a pre-approval to purchase a property at auction.

Never commit to buying a property until
the loan approval is *unconditional*.

The advantages of pre-approval are:

▸ You have an indication of how much you can borrow, so you know what price ranges to look at.

▸ It shows the seller and agent that you are a serious buyer.

▸ When you find the right property, you can quickly secure it after the lender is satisfied with the valuation, since they are already familiar with your financial situation and only have to verify this (if they have not already done so) and the property's value.

▸ You are not committed to the lender until you sign all of the final paperwork.

Make sure you negotiate the interest rate and all fees upfront during pre-approval when your bargaining power is strongest. The fees usually occur in three stages—application, maintenance and exit, under various names—so make sure you have them all covered. If you leave things until the unconditional stage, your bargaining power will evaporate because you will not have time to apply for another loan during the cooling-off period.

# 12 Research

Research is the most important stage in the buying process. Therefore, you should spend most of your time and effort on research. Research helps you answer the three 'W' questions and the big 'H' question: when to buy, where to buy and what to buy, and how much to pay. Research will also provide you with qualitative information to support your decision-making process, such as local information. An important part of the research process is befriending agents and picking their brains on the state of the local real estate market. Sometimes the research will only uncover bits and pieces of information, which might not be useful in themselves but the combination of many disparate pieces of information can give you a comprehensive picture.

## The 80/20 Principle

The 80/20 Principle of buying real estate states that you should spend at least 80 per cent of your time doing research and 20 per cent of the time physically inspecting properties. Most people spend almost 100 per cent of their time inspecting properties. As you become a more experienced real estate buyer, you will find that you will spend more time on research and less time on inspections. In fact, experienced real estate investors are comfortable buying properties sight unseen, after comprehensive research and building and pest inspections.

Spending all your time going to inspections is like firing all the time to try to hit a target. Experienced property investors, on the other hand, spend most of their time aiming. They only fire at the targets they want or think that they have a reasonable chance of hitting. If you follow the right sequence of doing research and then inspecting properties, not only will you use your time more efficiently but you will also purchase more effectively and save yourself money in the process.

## When to buy: the Buying Zone

You should only buy when the real estate market is in the Buying Zone, during the accumulation stage and early uptrend when market value is less than intrinsic value. Each state is a different property market with a different cycle, so use the median prices for the relevant state to determine the Buying Zone. Figure 12.1 shows that Sydney median house prices peaked at the end of 2003 and the accumulation stage started around 2006. However, the early uptrend was already well underway in the inner ring suburbs by 2007, while the outer suburbs were still in the distribution phase.

Figure 12.1: Sydney median house price trend[1]

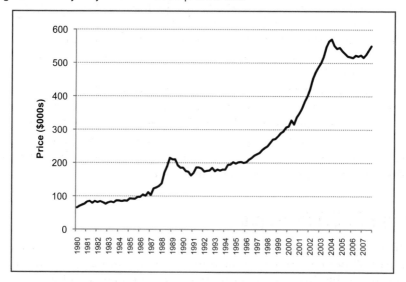

## Where to buy: drilling down to suburb level

You should aim to buy as close to the CBD and water as your budget will allow, because this is where the greatest capital growth occurs, driven by high demand and fixed supply.

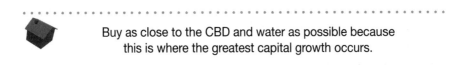

Buy as close to the CBD and water as possible because
this is where the greatest capital growth occurs.

The market cycle comprises all the individual suburb property cycles. The inner ring suburbs usually lead the property market cycle, followed by the middle ring and then the outer ring (this is the ripple effect). Therefore, even when the property market cycle is in the Buying Zone some suburbs might be leaving the Buying Zone, while others might not have arrived yet. You can finetune your entry at the suburb level by selecting the suburbs that are in the Buying Zone.

Figure 12.2 shows the quarterly trend in median house prices in one of the suburbs that I looked at. The suburb was in an uptrend from 1997 to 2003, distribution occurred in 2003 and 2004, followed by a short downtrend in 2004 and 2005, and accumulation appears to have resumed in 2006 and 2007. I decided to purchase a property in this suburb in 2007 because it was in the Buying Zone. Some data providers, such as RP Data, supply free suburb profile reports that show yearly median price trends over the last 10 years that are sufficient to determine the stage of the property cycle for each suburb using graphical analysis.

Figure 12.2: suburb median house price trend[2]

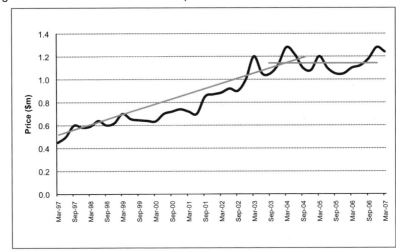

You might think that starting with the property market cycle is an unnecessary step, and instead go straight to the suburb property cycle. However, I do not encourage this because the suburb property cycle is more volatile; there are fewer sales, and median price trends can be masked by external factors such as council changes to suburb boundaries. You will get a more reliable picture of overall trends by looking at the market first, and then drilling down to suburb level.

You can also use suburb median price trends to optimise your suburb selection using graphical analysis. Figure 12.3 shows that while both of the adjoining Suburbs A and B were in the Buying Zone in 2007, Suburb A had already begun its uptrend, while Suburb B was still in the accumulation stage. (Coincidentally, the boundary between Suburb A and Suburb B is considered the boundary between the inner and middle rings.) The opportunity for capital growth over the next 10 years will probably be greater for Suburb B than Suburb A because prices have not taken off yet, and therefore Suburb B might offer a better yield.

It follows that if you miss the boat in a particular suburb you should look to the adjoining suburbs that are still in the Buying Zone. For example, say you only manage to save a deposit two years later in 2009. Suburb A would now be well into its uptrend and out of the Buying Zone. However, Suburb B would just be starting its uptrend and be within the Buying Zone. You want to buy in Suburb A but you have missed the boat, so you should look for properties in Suburb B, which is next to Suburb A and still in the Buying Zone.

Figure 12.3: comparing adjoining suburb median house price trends[3]

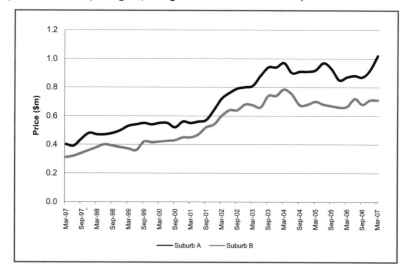

## What to buy

The most important buying consideration is to target properties with the greatest rental and sales demand: properties that are representative of the area and around the median price. You should also take into account changes in future demand, as this will drive the long-term yield of your property (both the capital growth and rental income).

## Appropriate for the area

As I discussed earlier, the property you are considering should be appropriate for the area to make it easy to rent out or sell if necessary. For example, a three- or four-bedroom house is the most common type of property in the outer suburbs of the capital cities, not a two-bedroom house or an apartment. Apartments are the norm in the inner suburbs of Sydney and Melbourne. In the outer suburbs, two-car garages are standard, whereas in the inner suburbs a parking spot is usually considered a luxury.

## Goldilocks principle

Investors should focus on median-priced properties that are not too expensive but not too cheap either. They have the greatest sales and rental demand. Expensive properties are unsuitable for a number of reasons. They are usually large and unique so rental demand is low, and they can remain vacant for months. The rental yield is also low, making it difficult to support the property. In addition, prices are more volatile. During boom times, prices can significantly overshoot intrinsic values. If you buy during these times, you could face large losses when the property market cools off. In contrast, in a downturn expensive properties are very difficult to sell or rent.

Very cheap properties are cheap for a reason. They are usually located in an undesirable location, such as next to a busy road or a railway line, and are too small or in poor condition. They are difficult to rent (and sell) and might attract tenants that do not pay the rent on time or look after the property. The property might also have structural problems that require remedial work before the property can be tenanted.

## Future demand

The future demand for housing will be influenced by the trends in Australia's demographics. Australia has around five and a half million baby boomers born between 1946 and 1964. Over the next 20 years, as the baby boomers move into retirement they will downsize their high-maintenance suburban homes to townhouse and apartment developments within their local community and in the inner suburbs. They will also drive demand for lifestyle property, such as townhouses and apartments near the coast and golf courses. These changes will probably show up in Adelaide first as it has a higher proportion of elderly people than the other cities.

The other major demographic trend is the increase in the number of Australians living alone and in single-parent families due to low birth rates and increased longevity, delayed marriage and high divorce rates. These small households will drive demand for small apartments near the city and in trendy suburbs, at the expense of large houses in the outer suburbs. Paradoxically, as household size shrinks, the size of new houses continues to grow. While they might cater for current demand, these houses are less suited to meet the needs of future demand. So why do *I* buy houses? Because catering for the future demand for townhouses and apartments requires land, and that is where my houses with their high land content come in.

## Desirable features

Ideally, the property will have some or most of the desirable features that tenants and other buyers look for:

▸ Within walking distance of transport (up to 10 minutes), but not next to it.

▸ Plenty of living space.

▸ Off-street parking.

▸ Room/space for a study or home office; there is increasing demand for this with the trend towards working from home.

▸ Light, with a north to rear aspect.

▸ Outdoor entertaining area. This can include a patio, deck, courtyard or balcony with room for a barbeque.

▸ Street appeal.

# Bird's-eye view

Once you have found a target suburb that is in the Buying Zone and is as close to the CBD and water as you can afford, you can start researching the suburb. Begin with a bird's-eye view of the suburb to get some perspective. Use an online map (see figure 12.4 for an example) or a street directory and look through the suburb, noting transport routes (railway lines and main roads), schools, shopping centres and parks. Some online maps allow you to zoom in and get a feel for the subdivisions in the suburb, such as the average block size. As you discover new things about the suburb (such as bus routes), mark them on your map. Talk to the local agents, find out where the blue-ribbon area and the best streets are, and highlight them on the map. Then get in your car and drive around the suburb to see all the marked features.

Figure 12.4: bird's-eye view of Spring Hill, Brisbane[4]

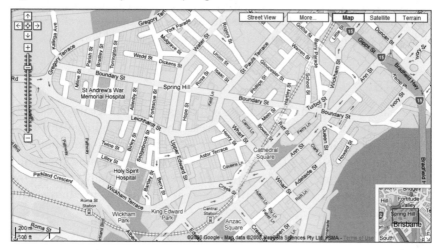

# Local information

Qualitative local information is useful for explaining price statistics, and will augment your decision-making process. For example, understanding the socioeconomic status of a suburb will help you buy the appropriate property for the area and avoid overcapitalising. Local information is also valuable for risk management when it highlights exceptions and problems.

You can source local information from:

▸ The local paper. Is the coverage of schools in the area positive (such as academic and sporting achievements and community service) or negative (such as vandalism and violence)? Is crime a major issue? Is the paper critical or complimentary of the council? What issues does the editor highlight? What are the concerns and complaints of locals in their letters to the editor?

▸ The council website is a valuable source of local information on planning, building and development, services, recreation and the environment.

▸ Real estate data providers supply free reports on the profile of a suburb, such as the age and sex demographics and household income bands, structure and occupancy (owner-occupied versus renting).

▸ Hairdressers, newsagents and other small businesses are a wealth of local information.

In addition, when you drive around the suburb you will get an appreciation of the profile of the land (level or sloping), architectural style, and condition and upkeep of the properties.

# Agents

The real estate agents should be your best friends because of their intimate knowledge of sales in the area. The way to achieve this is to change the usual real estate paradigm: get the agents to compete for your business, instead of competing for theirs. The more experience you have, the more you know and the more professionally you act (for example, by using their jargon), the easier it will be to change the paradigm.

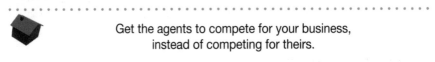

Get the agents to compete for your business,
instead of competing for theirs.

Approach a number of agents with a clear specification of the type of property you are looking for, such as the location, number of bedrooms, condition and price range. Give them a copy of your pre-approval letter to show that you are a serious buyer. (Do not tell them your budget because you do not want to reveal all your cards.) They will take you to inspect the listings they have that fit your criteria. Take the opportunity to ask questions, and learn as much as you can from the agent about sales and prices in the area. Let them know that you will also be talking to other agents and seeing their listings as well.

Each time you see another agent, you bring the knowledge gathered from all the previous ones. Eventually you will be able to deal with each agent on nearly similar terms, as if he or she were dealing with another agent. One technique you can use is to mirror the 'moves' of an agent and use them on another. For example, Agent A is selling a new property and points out that while Federation houses have an old-world charm, some are in below-average condition and may require substantial remedial work. When you inspect Agent B's listing of a Federation house, to justify why the price should be $50000 lower, you might point to some of the older parts of the building and ask the agent whether a building inspector would find that substantial repairs were needed.

To increase the competition for your business, you should have, or appear to have, at least one attractive alternative to your target property. Having an attractive alternative makes it much easier to walk away when the asking price moves beyond your budget or valuation. Ask each agent to help you assess the other properties. Invariably they will come up with a list of negatives, which you can mirror in your negotiations for these properties. Sometimes an agent might point out a crucial issue that you overlooked, which could potentially save you tens or even hundreds of thousands of dollars.

---

### Agents can be a wealth of information

I once looked at a house where the land sloped steeply down towards the back of the property and beyond. The owner had terraced it and put a pool on the lower level, which is where most people stopped their inspection. Everyone accepted that the steepness of the land detracted from the property's value, yet no one had thought about examining the back of the property in detail. Fortunately, an off-handed comment by another agent drew my attention to the lack of support for the land at the rear. He could not believe how the recent heavy rain had not caused a landslide. It would have cost a lot of money to install the necessary retaining walls, which no one had factored into the property's price.

---

Obviously, you have to bear in mind that the agent is required to act in the seller's best interests at all times, so you have to take everything they say with a grain of salt. However, the agent's duty is weakest when his commission is at stake. In multi-list sales (see 'Exclusive listing' in chapter 20), the agents will go out of their way to help you purchase the property because they are competing with other agents for the sale. For example, if another agent has a buyer with an offer, your agent will probably tell you the *minimum* price required to win the property so they can wrap up the sale before the other agent.

Finally, just before you decide to buy a property, check with some other agents if they think you are getting a reasonable deal. Even the ones whose listings you have inspected will grudgingly give you an opinion. Preface your question with something along the lines of you will consider them for the listing when it comes time to sell (and make sure that you do). Over time, as you develop a reputation as a property investor and you become acquainted with the agents, they will start to ask for *your* advice.

## How much to pay: recent sales

You should go through in detail as many recent sales in your target suburb as possible to get an understanding of current market values. That way, you will know how much to pay for a property. You can establish the market value of a property you inspect later on by comparing it to recent sales using various valuation methods (see 'DIY valuation' in chapter 14).

This is much more effective use of your time than inspecting properties for sale (whether online or physically), for two reasons. Firstly, you have the current market value (the sale price) to check against your valuation. It is like doing your homework and being able to check the answers in the back of the book to see if you were right or not. If you start by just looking at properties for sale, the only reference point you have is the asking price and this could be miles away from market value. Secondly, you can do this at your desk instead of pounding the pavement every weekend.

There are two sources of recent sales information. Firstly, the real estate websites such as realestate.com.au and Domain keep a few pages of recent sales for each suburb. This is a very good source of information because you can see a lot of the detail the buyer saw without actually being there, and best of all it is free. If the price is withheld, try asking the agent for the price range. The only drawback of this information is that it might not contain any sales near the street you are interested in.

The second source of information is a suburb report (such as from RP Data or Australian Property Monitors) of sales over the last 12 to 24 months in your target suburb or a street report of sales over a longer period in your target street. The drawback of this information is that you have to pay for it and the report only provides generic attributes of each property, such as land size, number of bedrooms and number of bathrooms. Try to persuade the agent to supply this information for free, if they are not doing it already.

# 13 Inspection

The research up to now has been at a high level, from the market down to the suburb level. The next stage of research is at the property level, where you inspect properties for sale in your target suburb.

## Online inspections

Start the inspection at home from one of the real estate sales websites, and cull it down to an inspection list of properties that meet your price range and other criteria. Real estate sales websites are much more useful than newspapers and real estate sales magazines because:

▸ You can view the properties in a list or on a map, which makes it easy to target a particular area in a suburb.

▸ They include more information on each property, such as additional photographs, maps and house plans.

▸ You can email the agent the four key questions below, and any others, as you go through each property.

▸ You can bookmark properties to refer back to and check what they eventually sold for.

▸ The websites contain recent sales with the original information, so you can assess what you would have paid for the property and compare it with the selling price.

## The four key questions

For each property on your inspection list, you need answers to four key questions to aid your decision-making. You can email the agent these questions as you browse through each property, or phone them or wait until the open inspection.

▸ *What price are the vendors looking for?* For private treaty sales where the asking price is not quoted, is negotiable, specified as a range or above a certain value, this will give you an indication of the price that you have to pay. It is usually a high price relative to the final selling price because it is the starting point for negotiations. (For auctions, it is usually much lower to attract as many bidders as possible.) Ask this question even if the asking price is quoted because you just might be able to start with a lower figure. If the agent questions your literacy, try: 'Seriously, what price are they looking for?'

▸ *How long has the property been on the market (including with other agents, and whether it was passed in at auction)?* The longer the property has been on the market, the more realistic the asking price. Your best chance of getting a bargain is with stale properties that have been on the market for a long time, for two reasons. Firstly, the vendor might be fed up or be forced by time constraints to accept the best offer. Secondly, there is less competition because other buyers might think that there is something wrong with the property or that the seller is asking too much.

▸ *Why are they selling?* The reason you should ask this question is to assess the likelihood of the vendors selling. For example, if they have already bought another property and taken out bridging finance, they are seriously looking to sell. On the other hand, some homeowners are just testing the market and are prepared to wait for months and even years. Some authors suggest that you look for 'motivated' sellers (such as mortgagee sales, deceased estates and divorce settlements) to get a good deal. These sellers might have other priorities over getting the very best price, such as a quick sale to split the proceeds (deceased estate and divorce sales) or to recoup their loan (mortgagee sales). The only problem is that most buyers are familiar with these situations, so there is usually a lot of demand, with the net effect being that the property will probably sell for around market value. And if you get a situation where two or more novices bid up the price, the property could easily go for more than market value.

▸ *What did the property last trade for?* This information will assist your valuation of the property if it last traded only a few years ago and no significant renovation and/or extension has been carried out on the property since that time. You need to make sure that the last sale price was reasonable, and take into account the stage in the property cycle that the property last sold at. This information might also help you understand the vendor's motivations and decisions.

## Open inspections

Draw up an inspection schedule (see table 13.1 for an example), sorted by time and proximity of the properties. Next, input the address of each property into your GPS as a waypoint, and off you go. (If you do not own a GPS, this is a good reason to buy one. They only cost around $100 to $200 these days.) Most open inspections take place on a Saturday between 10 am and 2 pm, with some also held on Sundays and Wednesdays. If you cannot fit a property in, arrange a separate inspection time with the agent for the beginning or end of the day, when you both have free time.

Table 13.1: inspection schedule

| Address | Time | Agent | Mobile | Reminder | Notes | Summary |
|---------|------|-------|--------|----------|-------|---------|
| G | 11:00 | JM | XXX | | Building cost? | |
| F | 11:00–11:45 | LC | XXX | Auction 10.30 am XX | | |
| X | 11:00–11:45 | DE | XXX | Offers by 5:00 pm YY | | |
| I | 12:00–12.45 | JM | XXX | | | |
| A | 12:00–12.45 | CC | XXX | | | |
| Y | 12:00–12.45 | HM | XXX | | | |
| J | 1:00–1:45 | DH | XXX | | | |
| Z | 2:30 | CD | XXX | | | |

The purpose of going to the open inspection is to:

▸ Identify issues you cannot see from the website (possibly due to selective advertising), such as the slope of the land, the setback of the house, the amount of natural lighting, the condition of the property and the level of traffic outside the property.

▸ Determine a valuation of the property based on the value of the land and building, considering its condition.

▸ Assess the level of interest in the property. This is done by examining the number of people who come back for subsequent inspections, not by the amount of traffic on the first open inspection.

▸ Ask the agent any questions (although if there is a large turnout you will be better off calling the agent afterwards). Make sure you do not show too much interest in front of the other buyers.

▸ Take as many notes as you want, and photographs (with the agent's permission).

If the property warrants a second look, bring your partner or a friend for a second opinion, and catch public transport and walk to the property. This will let you assess the property's proximity to transport, and the walk will give you a good feel for the neighbourhood. You only need to do this for the target property and the two or three attractive alternatives.

## After the inspection

After you inspect each property on your inspection list, summarise the key features of the property so you can quickly refer back to it later without having to be at the property:

▸ Location: each suburb has a blue-ribbon area that covers the best streets. These locations are in high demand from owner-occupiers and command higher prices than surrounding areas. People build bigger and more extravagant houses in the blue-ribbon area, which pushes up average prices even more. Proximity to transport is an important consideration. However, properties next to or near a railway line or main road sell at a large discount to similar properties in quiet streets. In addition, parents with children might only target the properties that fall within a particular school catchment area.

▸ Land: the features of land that determine its value are size, shape, slope and aspect (the four 'S's), for a given location and zoning:

▷ Real estate is about land, so the bigger the land the more valuable the property. The price per square metre depends on supply and demand. For example, if the average block size is 800 m², a subdivided dual occupancy (see chapter 19, 'Property development') block that is only 400 m² will sell for much more than half the cost of an 800 m² block. Similarly, a 1600 m² block could sell for more than twice the cost of an 800 m² block.

▷ The shape of the block determines the amount of frontage and what you can fit on the block. Rectangular is ideal, and the larger the frontage the more valuable (better street appeal and access). Battle-axe blocks have no frontage and therefore sell at a large discount.

▷ Sloping land is difficult and expensive to use (it usually needs to be terraced, which requires cutting and filling and retaining walls), and so sells at a discount. When there are no photos of the yard, a split-level house, often with a deck, indicates sloping land. It is usually better to have land that slopes down the back of the property instead of up because you can get good views of the garden or pool from the house (instead of a view of the roof from the back of the garden). Properties on the high side of the street are more valuable because they have better street appeal and drainage.

▷ A northerly aspect (for the southern hemisphere) to the rear is more valuable because this is where the kitchen and living/entertainment areas are usually located. Some property plans have been reorientated to take advantage of a different northerly aspect.

▸ House size: the description should be relative to the average property size in your target area. For example, in some areas a medium-sized house would have a separate lounge and dining room, four bedrooms, two bathrooms and a family room, whereas in others a medium-sized apartment might have a combined lounge and dining room, two bedrooms and a bathroom.

▸ Condition: use the same terminology that a building inspector uses to describe the property's condition. After you look at a number of properties, it will be easy to group the properties into four categories: new, above-average, average and below-average condition:

▷ New: built or renovated in the last few years.

▷ Above average: everything is well maintained, and the building work, finishes and fittings are of a high standard compared to properties of similar age and construction.

> ▷ Average: some items require repair or maintenance but there are no significant problems compared to properties of similar age and construction.

> ▷ Below average: there is a lack of maintenance and repair, the quality of the building work is low, and there may be defects that require substantial remedial work.

▸ Extras: for example, a pool and landscaped gardens usually add at least their replacement cost to the property in the right suburb.

# 14 Valuation

The most difficult decision for any property buyer is the price to pay for the property. No one wants to pay over market value (and sellers do not want to short-change themselves), but how do you determine market value? There are four main ways to establish market value:

▶ pay for a professional valuation

▶ pay for an automated valuation

▶ get a few agent valuations

▶ do it yourself.

Once you have a valuation, it is like going shopping because you know the price to pay. If the asking price falls to your valuation or the bidding stops at or below your valuation, you buy the property, otherwise you move on to the next one.

You should not be too concerned with coming up with a precise value. All you need is a reasonable range to begin negotiations with the seller. Start from the bottom of the valuation range, and be prepared to walk away as you approach the top of the valuation range. Finally, be systematic with your valuations by listing every property inspected, their features, and your estimate of the value.

## Professional valuations

If you are not familiar with market values, you can pay around $300 for a property valuation from a professional valuer. A valuer is a professional accredited by the Australian Property Institute (API) to determine the current market value of a property. The valuer assesses the market value of the property based on recent comparable sales, and supplies a valuation report that usually includes the following:

▸ A valuation of the property presented as the sum of the value of the land and improvements (the depreciated value of the building).

▸ The replacement value of the building for insurance purposes.

▸ Recent sales (including the price the property being valued last traded for) and their comparison to the property. The sales evidence includes a balance of inferior and superior properties.

▸ Opinion on whether the price represents fair market value for a lender valuation.

Most people who have not used a valuer before turn to family and friends to recommend one. However, a better option is to ask your lender to provide the details of the valuers on their panel. That way, you can get the valuer to value your property before you purchase it and then assign it to the lender for final approval of the loan (see 'Pre-purchase vs lender valuation', later in this chapter). Provided they have access to the property, the turnaround time is usually only a few days.

## Agent valuations

Agents can provide reliable valuations because they have a good feel for comparable sales in their everyday work and regularly provide valuation guidance for sellers. Note that an agent's valuation is called an *appraisal*, because only professionally accredited valuers can provide a formal property valuation. Obviously, you cannot depend on the selling agent because they have to act in the best interests of the seller and therefore their valuation will be biased upwards. Similarly, sellers looking for a valuation of their property should be wary of agents inflating values to win the listing.

The main advantage of agent valuations is that they are free and you can get a few different ones to help you triangulate a value. The disadvantage is the lack of detail that goes into an agent valuation because the agent will probably be unfamiliar with the specifics of the property and is unlikely to go inside to assess the condition of the property. Moreover, agents prefer to sell their own listings instead of doing valuations for other properties, so you need to befriend the agents and try to give them something in return, such as a referral.

# Automated valuations

Some of the property data suppliers have developed an automated valuation service costing around $60 to $80 that uses a formula to calculate the value of a property based on historical sales data and features of the property, such as the number of bedrooms. In effect, it tries to mimic the process used by valuers, but does it systematically. The drawback is that it cannot take qualitative factors such as the property's condition into account. The quantitative factors it does take into account include the last sale price of the property, the sale price of comparable properties and the distance to transport and other amenities. Automated valuations are widely used in the United States and United Kingdom, alongside and as a substitute for inspection valuations, but are still in their infancy in Australia.

# DIY valuations

Do-it-yourself valuations have the advantage of being cost-effective (it is not economical to pay for a valuation for each property that you inspect) and timely. When I started out, I supplemented my valuations with agent appraisals and the occasional paid valuation. However, as I became more experienced I mainly relied on my own valuations. The two main methods for estimating the market value of houses are the summation method and the comparison method, and the comparison method and capitalisation method are used for apartments. You should use more than one method as a cross-check of your valuation. In addition, you should do reasonableness checks, such as ensuring that your valuation does not exceed the asking price of similar properties that have not sold.

## Summation method

The summation method values the land and building separately and then sums the two components. Start by identify sales of vacant land or properties sold for land value only and use the market value of the land as your *reference point*. Subtract this land price from the sales price of properties on similar-sized blocks to calculate the building cost for houses of different sizes, construction and condition. Note that this is the depreciated cost, not the replacement cost of a new house.

For example, a 500 m$^2$ block of land recently sold for $350000. A medium-sized house in average condition down the street on a same-sized block sold for $500000. Thus, the depreciated cost of the building is $150000 ($500000 – $350000). You can extend this further by estimating the size of the house and calculating the depreciated construction cost per square metre. For example, if the previous property is 170 m², this gives a depreciated building cost of $880/m² ($150 000 ÷ 170). The property next door is on a same-sized block and in a similar condition, but the house is 200 m², so you might value it at $526 000 ($350 000 + $880 × 200).

## Comparison method

The comparison method values the property as a whole by comparing similar properties, and then adjusts for differences. Find a property that was recently sold that is similar in size (land and house), construction and condition to the property you are interested in. Next, adjust the sales price for each significant difference. For example, if the comparison property has a new kitchen that cost around $30 000 you would subtract this from the sale price of the comparison property to get the valuation of your target property. Alternatively, if the property you are interested in has a new bathroom that cost around $20 000 you would add this to the sale price of the comparison property.

For apartments and townhouses, use the comparison method on sales within the same complex or nearby similar complexes, adjusted for differences such as size, condition, parking spot(s), views and title (strata vs company). You can estimate the adjustments based on the sale price of apartments in the same complex with these differences. For new developments, make sure you also check the sale prices of established apartments in case the developer is selling the new apartments out of line with the price of established apartments. For example, if new two-bedroom apartments in high-rise complexes are selling for $400 000 to $500 000 compared to nearby two-bedroom apartments in low-rise blocks solidly built 30 years ago that are only selling for around $330 000 with much lower strata levies, you should question the market value of the new apartments.

## Capitalisation method

The capitalisation method values a property by applying a multiple to its maintainable income stream. The capitalisation method is less appropriate in valuing houses because they are more dissimilar than apartments. First, calculate the capitalisation rate (cash flow ÷ price) of similar apartments. Then estimate the cash flow of the apartment you are interested in and calculate its market value as: cash flow ÷ capitalisation rate. While there are many definitions of cash flow, the most important consideration is to calculate it consistently in your comparison properties and the one you are valuing. So if you calculate the cash flow of the comparison properties as net rent, that is how you should calculate it for the property you are valuing.

For example, a two-bedroom apartment in the same complex two floors below recently sold for $250000. It was previously rented out for $325 per week, giving a capitalisation rate of 0.0676 (325 × 52 ÷ 250000). The three-bedroom apartment that you are interested in is being rented out at $400 per week, so you might value it at $308000 (400 × 52 ÷ 0.0676).

# Valuer-General valuations

A fifth source of valuations is by the Valuer-General, which only assesses the value of the land and does not take into account the value of any structural improvements. State governments use the information to determine land tax and the local council uses it to calculate rates. For example, in New South Wales the Department of Lands carries out the valuation on behalf of the Valuer-General, and the information is readily available online for a nominal cost.[1] These valuations are infrequently updated and appear to lag market values, although they can sometimes exceed them (see table 14.1). The Valuer-General valuations are less reliable than the other methods, and even if they were similar to market valuations you would still need to estimate the value of the building.

Table 14.1: examples of Valuer-General vs market valuations of land

| | Valuer-General | | | | Market |
| House | 2004 | 2005 | 2006 | 2007 | 2007 |
|---|---|---|---|---|---|
| Low example 1 | $218000 | $218000 | $228000 | $207000 | $270000 |
| Low example 2 | $785000 | $839000 | $790000 | $790000 | $1100000 |
| High example | $310000 | $310000 | $310000 | $310000 | $290000 |

# Last sales price

If the property was sold not too long ago, the sales price could give you an indication of its current market value. You can get the price the property last traded for by asking the agent. If the seller subsequently renovated or extended the property, the last traded price might not be relevant in determining current market value. Note that this valuation method assumes that the purchase price was around market value in the first place.

## Pre-purchase vs lender valuation

Purchasing a property usually requires at least one paid professional valuation. Different orders in which this is done have advantages and disadvantages. You can pay for a *pre-purchase valuation* to be conducted *before* you buy the property. The main advantage is that this provides an independent assessment of the market value of the property to guide your purchasing decision. This can save inexperienced buyers and those buying in an unfamiliar suburb from overpaying tens and even hundreds of thousands of dollars. The disadvantage is that irrespective of whether you manage to purchase the property or not, the cost has to be paid. If you buy a property on the first few tries this would not be a problem, but it might take many attempts and the costs will add up.

Regardless of whether you pay for a pre-purchase valuation, the lender will still require a satisfactory independent valuation before providing unconditional loan approval. The *lender valuation* is usually conducted *after* exchange of contracts and is therefore less useful than a pre-purchase valuation, because if the findings are unsatisfactory it could cost you thousands of dollars to rescind the contract (by forfeiting the 0.25 per cent deposit to the seller), and you have also wasted the building and pest inspection. Even if you do not have to pay for the lender valuation because the lender waives the valuation fee, make sure you negotiate beforehand to get a copy of the valuation report. A lender valuation is usually conservative and can be below market value.

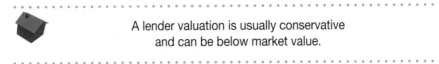

A lender valuation is usually conservative
and can be below market value.

The lender will only approve the loan unconditionally after they are satisfied with the valuation of the property. According to one lender, '95 per cent of the time, the valuation will be equal to the contract price', and the loan approval becomes unconditional. However, if the valuation is less than the purchase price, you have to cover the shortfall with either cash or equity. For example, if the purchase price is $500 000 but the valuation comes in at $450 000, for an 80 per cent LVR loan the lender will only lend $360 000 (80 per cent of $450 000), so you will need a deposit of $140 000 ($500 000 − $360 000) instead of $100 000 (20 per cent of $500 000). You also need to have sufficient funds to cover stamp duty and other costs.

If the lender declines the loan or requires additional security for the loan this is a clear sign that the property is overpriced. The reverse is not always true. If you have sufficient equity (for example, your LVR is only 60 per cent), but the valuation comes in below the purchase price, the lender might not tell you this because they still have sufficient security to proceed with the loan.

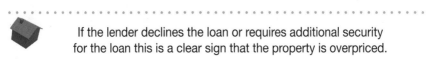

If the lender declines the loan or requires additional security for the loan this is a clear sign that the property is overpriced.

If you are an inexperienced property buyer you should consider paying for at least one pre-purchase valuation. Even if you do not succeed in buying the property, you can still use some of the information in the valuation report as a guide for subsequent purchases in the area. The most effective approach is to ask the lender if they will agree to you getting a pre-purchase valuation from a valuer on the lender's panel and then getting the valuer to assign the valuation report to the lender for unconditional loan approval. The net effect is that you only have to pay for one valuation, before you purchase the property.

# 15 Getting to *yes*

There are two main ways of selling a property: by private treaty, where the property is advertised at a fixed price or range until it is sold, or auction, where the property is sold to the highest bidder. A private treaty sale is like a private Dutch or reverse auction. The seller sets a high price, and progressively reduces the price until the property is sold. Auctions, on the other hand, start with a low price that progressively increases until the property is sold. With a private treaty sale, buyers generally pay what they can afford, unlike at auction where they can get carried away and bid beyond their financial capability. Bidding wars can occur with private treaty sales too, but the bidding is blind.

You should start with the three buying strategies, irrespective of whether you are buying by private treaty or auction: avoid other buyers, know what the property is worth, and have attractive alternatives. Then you can focus on the buying tactics, which have two parts: the opening moves, and the tactics that follow. The opening moves are the same for both private treaty and auction sales in that the offer or pre-auction offer should be made with reference to your valuation. However, the tactics that follow vary with the selling style; with private treaty, the tactics deal with the seller, and with auctions the tactics deal with the other bidders.

# Buying strategies

Buying a property is more difficult than buying everyday goods because not only do you have to deal with the seller you also have to compete with other buyers. Since the property does not have a definite price, you have to reach agreement with the seller before the other buyers to win the property. There are three strategies to effective buying: avoid competition, know what the property is worth, and have attractive alternatives. The first deals with the other buyers, and the last two deal with the seller.

> The three strategies to effective buying are:
> avoid competition, know what the property is
> worth, and have attractive alternatives.

You cannot get a good deal when other buyers are pushing up the price. To avoid competition with other buyers:

▸ Only buy during the Buying Zone of the property cycle when the market is gripped by fear (during the accumulation phase) or is just picking up (during the early uptrend). This is when the professionals buy because they have little or no competition and can get good prices.

▸ Target properties that have been on the market for a long time. However, make sure there is nothing wrong with them! Try to understand what the problem was. Were the sellers asking too much? They might be more reasonable now. Keep a look out especially for properties where the seller does not specify a price or only gives a price range. In these cases, the real estate websites cannot update for any price reductions and you might be able to snap up the property before other buyers become aware of it.

▸ Avoid auctions when the market is strong. There is less pressure if you buy by private treaty, and so you are more likely to make a sensible offer. An auction, on the other hand, is an emotional rollercoaster of competition, urgency and desperation. Buyers are whipped up in a bidding frenzy, and in the heat of the moment it is easy to get carried away and go over your budget. You should only buy at auction during the accumulation stage of the property cycle when competition is minimal. For example, in Sydney in 2007 there was frenzied bidding at auctions in the inner ring suburbs, with many properties selling way above their reserve price.

In contrast, in Sydney's south west, auction results, mainly mortgagee sales, were much weaker. It would have been much easier to pick up a bargain in Sydney's south west than in the inner ring suburbs because the competition was virtually non-existent. Another tactic is to target less busy periods, such as school holidays, Easter, December and January, and election dates, when there is less buying competition. In addition, vendors will want to wrap up the sale of their properties before the end of the Christmas–New Year break, and will be keener to sell.

▸ Keep an eye out for 'for sale by owner' properties where the owners are selling without an agent. There are websites dedicated to these sales, but the properties listed there tend to be in remote, less populated areas. The properties most buyers are interested in will usually be advertised in the traditional way by the owner sellers, such as sign boards, the real estate sales websites and letter box drops. These properties might receive less exposure than properties marketed by real estate agents if the owners do not put enough time into marketing their property. They might also be slightly cheaper because the owner is willing to split what would be the agent's commission.

▸ Make a pre-auction offer (after you have done your inspections and your solicitor has reviewed the contract) and be ready for immediate exchange. If the offer is good enough, some sellers will accept it instead of risking a higher price at auction. This is the 'a bird in the hand is better than two in the bush' principle. The key is to be able to exchange contracts right away. Not all the other buyers will be able to, so there will be less competition compared to when the property goes to auction.

Secondly, you have to know what the property is worth so you can walk away from the negotiations if the price does not come down to your valuation or quickly close the deal if the price reaches your valuation range. The same applies at auction; you continue to bid until you have won the property or the bidding exceeds your limit.

Finally, have attractive alternatives. If you don't have any alternatives and must have a particular property you might as well pay the asking price. On the other hand, if you have some attractive alternatives you can negotiate more rationally and walk away from the deal at any time, which greatly strengthens your bargaining power. Similarly, there will be less pressure to keep on bidding when the price exceeds your limit, because you can just walk away and turn your attention to your alternative properties.

**If you must have it, then you'll probably
end up paying the asking price**

One of my friends spent over 12 months looking for his perfect home. When he found the property, he did thorough due diligence on it, including parking outside for a couple of nights to check out the neighbourhood. With this kind of commitment, he had no attractive alternatives, and ended up paying the vendor's asking price (less a few thousand dollars due to the agent reducing his commission to $5000). The property had been passed in at auction, and remained on the market for months because the vendor would not budge from his reserve price, so my friend ended up paying above market value.

# Private treaty sales

Success with private treaty sales requires negotiation techniques that cover not just the offer and the negotiating tactics that follow, but also the psychology of the negotiation.

## Offer

A common misconception is that the party that makes the opening move in a negotiation will be the loser because the other party will take the opposite position, so that the final price will end up in between, but in the second party's favour. (If everyone had this attitude, no transaction would ever take place.) For example, if you offered $500000, the seller will counter with $510000, and then both parties negotiate to a price in between. On the other hand, if the seller asks for $500000, then you might counter with $490000, and then both parties negotiate to a price in between. In the first scenario, the final price ends up above your first offer, and in the second it ends up below the seller's original asking price. However, where the final price ends up compared to the buyer's or seller's original offer is irrelevant. What is relevant is how the final price compares with the property's value.

 Where the final price ends up compared to the buyer's or seller's original price is irrelevant. What is relevant is how it compares with the property's value.

In private treaty sales, the seller usually starts the negotiations with an asking price expressed as a number or a range, including 'offers above $X'. Sometimes they let the buyer start the negotiations by asking for expressions of interest or state that the price is negotiable. If the seller does not specify a price or a range is given, ask the agent for the indicative price. Since the vendors usually lead off, they will start with a high asking price. So even if you manage to bring the original asking price down by $100 000 (and claim to save $100 000), you could still overpay for the property.

The offer should be made with reference to your valuation, not the seller's asking price. Therefore, the only way to make a sensible offer is if you know the market value of the property based on comparable sales. Where you start depends on how much you want the property and the level of competition. For example, if you *must* have the property you might as well pay the asking price. If you would like to have the property but have one or two attractive alternatives, you could start near the bottom end of your valuation range and work upwards. If you would like to have the property but do not have any attractive alternatives, and the market is rising and you have already missed out on four properties in the area, you might be better off starting close to the top of your valuation range.

> The offer should be made with reference to your valuation, not the seller's asking price. Where you start depends on how much you want the property and the level of competition.

To avoid competition, always put a time limit on your offer to prevent the agent from shopping around for other buyers. You should also make the offer when it is difficult for the agent to contact other buyers. For example, offers late on Saturday that expire at 5.00 pm on Sunday are ideal because the agents usually do not work on Sunday, and in any case it will be more difficult to reach the other buyers on a Sunday. In contrast, if you put in an offer on Friday evening the agent has all of Saturday's open inspection to inform the other buyers of your offer. A property might have no previous interest, but an offer on the table will draw buyers in because the offer convinces them of the property's value.

> Always put a time limit on your offer.

Some real estate investment courses recommend making hundreds of low-ball offers to buy below market value. They rationalise that most sellers will reject your offer, but one or two might accept it because they are 'motivated sellers' or have no idea of what their property is worth. This might work if the owner is desperate to sell quickly and there are no other buyers, but in practice many buyers target 'motivated sellers', so the possibility of buying at a large discount to market value is illusory. Also, if you believe that there are owners trying to sell their property who have no idea of what it is worth, you probably also believe in Santa Claus.

Not only is low-balling a waste of time, it can also be detrimental to your prospects of securing a property for a reasonable price. If you make a silly offer, you might offend both the seller and the agent and they could shut you out from further negotiations. Even if you come back with a reasonable offer, they might not take you seriously. You need the seller and the agent to be on your side if you are going to beat the other buyers. Another risk with low-balling is that the agent will use your low offer as the starting point for the property's price guide, which will draw in bargain hunters. If you are insistent on low-balling, only do it during the accumulation stage of the property cycle. There is nothing more futile than low-balling in a rising market, because you will miss out again and again while property prices keep rising.

Not only is low-balling a waste of time, it can also be detrimental to your prospects of securing a property for a reasonable price.

## Negotiating tactics

If the seller rejects your opening offer, ask him or her to make a counter-offer before you raise your offer. For example, if they say your offer needs to be higher, ask them by how much. Otherwise, you will just compete against yourself. By law, the agent is required to pass all offers to the seller for consideration. If you feel that the agent is not doing this, send a copy of the offer to the seller or the solicitor (the details are on the first page of the contract). If you have to raise your offer, try asking for a concession in return. Be prepared for a lot of to-ing and fro-ing before you agree on a price. However, do not drag negotiations on too long in case another buyer enters the fray.

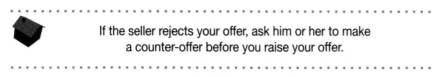

If the seller rejects your offer, ask him or her to make a counter-offer before you raise your offer.

If the agent tells you that you have to beat a higher offer from another buyer, there is no way you can tell whether this is genuine. The best you can do is to question the agent in detail to check for consistency.

You can also get a friend to pose as another buyer to see if the agent gives the same story. If the asking price is well within your valuation range, it is likely that there *is* another buyer. If there is really another buyer, consider making a knockout offer (provided it is still within your valuation range) to scare off the competition. So instead of increasing your offer by $2000, you might raise the stakes by $10000, depending on the value of the property.

Consider making a knockout offer to scare off the competition.

Some sellers need to settle quickly because they may have already bought another property or they want to divide up the proceeds of the sale. In these situations, you will have a significant advantage over other buyers if you can exchange contracts immediately. An offer with the signed contract and deposit cheque can prove to be irresistible to some sellers. Furthermore, when there is not much difference between two offers, the buyer that can close the deal first will usually get the sale. Sometimes the seller will give you the opportunity to match a higher offer if you can exchange contracts right away.

You have a significant advantage over other buyers if you can exchange contracts immediately with sellers under time pressure.

Note that in addition to the price you can also negotiate the terms of the contract, such as the inclusions and the settlement date (including access before settlement to start renovating). If you try to negotiate, or agree to a non-standard settlement date, make sure you understand the time value of money. For example, if you could defer paying for a $500000 property by an additional three months and you could invest the money at 7 per cent per annum, this is equivalent to paying $491600 ($500000 $\div$ $1.07^{0.25}$) now—an $8400 saving.

### Negotiation 101: negotiate with reference to your valuation, not the asking price

A few years ago, some colleagues and I went to conduct due diligence on a potential acquisition in an Asian country where the currency was close to parity with the Australian dollar. One colleague, a mergers and acquisitions specialist, arrived a week early to have a short holiday with his family. One day, while the family was wandering about the city, his daughter jumped on a rickshaw. My colleague was reluctant to get on because he knew how expensive they could be, especially for tourists. However, he could not resist his daughter's protests and the family went for a short ride around the block. When they got off, he asked the driver how much it cost. When the driver said, '$300', my colleague's first reaction was, '@#$&!'. After he calmed down, he countered with $100, to which the driver replied, 'Okay, $100 each for the two adults and the child is free.' After some more haggling, he managed to get the ride down to $100!

My colleague's biggest mistake, apart from telling me the story, was that he made his offer with reference to the seller's asking price and not his valuation. Even though he did not know what the right price was, he should still have started with what he thought was a reasonable price, like $10. Note how the driver did not accept the $100 when my colleague made the counter-offer (because he knew the importance of psychology in a negotiation), but made my colleague negotiate some more to earn the $100 price. If he had accepted the $100 right away, my colleague would have felt ripped off. Also, note that a 66 per cent discount from the asking price does not constitute a bargain.

A week after the incident, the rest of the due diligence team arrived. At the end of the first day, the mergers and acquisitions specialist acted as tour guide for myself and the lawyer on the team and took us to the food area of the city. The prices were very reasonable, so for dinner we chose a few dishes, including chilli crab, which is a delicacy of the area. However, when it was time to pay we were shocked at the price of the crab. When we insisted that there was no way the crab could have weighed more than two pounds, it fell on deaf ears. Reluctantly we paid. Our mistake was that we only negotiated on the price but left the terms (weight) open and were taken advantage of by the seller.

While the amounts in these examples were small, when you deal with real estate they are much more significant and can cost you tens or even hundreds of thousands of dollars. The key lessons from this trip, which are just as applicable to real estate, are: always negotiate with reference to your valuation and not the seller's asking price, and do not just negotiate on the price and get screwed on the terms.

## Psychology of negotiations

Do not underestimate the importance of psychology in a negotiation. You have negotiated successfully if you can make the other party feel good about the deal (and obviously you have to feel good too). Even if you think the asking price is reasonable, do not accept it right way, because if you do the seller will think that he or she underpriced the property. If you start a bit lower and move up a little, the seller will think that he or she got something extra out of you. Otherwise, the seller might wonder if he or she could do better and perhaps withdraw from the deal at the last minute.

# Auctions

Success with auctions requires a good understanding of how they work, judicious use of pre-auction offers and application of good bidding tactics.

## How auctions work

The English auction is the predominant sales method in high-demand suburbs. Participants bid openly against each other, with the winning bidder paying the highest price. Typically, the agent runs a marketing campaign and open house inspections in the three to four weeks leading up to the auction. They are required to quote a realistic price guide for the property, but invariably the property sells for more. Sometimes this is due to a rising market, especially if the price was quoted using historical sales data. However, sometimes agents deliberately underquote by up to 25 per cent to attract more bidders. Obviously, the gap can also result from the combination of underquoting and strong bidding.

Underquoting is costly for buyers because each bidder pays for a building and pest inspection, yet some will not even be able to afford the reserve price. You could ask the agent whether the price guide quoted is similar to what they advised the sellers of their property's worth. However, the best defence against underquoting is to know the property's market value based on comparable sales. Then you can turn underquoting to your advantage, because on the day of the auction there will be fewer bidders prepared to pay the property's true value. In addition, even though you are competing with the other bidders, it makes sense to share the cost of the building and pest inspection. So get together with the regular faces you see at each auction and suggest sharing the inspection costs.

The best defence against underquoting is to know the property's market value, and use it to your advantage.

The best way to really understand how auctions work is to attend a number of them as a spectator and familiarise yourself with the process and atmosphere. Then follow the auction result for each property that you inspect. Record the agent's initial price guide and any updates throughout the marketing campaign, then attend the auction or check the newspapers and compare the winning price with the price guide(s) to see if there are any patterns by office or agent and over time.

The bidding process varies slightly by state, so make sure you check the details with the agent beforehand. On auction day, in some states, such as New South Wales, only the buyers that have registered their details with the agent (name, address and ID) and are given a bidding number can bid. The vendor sets the undisclosed minimum price that they will accept, called the reserve price, before the auction. When the bidding exceeds the reserve price, the auctioneer announces that the property is on the market, and the winner of the auction is the highest bidder.

If the bidding does not reach the reserve price the property is passed in. The highest bidder is offered the opportunity to negotiate with the seller to achieve a sale. So if you feel that the property is going to be passed in, try to get the last bid in so you can be first to negotiate. You will be in a much stronger bargaining position because the vendor has outlaid a substantial sum towards the marketing campaign and will want to recoup costs by achieving a sale.

The vendor is allowed to make one bid, which must be announced by the auctioneer. The vendor bid is usually used to start the bidding or towards the end of the auction to try to reach the reserve price. If the property is passed in after a vendor bid, this gives you an indication of the price the vendor is looking for. A dummy bid is a non-genuine bid made up by the auctioneer or by someone planted in the crowd, and is illegal.

With auctions, you need to organise your finance approval and inspections beforehand because there is no cooling-off period and the successful bidder has to sign the contract and pay a 10 per cent deposit immediately after the auction.

The sealed-bid auction is less common than the English auction. Bidders are asked to submit one bid simultaneously (or by a certain date), so that no bidder knows the bid of any other participant. While a sealed-bid auction does not have the competitive pressure of an English auction, you have to put in your best offer if you want the property because you cannot see the other bids. Some pre-auction offers are conducted as a sealed-bid auction.

## Pre-auction offers

You should try to put in a pre-auction offer instead of waiting for the property to go to auction because there is the risk that the property will sell for more than the vendor's expectations. You can submit an offer by completing the front page of the contract of sale with your offer price with the 10 per cent deposit and waiving the cooling-off period (see 'Exchange of contracts' in chapter 16). Obviously, you can make the offer subject to finance or some other condition. However, if you do this the vendor will just ignore the offer and proceed with the auction. Make sure you specify a deadline to encourage the vendor to exchange contracts as soon as possible and avoid tying down your funds for too long. Note that the vendor will usually seek offers from other interested buyers and the property remains on the market until contracts are exchanged.

If the market is strong and you are worried about missing out at auction, you should put in your best offer. An offer has to be very attractive for the vendor to sell the property before auction because of the cost of the marketing campaign. The catch-22 is that if there are signs of interest in the property (many pre-auction offers) the agent will recommend that the vendor take the property to auction to try to get a better result.

## Bidding tactics

The most important rule in bidding at auction is to avoid auctions where there is excess demand, because prices could go through the roof. The best auctions are mortgagee auctions after a series of interest rate rises where there is plenty of supply but very little demand. The second most important rule in bidding at auction is to set a predetermined budget based on your valuation, and be prepared to walk away when the bidding exceeds it.

Most experienced auction bidders would agree that the third most important rule is to bid confidently to give the impression that you are an experienced buyer and have a lot of money. This might scare off the competition and save you some money. Some of the tactics that convey confidence include:

▸ Positioning: stand at the front of the auction by the side of the auctioneer so you can be seen by the other bidders.

▸ Timing: wait until the property is on the market and the bidding dies down, and just before the auctioneer says, 'sold', start bidding to give the impression that you are just starting when everyone else has run out of money.

▸ Increment: bid in large increments, or throw in the knockout bid.

▸ Pace: bid rapidly and keep the flow of the auction going until you either win the auction or reach your limit. Do not stop to consult with your partner because the other bidders will assume that you are nearing your limit. It will also stop you from going over budget by removing the temptation to add 'just another $5000' to the limit.

▸ Showmanship: bid loudly. Bid with authority. Do something unconventional—I will leave this up to you.

Familiarise yourself with how auctions work by attending a number of auctions in advance, ideally with the same auctioneer who will be conducting your auction so you are accustomed to his or her mannerisms. Study the tactics of other bidders; they might end up bidding at the same auction as you. Remember that this is very different from the real thing because you do not have any emotional or financial stake in the outcome.

---

### The knockout bid

An Artarmon property sold for a 'whopping' $2 210 000, $335 000 above the reserve of $1 875 000. Eight bidders registered for the auction. The opening bid of $2 000 000 knocked out six bidders right from the start. The second bidder upped the ante to $2 110 000. Bidding increased in increments of $10 000 until the hammer fell at $2 210 000.

*North Shore Times*, Friday, 16 November 2007

---

# 16 Closing the deal

In a private treaty sale, after the seller accepts your offer there are four remaining steps before you can collect the keys: holding deposit, exchange of contracts, conveyancing, and settlement (see figure 16.1). These steps apply in all states and territories, but the details vary from state to state. Your solicitor or conveyancer will provide further details specific to your purchase. The first step does not apply to auctions and is sometimes bypassed in private treaty sales when the market is rising.

Figure 16.1: steps to settlement after acceptance of offer

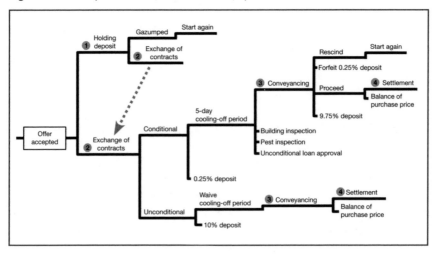

# Holding deposit

The agent will ask you to pay a holding deposit of a few hundred dollars to show that you are serious about the purchase. However, *this does not secure the property*. The property remains on the market until contracts have been exchanged. Before exchanging contracts, you might want to take the contract to your solicitor to check. Some people also carry out a building and pest inspection and get unconditional approval from their lender.

The advantage of a holding deposit is that if either party changes their mind, the holding deposit is refundable. The disadvantage is that the seller can gazump you by exchanging contracts with another buyer with a higher offer. Gazumping is more likely to happen when the market is rising. You will lose any money spent on the building and pest inspection, not to mention the time to find another property (this is what happens when you miss out at an auction).

# Exchange of contracts

Exchange of contracts refers to the buyer and seller signing their duplicate copies of the contract for sale and then exchanging them. You secure the property and 'close the deal' by signing the contract and paying a deposit. There are two types of exchanges. Under a conditional exchange, a deposit of 0.25 per cent to 10 per cent of the purchase price is payable. In most states, you have a five-day cooling-off period to rescind the contract if you decide not to proceed with the purchase, but at a penalty of 0.25 per cent of the purchase price (see table 16.1, overleaf, for the differences by state and territory). If you want to rescind the contract you must do it in writing. The balance of the deposit has to be refunded within 14 days. Note that if you are the successful bidder at auction you must exchange contracts and pay the 10 per cent deposit on the spot. There is no cooling-off period.

The advantage of a cooling-off exchange over a holding deposit is that it locks the seller in. The disadvantage is that it costs a lot of money to rescind the contract if you change your mind, or the building or pest inspection is unfavourable or your finance is not approved. The cooling-off period is used to conduct the building and pest inspection (usually ordered by the solicitor) and get unconditional loan approval. The pre-purchase loan approval is conditional on satisfactory valuation of the property, so the lender will have to get a valuation done during this time. If your solicitor or conveyancer has not seen the contract, this is the time when they go through it to check for any irregularities and do various searches. You might have to ask for a few days' extension of the cooling-off period to get everything completed.

Table 16.1: cooling-off periods and penalties

| | Cooling-off period* | Penalty for cooling off** |
|---|---|---|
| New South Wales | 5 days | 0.25 per cent |
| Victoria | 3 days | Higher of $100 or 0.2 per cent |
| Queensland | 5 days | 0.25 per cent |
| Western Australia | 0 | N/A |
| South Australia | 2 days | 0*** |
| Tasmania | 0 | N/A |
| Northern Territory | 3 days | 0.25 per cent |
| Australian Capital Territory | 5 days | 0.25 per cent |

\* There are some circumstances in which the cooling-off period does not apply.

\*\* Percentage of purchase price.

\*\*\* The deposit is usually paid after the cooling-off period. If a holding deposit (no more than $100) was paid, it is forfeited.

Under an unconditional exchange, such as with a pre-auction offer, you give the seller a section 66W certificate in New South Wales or a lawyer's certificate in Queensland, the Northern Territory and the Australian Capital Territory waiving the cooling-off period, and pay the 10 per cent deposit. In Victoria (if the property is purchased within three days of an auction, the cooling-off period does not apply) and South Australia, you waive the cooling-off period by obtaining legal advice. The contract cannot be rescinded.

# Conveyancing

Conveyancing is the legal transfer of the property from the seller to the buyer. It is better to use either a solicitor or a conveyancer instead of trying to do it yourself with a DIY kit because the solicitor or conveyancer will carry professional indemnity insurance. The typical conveyancing cost is around $1000, including disbursements.

The conveyancing process can include the following[1]:

▸ Examining and exchanging the contract of sale.

▸ Organising building and pest inspections.

▸ Organising payment of the deposit and stamp duty.

- Overseeing the change of title with the Land Titles Office.

- Checking that the seller is legally entitled to sell the property and the property does not have money owing on it, such as unpaid rates and taxes.

- Checking if any government authority has an interest in the land or if any planned development could affect the property (for example, the local council, Roads and Traffic Authority or utilities).

- Checking construction work (building, extending or altering) complies with council requirements.

- Calculating adjustments for council and water rates.

- Attending settlement.

## Contracts

The contract for sale includes the following items:

- Details of the seller and buyer, and their solicitors.

- Deposit requirements and settlement period.

- Inclusions and exclusions of the sale, such as curtains and dishwashers. Never assume that everything you see is included in the sale. Only essential items attached to the building are always included, such as the hot water system. Things that can be removed easily, such as a garden bench, are usually excluded.

- Title documents.

- Planning and zoning certificate from the local council.

- Sewerage diagram.

## Building inspections

A building inspection is a visual examination of the accessible areas of the building to determine its condition and look for structural defects. The building inspectors, who usually have extensive building experience, supply a comprehensive report. If there are structural defects, you have to decide whether to proceed with the purchase. You might be able to negotiate a lower price to pay for the rectification. The building inspection report also provides useful reference for later repairs and maintenance. You should arrange the inspection time so you can accompany the inspector and ask questions.

Most people use the building and pest inspectors recommended by their solicitor. The inspections usually cost a few hundred dollars each. Make sure the building and pest inspectors have paid-up professional indemnity insurance, and do not use those suggested by the agent in case there are any conflicts of interest.

A building and pest inspection are part of the cost of buying real estate. Nearly everyone who is not a mechanic would get a mechanical inspection before buying a used car. Yet many people try to save a few hundred dollars and skimp on a building and pest inspection when they purchase a property that costs many times more. This is false economy, because it could cost tens of thousands of dollars to rectify structural and pest damage.

> A building and pest inspection are part of the cost of buying real estate.

A building inspection typically covers the following:

▶ The exterior and interior of the building.

▶ The roof and roof-space.

▶ The subfloor area.

▶ Electrical and plumbing services.

▶ Site drainage.

▶ Outbuilding structures, fences and retaining walls.

## Pest inspections

A pest inspection is a visual and auditory examination of accessible wood structures in the building for wood-destroying insects, such as termites (white ants) and borers, and fungal decay. A pest report contains information on current and past infestation to a building. It also makes recommendations on how to make the property less attractive to termites and reduce moisture and dampness.

## Unconditional loan approval

The lender's valuer will require access to the property during the cooling-off period to conduct the valuation. Most of the time the valuation comes in at the purchase price. However, if it falls short you have to cover the difference with your own funds or equity. Alternatively, you can rescind the contract and forfeit the 0.25 per cent deposit if you are still within the cooling-off period. Since there is no cooling-off period if you buy a property at auction, make sure you do not get carried away with the bidding in case the lender valuation is below your purchase price.

## Balance of 10 per cent deposit

The balance of the 10 per cent deposit is paid before the expiration of the cooling-off period if the building and pest inspections are in order and finance is unconditionally approved. The deposit is held in a trust until settlement, with the interest split between the seller and buyer. If you fail to complete the contract after the cooling-off period, you forfeit the 10 per cent deposit and might even be liable for any losses suffered by the vendor above this amount.

# Settlement

Depending on the state or territory, settlement normally occurs 30 to 90 days after exchange of contracts (not the date of the expiry of the cooling-off period). It is one of the main terms negotiated between the seller and buyer. Sellers who have already bought another property might ask for a quicker settlement. Alternatively, sellers might want a delayed settlement of a few months while they look for another home to buy. Buyers might seek access before settlement so they can start to renovate the property.

At settlement, the buyer pays the balance of the purchase price to take ownership of the property. The final amount includes adjustments for water and council rates. The lender retains the certificate of title until the mortgage is repaid. You should arrange a final inspection with the agent to ensure that the property is in the same condition as it was when purchased and that the vendor has left all of the inclusions in the contract with the property.

Finally, make sure you take out building insurance before settlement and contents insurance before you move in. The lender will want to see a copy of the building insurance policy before providing the funds. General insurance companies sell building and contents insurance under different brands in different states. The three largest retail general insurers are IAG, Suncorp and Allianz (see the resources section for more details).

# Part IV: Managing your properties

After buying a property at the right time, managing your properties is the key to making money in real estate because it maximises your yield and minimises your costs from spending time in the market. There are a number of aspects to managing your properties, including:

▶ Keep properties occupied with tenants paying market rents, while minimising your expenses.

▶ Renovating to increase the rental income, and perhaps the value of your properties.

▶ Property development to increase the value and rental income of your properties.

▶ Selling your property if necessary.

# 17 Property management

Now that you have an investment property, you need to find a tenant to help you service the loan. First, you have to understand the tenancy laws specifying the rights and responsibilities of the tenant and the landlord. Next, you have to understand the property management functions so you can decide whether to do it yourself or hire a property manager. I recommend that most people go with a property manager. In addition, you should keep good records and regularly review your portfolio using the **SYSTEM T™** framework.

## Tenancy laws

Landlord and tenant rights and responsibilities are governed by the Residential Tenancies Act in each state and territory, and can be quite different. Fortunately, each state and territory provides a handbook that explains these rights and responsibilities in plain English. See the resources section for links to these handbooks, which are usually called the *Renting Guide* or *Renting Book*.

With each tenant, the landlord is required to provide a tenancy agreement in writing which sets out the terms of the agreement, such as:

▸ *The length of the tenancy.* The tenancy agreement initially specifies a fixed term such as six or twelve months. In New South Wales, at the end of this term the tenancy becomes a continuing agreement with the same terms and conditions, unless terminated by either party or they sign another fixed-term agreement. In the other states, it becomes a periodic tenancy. You should encourage the tenant to sign a fixed-term agreement after the initial one to give both parties more certainty and reduce the vacancy rate. Make sure the tenancy agreement does not end in December or January as it can take a long time to find a new tenant over this period. If tenants break a tenancy agreement early, they can be liable for the rent until new tenants move in or the tenancy agreement finishes, a reletting fee and advertising costs.

▸ A *condition report*, which notes the cleanliness, general condition and working order of items at the start of the lease. The landlord or property manager fills out three copies and gives two copies to the tenant to agree or disagree with each item, sign, and return one to them, and they keep the other one for themselves.

▸ *Entry costs*, which include the reservation fee, rental bond and advance rent. The reservation fee is usually just one week's rent, while the rental bond and advance rent are usually four weeks' rent and two or four weeks' rent respectively (with minor variation in some states/territories). The rental bond acts as security for the landlord against any money owing for unpaid rent or damage to the property, and must be deposited with the relevant authority by the specified time.

▸ *Rent*, which is the charge tenants pay for usage of your property. The tenancy agreement specifies the level of rent and the payment method. Unless specified in the tenancy agreement, the rent can only be increased after the fixed-term agreement has expired, and the landlord has to give the tenant 60 days' notice in writing (with minor variation in some states/territories). The notice needs to specify the new rent and the date from which it applies. In some states, the frequency of increases is restricted to six months.

If the tenant thinks that a proposed rent increase is too high they can negotiate or apply to have it reviewed by a tribunal which will take into account factors such as rents on comparable properties, the extent of the increase and the condition of the property. You should increase the rent every year to avoid a sharp increase to catch up to market rents when they take off.

If the property is vacant for more than two weeks, consider dropping the rent by $10 a week to get a tenant in. This costs $520 a year, and compares favourably to the rent forgone for a property, rented out for $300 a week, that remains vacant for two weeks. You can always increase the rent at the end of the fixed-term period in line with market rents.

> You should increase the rent every year.

▸ *Access.* Notice to gain access to the property for inspections, repairs, valuation and to show the property to a prospective purchaser or tenant varies between states. You usually require a minimum notice of 24 hours, and in some states the landlord or property manager needs to give the tenant seven days' notice for general inspections and can do no more than two or four a year. Access for repairs and access to show the property to a prospective purchaser or tenant require one or two days' notice.

▸ *Repairs.* The landlord is responsible for ensuring that the premises is clean and in a reasonable state of repair. The landlord is responsible for urgent repairs (such as a burst pipe, leaking roof, the breakdown of essential services such as hot water or heating, or anything that causes the property to be unsafe or not secure), to be fixed as soon as reasonably possible. If the landlord cannot be contacted, in some states the tenant can spend up to $1000 on urgent repairs and be reimbursed by the landlord within 14 days. The landlord is also responsible for installing smoke alarms.

▸ *Rates and charges.* The landlord is responsible for paying council rates and water and sewerage service charges. Where specified in the tenancy agreement, the tenant is responsible for paying for water usage. The tenant is responsible for all electricity, gas, telephone and internet connection and usage charges.

▸ *Ending the tenancy agreement.* A tenancy can be terminated by either the landlord or the tenant giving written notice to the other party. The notice period varies by state and territory, and for the landlord is around 14 days at the end of a fixed-term agreement or 60 days otherwise.

▸ The *final inspection,* which is used to assess whether any repairs or cleaning up are required at the end of the tenancy to bring the property back to the condition set out in the condition report, subject to fair wear and tear. The tenant pays for any damage, usually by a deduction from the bond. At the end of the tenancy, a claim for refund of bond money is submitted to the relevant authority to be refunded to the tenant or (partially) claimed by the landlord or agent to cover rent owing and/or damage to the property.

## Property management functions

The objective of property management is to maximise your returns from spending time in the real estate market by keeping the property occupied with tenants paying market rents while minimising your expenses. The key functions of property management are:

▶ advertising the property

▶ showing the property to potential tenants

▶ conducting background checks on potential tenants

▶ collecting the rent and paying bills

▶ keeping records

▶ conducting periodical inspections of the property

▶ handling repairs

▶ evicting tenants for not paying the rent and/or damaging the property (this is rare).

## Advantages of using a property manager

The most important decision to make is whether you will manage the property yourself or hire a property manager. For most property investors, I recommend using a property manager. Property managers typically charge between 5 and 7 per cent of the gross rent plus GST, and one week's rent for finding a new tenant. You might be able to negotiate a lower rate if you have more than one property with the manager.

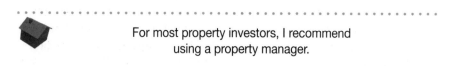

For most property investors, I recommend using a property manager.

The main advantages of using a property manager are:

▶ *Opportunity cost:* if you are a high-income professional, for example, you are better off spending more time at work and hiring a property manager. Even if you only have a low-paying job, the ad hoc nature of managing just one or a few properties might still make it more economical to use a property manager.

▶ *Expertise:* property management is what they do for a living and their superior knowledge of the rental market and tradespeople can get you higher rents for a lower cost. They also have more experience in screening tenants, which could save you a lot of money in rent arrears, vacancies and repair costs.

▶ *Economies of scale:* the number of properties that they manage allows property managers to plan and organise their day instead of managing on an ad hoc basis. They are also available throughout the day and for after-hours emergencies. Unless you manage your investment properties on a full-time basis, you will not be able to provide this level of service. For example, if you can only show potential tenants the property on the weekend, you miss out on a pool of potential tenants and your property could remain vacant for longer.

▶ *Systems:* property managers have established systems for collecting rent, paying bills and producing accounts. If you manage a property yourself, you will have to do everything manually or set up your own systems.

▶ *Impersonal:* property managers are the gatekeepers between yourself and tenants. If you do not enjoy dealing with people and solving their problems or are not assertive, having someone else do it is a blessing. It is also easier to make a business decision such as putting up the rent or evicting a tenant in arrears if you do not know the tenant personally.

▶ *Proximity:* if you do not live close to the property, it will not be worthwhile managing the property yourself because there are times when you have to be at the property to show it to potential tenants, let tradespeople in or conduct inspections.

While property managers are efficient at managing properties, they are not always effective. (Efficiency is about doing things right; effectiveness is about doing the right things.) To improve the effectiveness of property managers, you need to treat your relationship as a partnership: the property manager handles the administration of your properties while you make the strategic decisions such as doing deals, making the major financial decisions and finding cheaper loans. By paying someone else to take care of the operational issues, you free up your time to handle the big-picture issues.

There are some situations where using a property manager might not add any value or be so clear-cut. For example, if you have a spare bedroom or granny flat to rent out, you are probably better off managing it yourself because the proximity removes most of the advantages of a property manager. If you own a few blocks of apartments, you probably have the expertise and sufficient economies of scale to manage them yourself and there are fewer reasons to use a property manager. Finally, if you have had the same good tenant for many years, you might want to manage the property yourself. You could negotiate a win–win situation where the tenant takes care of all the minor repairs in exchange for smaller increases in the rent.

If you decide to manage a property yourself, make sure you get a copy of the 'Renting Guide' handbook for your state/territory to familiarise yourself with each party's rights and your responsibilities. In addition, consider taking out landlords' insurance to give yourself some added security.

## Choosing a property manager

If you do not know where to start, ask family, friends and other property investors to recommend a property manager. Interview the property manager and ask how they carry out each function. Also, ask for a list of clients, and ask how proactive the property manager is in recommending rent increases, managing problem tenants and their responsiveness such as giving regular updates on the progress of a repair job and returning calls promptly. (You can also use this referral process to find tradespeople for repairs.) To make sure that the property manager does not become complacent in their job, specify in the management agreement that you can cancel the arrangement with 30 or 60 days' written notice, or immediately if they breach any conditions in the property management agreement.

An important factor in choosing a property manager is whether your property falls within their service area. This makes it much easier to tenant the property because the real estate office is an important source of enquiries for properties for rent. It will also be more convenient for the property manager to go to your property, to let tradespeople in for example.

**Choose a property manager whose service area covers your property**

One day the property manager that I used for many years with two of my properties decided to buy a real estate office two suburbs away. She went from being a property manager to the owner of a real estate office, with responsibility for both sales and property management. I did not have a problem with this as she had hired another person to look after the property management side. When one of my properties became vacant, the property manager assured me she would find a new tenant quickly. However, after two weeks it became clear how difficult it was for her to find a tenant for a property outside of her service area, so she asked some of the agents in her former service area to help her find a tenant and offered them a referral commission. Despite our long relationship, I decided to change property managers a short while later to avoid the possibility of lengthy vacancy periods in the future.

Make sure that the property manager does a proper job of managing your property. This means that it must be a standalone business from the sales side of real estate agency. Some real estate agents operate the property management business as a loss leader for their sales business, hoping to recoup some of the money when you come to sell your property. You can check this by asking for the property manager's experience and the number of properties managed by each person (their workload), and comparing it with other property managers in the area.

## Keep good records

Keeping good records is an important part of property management. You have to do it for tax purposes. You also need good records to track your performance. For example, if you lose money every year for 10 years, perhaps you should consider investing in another asset class. I keep a folder for the transaction and financing details of each property, a filing cabinet for statements and a scrap book for receipts. I summarise the financial information into a spreadsheet for my tax return and analysis each year.

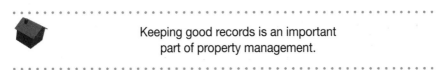

Keeping good records is an important part of property management.

Another important reason to keep good records is for warranty purposes. Many electrical items have up to five years' warranty on some of the parts, such as the compressor in air conditioners. When you have a repair problem on an electrical item, first check your records to see if it is still under warranty. Just this simple step can save you thousands of dollars. Even if it is outside of the warranty period, it might be cheaper to get it fixed by the manufacturer's service technicians, instead of a general technician recommended by the property manager.

> **Warranties save money**
>
> When the air conditioning system in one of my investment properties stopped working, the property manager promptly got two quotes to replace it. They both came to around $2500. When the property manager asked me what I wanted to do, I replied, 'Let me think about it.' I went home and checked my records. The air conditioner was still under warranty. I called the property manager back, gave him the details of the manufacturer, and asked him to take care of the warranty claim.

# Review your property portfolio

At the end of each financial year I do a comprehensive review of my property portfolio by going through each component of the **SYSTEM T™** framework.

## Security

I start by assessing the long-term demand for properties where I am invested. For example, a number of years ago I built some properties in an area that was predominantly bushland and farms because the area had only recently been rezoned to residential. One year later, as I drove by I noticed that houses were popping up everywhere, but around 80 per cent of the land was still vacant. However, five years later the whole area had changed completely. I actually got lost trying to find my properties. There was a sprawling new shopping centre and two new schools, some roads had been widened and many now had traffic lights and roundabouts, and there was no more vacant land. This is a positive sign.

If, on the other hand, I had noticed that there was an increase in 'for sale' and 'for lease' signs, I would investigate further to see whether this was a short-term aberration or due to some longer term structural change in the area. I certainly would not wait until the population started to decline and the houses were being vandalised and boarded up before selling out of the area.

I also examine the economic outlook and its potential impact on interest rates. For example, when the Australian economy was booming over 2006 and 2007, I built up my cash holdings in preparation for higher interest rates. While I did not foresee the subprime market collapse in 2007 and its impact on the cost of funding of lenders and hence interest rates over 2008, I was not unduly affected by it due to the precautionary measures I took over the previous two years.

## Yield

To maximise my yield, I review the rents on my properties to make sure they are in line with the market. I also ask my property managers to ask the tenants whether they need anything. Some have asked for dishwashers, air conditioners or awnings, which I install for them. This does two things. Firstly, I have happy tenants who want to stay in my properties, which reduces my holding costs (advertising costs, re-letting fees, vacancies and minor repair costs—long-term tenants are more likely to cover these out of their own pockets) and increases my net yield. For example, I have tenants who have been with me for nearly 10 years (and are paying market rents). Secondly, these costs can be recouped with a slightly higher rent in a few years, so they pay for themselves.

In between long-term leases, I might update the property cosmetically by giving it a new coat of paint or changing the carpets, provided I can expect to recoup these costs in a few years with a higher rent. I also review the performance of my property managers. For example, have they been proactive in making recommendations, have they responded quickly to my queries, and most importantly should I continue paying them?

## Spread

The way I assess the spread of my portfolio is to look at a pie chart (this is easy to set up in a spreadsheet) of the values of the properties in my portfolio by area. I do not just look at the spread of my properties, but also the spread of all my investments. For example, if I am overweight in a particular area or in real estate or shares, I will rebalance my portfolio over the long term.

## Time

I analyse whether the property market in each state is in the Buying Zone or the Selling Zone, and where they are in the zone, so I can plan my next investments.

## Equity

If the market has risen or I have done some cosmetic renovations to increase the value of a property, I will revalue my properties so that I can draw down the equity to invest in another property if the property market is in the Buying Zone or in shares. Obviously, you should only get a valuation if you are going to do something with the equity; otherwise, you just increase your holding costs for nothing.

## Magnification

I am on constant look-out for a cheaper loan. This is the easiest way to make (actually save) money. Yet few people think about the interest cost of the mortgage on their property when they think about property management. However, it is the biggest cost for most people. With rental yields at 4 per cent per annum or lower, a 1 per cent saving on the mortgage interest can make a significant difference to the profitability of a property.

I systematically check comparison tables of home loans in the newspapers and on the internet to make sure that I have one of the cheapest loans. In addition, I sometimes drop into the offices of a mortgage broker, and to avoid wasting my time and theirs, I tell them 'I have N property loans worth $X, at i per cent per annum' (substitute for your actual amounts). I then give them my business card and say, 'Only contact me if you have a better rate.' You should make sure that the 'better' rate is not a honeymoon rate that reverts to a higher rate later on.

## Tax

I file and summarise my income and expenditure records to make sure that I declare all income and claim all appropriate deductions.

# 18 Renovations

The renovation shows on TV have created a myth about how ordinary people can buy a run-down property, renovate it and flip it for a handsome profit. In reality, it is very difficult to make money this way, even when the market is rising. If it were this simple, you would see many more tradespeople getting into the game either by themselves or in partnership with equity investors. There are two types of renovations: structural renovations and cosmetic renovations. I suggest that you just focus on cosmetic renovations to increase the rent on your property.

## Structural renovations

Structural renovations involve buying an old, neglected property and making major changes to the structure (or 'bones') of the property, which can take months or even years. I do not encourage structural renovations for the following reasons:

▸ There is strong demand for 'renovator's delight' properties in the inner and middle suburbs, possibly due to the influence of renovation shows, but also because many people want to put their own stamp on a property. So you might already be starting from behind even before you begin the renovations because you paid a premium price for the property.

▸ Structural renovations are expensive and time consuming. For example, adding a second storey costs in the hundreds of thousands of dollars and can easily take six to twelve months to complete, while a new kitchen or bathroom can cost many tens of thousands of dollars and take weeks or even months to complete.

▶ Many people forget about the opportunity cost of structural renovations, which when added to the cost of the renovations can turn an apparently profitable project into a very unprofitable one. This includes the interest and holding costs of the property while you are renovating and the cost of your time (and family and friends that help you out). There is also the inconvenience of the intrusion, noise and dust, which are hard to put a value on.

▶ Structural renovations require specialist knowledge and skills. Most people do not even know the right tradespeople to hire or the order in which to do it (carpenters, bricklayers, plumbers and electricians, plasterers then painters), let alone know how to do the building work themselves. In addition, the people smart enough to outsource the work are unlikely to have any experience in managing all the different tradespeople.

▶ Even small structural renovations may need council permission, while larger ones will need a development application (see 'Property development' in chapter 19).

▶ Murphy's Law: anything that can possibly go wrong will go wrong. The 'tradies' will underquote on cost and time, they will not turn up on time, they will not have the skills to do the job properly, they…well, you get the idea.

Before you embark on any major renovation work, get feedback from real estate agents and valuers on the needs of the market and the value you can add to the property to avoid overcapitalising. This also helps you work backwards to calculate your walk-away purchase price: expected value after renovation less renovation cost, opportunity cost and profit margin. Sometimes you might find that it is cheaper and more profitable to knock down the property and rebuild.

You should consider engaging an architect to draw up the plans and even project manage the work. This typically adds 10 per cent or more to the renovation, but you can expect a more innovative design, better use of light and space, and better flow and interaction of the spaces. Alternatively, draw up a list of your requirements and get two or three licensed builders to provide a fixed-price quotation for the job.

Before you hire anyone:

▶ Check that they do not have too much on their plate and can spend the bulk of their time on your project.

▶ Check references: What was the quality of the work like? Was it completed on time and on budget? Did they turn up when they said they would? Were they easy to deal with?

▶ Sight examples of recent work.

▶ Check that the builders have homeowner warranty insurance.

Adding another bedroom usually yields the best return on your outlay. For example, if you own a two-bedroom apartment, and one of the bedrooms is larger than normal, then it is cheaper, easier and more profitable to divide the large bedroom into two and market the property as a three-bedroom apartment, rather than adding an ensuite to the bedroom and marketing the property as a more upmarket two-bedroom apartment. The difference in value between the two properties can be around $50 000 to $100 000.

It is hard enough to make a return from renovating a property to keep, let alone one to flip because the transaction costs and capital gains tax (unless it is your primary residence) can wipe all of your profits, and more. A better strategy is to get the property revalued after it has been renovated and borrow against the increase in equity to fund the next job. As a bonus, the renovated property will support a higher rent.

Another strategy is to buy a run-down property, renovate it while living in it, and then sell it and use the proceeds to repeat the process until you reach the home of your dreams. This has the benefit of not incurring capital gains tax since your principal residence is exempt. The drawbacks are the significant transaction costs, the opportunity cost of your time and the inconvenience. Most importantly, you need to recognise that this is a lifestyle strategy and not a wealth-building strategy, because at the end of the process you will not have a portfolio of properties to fund your retirement, just one property to live in or sell.

Timing is critical to a successful structural renovation, especially if you are looking to flip for a quick profit. Make sure you start before the uptrend is well underway to give yourself time to complete the job and sell the property while the market is still rising. Novices that jump on board at the end of the cycle face huge losses when they are hit by the double whammy of high labour and building material costs and falling property prices.

## Cosmetic renovations

The only renovations that I recommend are cosmetic renovations that do not involve touching the structure of the property. These either give the property a facelift or add some functionality to increase the rent. The best time to carry out a cosmetic renovation is right after you buy the property. Talk to the property manager before you start and ask them to give you an estimate of the additional rent you can expect. You should only proceed if the renovation is rental positive.

A renovation is rental positive if the rental yield increases as a result of the renovation, otherwise it is rental negative. In other words, the renovation is rental positive if the marginal rental yield (additional rent as a percentage of the renovation costs) exceeds the existing rental yield. For example, if a $300 000 investment property currently earns a 5 per cent rental yield ($15 000 per annum) and you spend $20 000 renovating the kitchen to earn an extra $10 in rent each week, the renovation is rental negative. The 2.6 per cent ($10 \times 52 \div 20 000$) marginal rental yield is less than the 5 per cent current rental yield. By undertaking the renovation project, you reduce the rental yield on the property from 5 per cent to 4.85 per cent $[(15 000 + 10 \times 52) \div (300 000 + 20 000)]$.

Only proceed if the renovation is rental positive.

Examples of rental positive cosmetic renovations include:

▸ Mow the grass and tidy up the gardens. You will be surprised what a difference this can make. Try leaving your grass unmown for two or three months and you will understand. Do not bother bringing your lawn mower along; just hire someone to do it for you.

▸ Give the house a new coat of paint. Use white on the inside to give the impression of more space. A fashionable trend is to paint a feature wall a strong contrasting colour. For the outside, use a contrasting colour for the trims such as quoins, doors, window frames, gutters and down pipes. If you have never used a paintbrush, hire someone to do it for you. Do not worry if you have no colour coordination; just get a project home builder's catalogue and copy the colour combinations of a facade that you like. In general, if you are short of ideas or not quite sure how something looks, just visit the display homes of project home builders.

▸ Replace worn out and stained carpet. Nylon commercial carpet is a good option. It is long wearing, inexpensive and fashion neutral. If you are not experienced with choosing colours, stick with a safe neutral colour such as grey or greyish blue. They go well with off-white walls and do not show stains and soils.

▸ Check underneath the carpets to see if there are floorboards. If there are, rip out the carpets and polish the floorboards.

▶ Re-enamel or resurface bathroom tiles. You can achieve the look of a traditional bathroom renovation at a fraction of the cost and time.

▶ Install inexpensive light coverings to raise the look of a property a notch.

▶ Change the handles on doors, kitchen and vanity cabinets and tap fittings.

▶ You might have second thoughts about installing a dishwasher because it seems like overcapitalising. However, it can be useful in attracting higher rental tenants.

▶ Install a new garage door, with automatic opener, in a contrasting colour to the bricks. This is not only functional but is an inexpensive way of improving the facade of the property. It is better value (and cheaper to maintain) than, say, bagging and painting the exterior.

▶ Resurface the driveway and other concrete surfaces with spray-on concrete in various stencilled patterns. This is a cost-effective way to brighten up and improve the attractiveness of your property.

▶ Landscape the gardens. Put in flowerbeds covered with bark, not pebbles, which are expensive and heavy. In many parts of Australia, the soil is clay and very hard to work with. Use gypsum to break up the clay and plant clay-loving flowers such as geraniums. Shade sails are an attractive and cost-effective way to cover a patio.

▶ Install a split-system air conditioner. In many parts of Australia, the heat can be unbearable in summer. A split-system air conditioning unit solves the problem for around $1500 including installation costs. Alternatively, consider installing awnings or ceiling fans, depending on the area.

### Focus on renovations that pay for themselves

I installed a split-system air conditioning unit at one of my properties which cost $1600 all up and increased the rent by $15 per week. The air conditioner was rental positive, with a marginal rental yield of nearly 50 per cent ($15 \times 52 \div 1600 = 48.75$ per cent), and it paid for itself in only two years [$1600 \div (15 \times 52) = 2.05$].

Some of these renovations do not increase the rent directly, but improve the presentation of the property to attract higher rents. You might feel more comfortable starting with the necessary renovations first. For some items, you might be able to negotiate with the tenant to split the cost.

## You might be able to share the cost

One of my tenants paid for a dishwasher to be installed himself. When he left a year later he asked if I would waive a week's rent for the dishwasher; I readily agreed, because I would have paid for it myself anyway as I have found that a dishwasher usually pays for itself within a year or two in extra rent.

Always get at least a second quote to make sure you are not overcharged. Also, try to renovate as many of your properties at the same time as possible. You will use your time much more effectively and you will be able to negotiate the best volume discounts.

With electrical appliances, it can be more effective to buy a less flashy but reliable brand than paying top dollar for a leading brand. For example, some whitegoods are identical except for a different label and some styling, yet they can sell for many hundreds of dollars difference. Avoid the bells and whistles, such as an LCD display. Extra features add no tangible benefit, but often require more frequent servicing and are expensive to replace as they cannot be repaired. Instead, you are better off spending the money on something with a long warranty period.

Sometimes technicians from the manufacturer of an electrical item will dispute a warranty claim due to incorrect installation. You can avoid this situation by negotiating a total price with the retailer that includes installation. That way, if there is any dispute with the warranty, the manufacturer and retailer can sort it out between themselves and one will have to bear the cost.

## Sexy vs boring

My theory of business is that the boring things make you money while the sexy things lose you money, and I apply this religiously to my real estate portfolio. So you will not find me undertaking grand renovations.* Instead, you will find me constantly trying to reduce my expenses (interest and holding costs), and occasionally spending a few hundred or thousand dollars on cosmetic renovations or new appliances to increase my rent. You will also not find me installing the latest appliances with their computer panels and LCD displays that break down like clockwork and cost around half of the appliance's price to replace. Instead, you will find me installing the cheaper but much more reliable models of the same appliances, without the computer panels where possible. You will also not find me attending every new open house, which can be very exciting. Instead, you will find me at my desk poring over price charts, recent sales and other statistics.

\* Note that while I do not undertake grand renovations, I like to buy houses where I can get quite a lot for my money — the type of houses where the owners have spent a lot of time and money on grand renovations but are unable to fully recoup their investment when they sell. This is consistent with my value approach to investing in real estate of buying when market value is less than intrinsic value.

# Extensions

When people outgrow the family home, perhaps with another child on the way, they usually decide to either extend the property or sell and look for a bigger home. The main advantage of extending the property is the saving on stamp duty and transaction costs, which are in the tens of thousands of dollars. There are also non-financial advantages such as not having to make new friends and avoiding disruption to the children's schooling. However, the cost of an extension is significantly more than the cost to build from scratch.

If you need more room consider adding a studio or granny flat at the back with a self-contained bathroom and kitchenette. It is easier and usually cheaper to build a separate structure, and it is also much less intrusive. When the children move out of home, you could rent it out or use it as a home office. The disadvantage is that it requires a bigger footprint than extending upwards. In contrast, adding a second storey gives you more room for a courtyard, garden or pool, but can add up to 30 per cent to the building costs.

A third option that most people do not consider is to keep their old home, rent it out, and buy a bigger one. If you can afford to service a second property, you should investigate this option to build your property portfolio. The advantage of this option is that you will have two properties working for you. However, you will incur stamp duty and transaction costs to buy the new property and you might need to service the rental property in the short to medium term before it becomes self-funding. The disadvantage of this arrangement is that it is usually not very tax efficient because you will have paid off more of the mortgage on the first property than the second one, but you will be renting out the first property and living in the second one as your primary residence.

# 19 Property development

Property development typically involves the purchase of land, and construction, marketing and selling of property. It operates on the principle that the more dwellings you can fit on a block of land, the greater your yield, since the cost of the land is fixed. The property development options available to most private property investors include:

▸ Building a new dwelling on a block of land.

▸ Dual occupancy, which involves the building of two dwellings on a block of land.

▸ Small-scale developments that involve the consolidation of two or more blocks of land to build six or more townhouses or apartments.

However, with the potential for greater return comes greater risk. Property development requires a larger outlay than traditional real estate and takes much longer to generate cash flow. This is why property development is the easiest way to go broke with real estate.

## Buy land and build

Instead of buying an established property, you can buy land and build a house. This strategy can save thousands of dollars on stamp duty because you do not have to pay stamp duty on the value of the house. Buying land and building is becoming more difficult in the major capital cities due to the shortage of vacant land.

While you have the flexibility to tailor the house to your liking, for investment purposes it only makes sense to build project homes. Project homes are standardised and much cheaper to build than architect-designed homes, so there is less chance of overcapitalising. Furthermore, project homes are of brick veneer construction, which reduces construction costs.

You can think of buying land and building as being in between buying an established property and buying off the plan. You pay for the land upfront and make progress payments to the builder after each stage is completed. The downside is that you can tie up your capital for six to twelve months without any rental income, and the interest cost during the construction stage is not tax deductible (it has to be capitalised). This is usually offset by the increase in the value of the land during the construction stage.

One of the most underestimated advantages of buying land and building is that search and inspection costs are minimal. Blocks of land are much more similar than houses and apartments, and therefore trade within a smaller price range for a given location and size. This means that there is less negotiation involved. There is also no need for building and pest inspections. In addition, the costs are relatively transparent. You can compare construction prices between different builders and overall costs against house and land packages.

The main disadvantage of buying land and building is that you can usually only acquire land in the outer suburbs, with other new developments. So not only will capital growth be lower due to the distance of the properties from the CBD and water, but the supply of new properties will usually restrain capital growth for a number of years.

The cost to build a brick veneer project home ranges from $150 000 to $300 000. As a rule of thumb, double-brick homes cost twice as much to build. Until recently, the land component was usually cheaper in the capital cities apart from Sydney and Melbourne. However, the property boom in the smaller capital cities from around 2003 onwards pushed land prices up so that in most parts of Australia the land component is now at least as expensive as the cost of the project home. In some areas in Sydney, the land component can be up to three times the cost of the project home.

To start the process, first get approval for a construction loan, which is used to finance the buying of the land and the construction. Standard loans have one drawdown to pay for the property. A construction loan, on the other hand, usually has six drawdowns. The first one is for settling the land, and the remaining five progress payments are for the completion of each stage of construction. The lender sends a valuer out to inspect each stage of work before making the progress payment to the builder.

Next, visit some display home centres to see different builders and their designs. Make sure you speak to previous clients about their experience with the builder. When you have settled on a builder and design, get a fixed-price quotation from the builder. If you want to avoid overcapitalising, minimise the number of variations from the standard contract because the cost of the variations can add up very quickly.

Whether you should choose a single-storey or a double-storey design depends on the location. A single-storey house is usually cheaper to build than a double-storey house by around $50 000 to $100 000. Single-storey houses are suited to the outer suburbs, where the rent needs to be affordable. You would overcapitalise with a double-storey house since the extra rent would not be commensurate with the additional costs. In more well-off areas, land sizes are smaller, so the small footprint of a double-storey house is more appropriate. You should choose a plan where the floor area of the first storey is the same as the ground floor to maximise land usage. This usually requires the double garage to be tucked under the first floor.

It's usually best to buy the land *after* the builder inspects it to ensure that it will fit a standard design. The builder will also conduct a soil test; the type of soil (clay, sand or rock) determines the cost of the foundations. Sometimes the builder will charge a non-refundable deposit of $1000 to $2000 for this preliminary work. Obviously, there is nothing stopping you from buying the land first and then shopping around for a builder and house design. However, you should take into account the opportunity cost of holding a vacant block of land.

The builder commences construction after you have completed the colour selection process. This involves selecting the colours, designs and finishes for the various items inside (such as the colour of the walls, kitchen cabinets and vanities) and outside the house (such as bricks and roof tiles), with the guidance from the builder's colour consultant. Select colour combinations and designs that will appeal to the majority of people, rather than your individual taste.

Construction involves five stages:

‣ Slab: laying down the concrete foundations.

‣ Erecting the frame.

‣ Lock up: completion of the exterior of the building (walls, roof, doors and windows).

- Fixing: completion of the interior of the building (walls, ceiling, flooring, kitchen and bathroom, including the electrical wiring and plumbing).

- Completion/handover: painting and installation of the appliances and issue of the occupancy certificate by council. At the final inspection, the builder hands over the keys.

Before you or the tenant moves in, the gas, electricity and phone lines need to be connected. Do not forget to take out building and contents insurance on the property after completion.

After the builder hands over the keys, there is a 90-day warranty for any problems and blemishes that were not evident during the final inspection. The builder will only rectify structural problems after this time. The structural warranty period is specified in the contract, and is usually seven years.

The main risk of buying land and building is the builder going bankrupt in the middle of the job. You can reduce this risk by checking how long the builder spent on recently completed homes, as well as the ones under construction. A builder with financial problems will not be able to pay their tradespeople, which will cause the construction process to drag out.

Make sure the builder has homeowner warranty insurance to protect yourself against loss from the builder's failure to fix or compensate for defective work, or incomplete work if the builder goes bankrupt, dies or disappears. Builder's warranty insurance is compulsory when a builder undertakes residential building work, such as the construction of a new home or renovation of an established property valued over $12 000. Also, never pay the builder the total cost up front. You reduce the risk and cost of the builder running off with your money by only making payments after the completion of each construction stage. If you take out a construction loan, you will find that the lenders are very strict about this.

The standard project home does not include floor coverings (except for the wet areas), blinds, turf, driveway or fences. You can either get the builder to include these in the package or you can arrange for them to be done yourself. Using the builder takes the hassle out of having to coordinate different tradespeople. The downside is that for their efforts the builder adds a large profit margin. It might be much cheaper to hire the tradespeople directly. You should resist the temptation to do all the work yourself. Things like laying the turf and planting shrubs and flowers are light and manageable. Levelling the front and back yard, building retaining walls, concreting the driveway and patio and laying tiles is specialised work and can be back-breaking. They are best left to the professionals.

An alternative to buying the land and then finding a builder is to buy a home and land package from a developer/builder. You should also do your research on the total cost of this option. If the cost of buying land and building a house were more than the cost of a comparable house and land package offered by a developer, or significantly more than the cost of an established house, you would be silly to go down the DIY option. If you decide to buy a home and land package from a developer, try to structure it so that you buy the land from the developer first, to save on stamp duty, and then enter into a building contract.

# Dual occupancy

Dual occupancy involves the development of two dwellings on the one lot. The dwellings can be attached to one another, where they are known as a duplex, or detached. Generally, around 70 to 80 per cent of houses are owner-occupied, while the same percentage of apartments are rented. On the other hand, dual-occupancy dwellings have the same proportion of owner-occupiers and renters. The main advantage of dual occupancy is that you get two lots of rental income or two medium-valued properties for a less than proportionate outlay. You might even be able to turn a negatively geared investment into a positive-cash-flow investment.

At its simplest, dual occupancy involves the addition of self-contained accommodation to an existing property. For example, some families have converted an unused garage into a 'granny flat' by adding a small bathroom and kitchenette. Next in complexity are duplexes built on large blocks of land, which allow you to live in one half and rent out the other half. At the other end of the spectrum, the owners of large corner blocks have built two separate dwellings and sought council approval to subdivide the land, so that each dwelling can be sold separately.

First check with the council (talk to the town planner on duty and read the development control plan on the council website) to see if there are any development restrictions such as:

▸ Zoning: dual occupancy might not be permitted in some zones.

▸ Minimum lot size: for example, in some councils a minimum of 600 m² to 800 m² is required for dual occupancy.

▸ Subdivision: the lot size, shape and access determines your subdivision options. In some councils, subdivision is not permissible for small lots, while only lots above a certain size with dual street frontage can be subdivided by Torrens title. The remainder can be subdivided by strata title.

▶ Construction restrictions, such as minimum plot ratio (the ratio of the floor area to block area is no more than 50 per cent, for example), setback (distance from a boundary), streetscape, privacy, landscaping, height (rear dwellings are usually restricted to one storey) and heritage conservation restrictions.

Then you need to submit a development application to the council (see 'Council application' later in this chapter), which can take around three months to assess.

You should only proceed with a dual occupancy development if it makes financial sense. Speak to a few agents to get an estimate of the value of the completed development and compare this with your costs. Also, ask the agent's property manager to estimate the rents you can achieve once the development is completed. This lets you check if the development is rental positive. That is, the additional rent divided by the development costs is greater than current rental yield.

### Doubling your returns (as in x2)

An investor sold a three-bedroom inner city terrace for $1 300 000 in 2003. He bought the block in 1997 for $420 000, split it in half and built the terrace at a cost of $450 000. By subdividing the block, the investor doubled his money in six years [1 300 000 ÷ ($420 000 ÷ 2 + $450 000)].

## Duplexes

Duplexes are much cheaper to build than two detached dwellings. Some project home builders also build duplexes and have a variety of designs to suit most blocks. However, there are fewer of these builders, so there is less price competition than for project homes. It might be more cost-effective to hire a licensed builder to supervise the project. Make sure they have experience in building duplexes, preferably in your local area. Alternatively, you might be able to convert a large house into a duplex and make significant savings in building costs. In the inner city you can sometimes find double-storey houses that have been converted into duplexes with each dwelling on its own level.

Duplexes are best located in the middle suburbs because the outer suburbs are dominated by houses, while the inner city is dominated by apartments. The most appropriate design is usually three bedrooms, two bathrooms or a bathroom and an ensuite, and a single garage. Double-storey duplexes have the advantage of a smaller footprint to maximise the use of smaller blocks. However, they cost more to build and eliminate the retirement market who do not like stairs.

## Subdivision

Initially your dual-occupancy development will be on one title, so you can only sell the dwellings together. However, you might be allowed to subdivide the development into two titles, which increases the value of the development because then you can sell each dwelling separately. You can achieve returns on investment of around 10 times the subdivision costs (not the development). For example, the subdivision costs might be around $10000 (surveyor's fees, council development application fees, legal and Land Titles Office lodgement fees and the cost of installing water meters, and so on), but this could increase the valuation on your properties by $100000. Even if you do not have any plans to sell the properties, you can still draw down the increase in equity to grow your property portfolio.

There are two types of subdivisions. Torrens title is the most valuable because the lots are completely separate, with no common property and hence no owners' corporation to worry about. The resulting properties are like houses on small blocks of land. However, Torrens title is usually restricted to detached dwellings on large corner blocks (or blocks with dual frontages) with minimum frontages, and where the dwellings face different streets. Strata title subdivision of dual occupancy developments is more common for smaller blocks. Each dwelling has a separate title, but also shares common property such as the driveway. While not as attractive as Torrens title, it allows you to sell the dwellings separately. The resulting properties are like townhouses.

# Small-scale developments

Small-scale property developments are very risky. They require a much larger investment (both equity and debt financing) than normal residential property, and can take up to two years before they generate cash flow, and by then you might have run out of funds. This is compounded by the poor timing of inexperienced investors, who try to become property developers at the top of the cycle, pay top dollar for development sites and end up broke when the property market turns. The property development process includes financing, site acquisition, council application, construction and marketing.

Before you embark on any development, you need to conduct a feasibility study, which is a cost–benefit analysis of the project. Most people speak to the local agents to get a feel for potential sale prices and incorporate this into their analysis. However, it is very easy to come unstuck this way, even if you build a contingency factor of 5 or 10 per cent into your projections, because by the time you complete the development prices could have fallen by 20 per cent. Instead, you should take into account a range of future market values based on the stage of the property cycle and a conservative estimate of construction times and only proceed if the development is profitable under these scenarios.

## Finance

A common financing option for property developments is a commercial construction loan with progress payments. Other options include joint venture financing with profit share. You should involve your lender as early on as possible to take advantage of their experience with other development projects. They will help you assess and improve the viability of the project. The lender's lending criteria includes your and the builder's experience, the marketability of the development and the economic outlook. They will usually only lend to a maximum of 70 per cent of valuation or 80 per cent of costs. The interest rate is commonly expressed as a base indicator rate plus a risk margin. Pre-sales allow you to borrow more and at more attractive interest rates, but are very difficult to achieve unless you have a track record.

## The Monopoly® principle

The first step is to get set with the land without having to pay too much of a premium. The key is to buy old properties on large adjacent blocks *discreetly* that you can consolidate later on, subject to zoning changes. This is the Monopoly® principle, where the goal is to buy all of the (adjacent) properties in a colour group and build houses and hotels that generate higher rents. If you do not have enough money, try to buy adjacent properties with a relative. For example, you can buy the property next door to your parents when it comes up for sale. However, it is important that the properties make an adequate return in their own right. Otherwise, you are just speculating.

### Play Monopoly® with your family

The parents of one of my colleagues lived in Paddington. They bought their terrace many years ago after they arrived in Australia. When the property next door came up for auction in 1995, they helped my colleague buy it with her brother, without any inkling that they would become property developers one day. Five years later, as Sydney property prices started to boom and the council became more receptive to high-density living, the family consolidated the two blocks and built six townhouses.

The combined properties are worth more than the sum of the individual properties due to their ability to support proportionately more dwellings. If you can get set with the land for the cost of the individual properties, you build a margin of safety into the development, which turns into an extra profit margin on completion if everything turns out as expected. Alternatively, you can just sell the land in one lot, pocket the profit and let someone else bear the risk. If you cannot buy the land with a margin of safety built in, there is the risk that you overpay for the strategic value of the land and will not be able to recoup your outlay. This usually happens near the top of the market when there are many budding developers chasing a limited number of development opportunities.

## The key to successful property development is to get set with the land

In the late 1990s, an electrician bought a run-down house and rented it out. When the property next door came up for auction in 2003, he outbid the owner on the other side of the property with $325000. A year later he consolidated the blocks to build six townhouses. In 2005, two owners on the same street devised a profitable strategy. Being neighbours, they decided to put their properties up for sale together. Despite the property market moving sideways over 2003 to 2005 in that area, the two managed to sell their properties to a developer for $500000 each. They secured an additional $175000 (over 50 per cent more) each for their properties, which only consisted of land value, due to the combined strategic value of the land.

When the developer completed the townhouses two years later, the market had turned and, despite dropping the selling price by over $100000 each, he still could not sell any of the properties. Eventually he rented the townhouses out to try to cover his holding costs. With hindsight, he had significantly overpaid for the land and undertaken the development project at the wrong time.

Most developers and investors take a different approach to mine. They start by looking at the available development sites and the current and future development opportunities. The problem with this approach is that other developers and investors are doing the same thing and so everyone ends up competing for the scarce development sites and bid up the prices. The drawback of my approach is that it requires a much longer horizon, and development opportunities might never happen. However, my approach is to invest in real estate first, and only undertake development opportunities as they arise.

## Council application

Next, you have to get council approval for your development. Your architect (or a surveyor or ex-council town planner acting as a consultant) will be able to guide you through this process. First, familiarise yourself with council controls, policies and guidelines and the state's environmental planning policies. Then discuss your proposal with the council town planner as early as possible in the design process to ensure that you have their support for your development application (also known as a building application in some states).

You need to prepare and submit a number of different plans for your development proposal:

▸ Site plan, with orientation and property details such as boundaries, landform, access and existing developments.

▸ Floor plans.

▸ Elevations and sections.

▸ Reduced plans (A4 size), so council can provide copies to the people affected by the development, such as neighbours, to see if they have any objections.

▸ Survey plan, showing the exact location of buildings and other features.

▸ Landscape plan.

▸ Stormwater drainage plan, showing management of stormwater runoff.

▸ Shadow diagrams.

▸ Subdivision plan, showing existing and proposed boundaries and easements and rights of way.

▸ Waste management plan during the development.

▶ Environmental site management plan.

▶ Environmental effects of the development and how they will be mitigated.

After you lodge the development application and pay the relevant fees, the council will determine the application and approve or reject it. This lengthy process depends on the complexity of the development proposal and the objections from neighbours, and can require the submission of amended plans. For example, in one townhouse development application, the neighbours complained about the excessive overshadowing, so the developer had to increase the setback to bring shadow lengths within acceptable limits. If your application is approved, the development needs to be carried out according to the conditions of consent. Lastly, you have to apply for and receive a construction certificate before you can commence building.

When you receive approval for your development, you can apply for council approval for subdivision of the land. The process is similar to the development application for construction: apply for a development application for subdivision, submit plans and pay council fees. Councils generally prefer to know how the site will be developed before they approve subdivision of land, so they are less likely to support the development approval for subdivision of a vacant lot. Once you receive approval for subdivision from the council and satisfy the conditions of the consent, you need to lodge subdivision plans (prepared by your surveyor) with the council, and when they are satisfied you can then register the plans with the Land Titles Office.

## Construction

The construction process can take as long as the development approval process. First, you have to prepare detailed working drawings and a schedule of specifications so builders can quote for the project. Building costs are of the order of $1000/m^2$. Prices and construction time fluctuate with the supply and demand for tradespeople. For example, you might have to wait for weeks for a builder to finish the last job when the market is booming. In addition, prices in the inner suburbs will be higher than the outer suburbs because there are fewer builders that specialise there.

You can find recommendations for builders from the construction sites or ask the council for details of the main builders in the area. After you conduct due diligence on the builder (in particular, the quality of their work on recent projects and feedback from clients on meeting cost and time budgets), draw up a fixed-price contract for as much of the building work as possible. If you forget to include something, this can be added as a variation to the contract and quoted separately. The builder is paid after the completion of each stage specified in the contract. You should also include penalty clauses for construction delays in the contract based on your opportunity cost.

## Marketing

Ideally, you should keep all of your properties. However, you will probably be short of funds on completion of the project and need to sell at least one or two to pay down the interest on your construction loan (for example, you might have capitalised the interest for 12 months). The large developers typically conduct project marketing at the start of the development to achieve a certain percentage of off-the-plan pre-sales to satisfy their financing condition (usually at least 33 per cent). However, for small developers marketing involves appointing a real estate agent to sell or lease the properties after the development reaches lock-up stage or completion. Make sure the agent has a track record in selling new developments.

# 20 Selling

You should avoid selling any of your properties if possible to maximise your time in the market. You also save on transaction costs and capital gains tax (on investment properties) when you do not sell. However, if long-term demand declines you should sell because your yield could be negative for many years, and you might end up having to service the property yourself. If you get a great offer, this might be another reason to sell, although you should assess it on its merits. If you have to sell, the best time to do it is in the Selling Zone, when market value is greater than intrinsic value. Unfortunately, most people are forced to sell at the wrong time.

To sell a property, first decide whether you are going to do it yourself or use an agent. You should defer this decision until after you listen to a few agents' listing presentations to understand how the selling process works. (I provide some guidelines on how to choose and manage an agent.) Next, get a valuation of your property to help you price the property. Then you have to decide on whether to sell by private treaty or auction. After you select the selling method, you can set the starting price for a private treaty sale or the price guide for an auction. Now you can start to find buyers for your property using a number of different marketing and advertising methods. You should remember that most buyers live in or around the area, and they come into the area to buy, so the focus of your marketing should be in the area. Finally, you need to present your property in the best light to maximise your selling price.

# Avoid selling if possible

Selling a property is like killing the goose that lays the golden eggs. Not only do you put an end to the golden eggs (the capital growth and rising rental income), but you incur transaction costs (up to 10 per cent for a round trip) and capital gains tax (on investment properties) that take a large chunk out of your yield. There is also the time it takes to find and buy a replacement property later on. You should avoid selling your properties if possible by investing for the long term, planning for different contingencies and not overextending yourself, especially in the first few years.

> A farmer and his wife had a goose that laid a golden egg every day. They supposed that the goose must contain a great lump of gold in its inside, and in order to get the gold they killed it. Having done so, they found to their surprise that the goose differed in no respect from their other geese. The foolish pair, thus hoping to become rich all at once, deprived themselves of the gain of which they were assured day by day.
>
> *Aesop*

Some possible ways to avoid selling include:

▸ If you want to see how much money you have made just pay for a valuation. You do not want to do this too often because you should try to minimise all holding costs.

▸ If the property market has moved sideways for many years, be patient for a few more years. The uptrend might be just around the corner.

▸ If the rental income is insufficient to service the property and you are stretched, try drawing down some of the equity with a loan to buy some more time.

▸ Divorce is not a reason to sell. You should try to keep the family home as a joint investment. It saves on transaction costs, and more importantly will help both parties get back on their feet financially. At the right time, one party can sell their half to the other and use the proceeds to buy another property. That way, both parties will be able to own a property down the track.

Say that you bought a property in the Buying Zone. Even if the market rises strongly, you will be better off just drawing down the increase in equity as a loan, instead of selling. You get a similar amount of cash as selling, but you do not incur the transaction costs—including the buying costs to get back into the real estate market at a later date—or capital gains tax. You do not get more cash because you have to leave some equity behind (20 per cent of the property value).

However, by holding on to the property you will give back some of the gains when prices pull back from the peak in the downtrend (see 'The real estate cycle' in chapter 6). But this is usually a better option than selling because the pull back in prices is unlikely to be more than what you give up in transaction costs and capital gains tax when you sell. The reason why property prices do not fall as much as share prices is because 70 per cent of property owners are owner-occupiers who do nothing when prices fall, which dampens the drop.

Finally, it takes a lot of time and effort to find a good investment property or home, so you need to consider this when you decide to sell a property. There is also the risk that you might spend the proceeds instead of investing in something else.

## Drawing down equity is usually better than selling and buying back

During the uptrend of the last property cycle, the value of one of my investment properties rose by over 130 per cent four years after I finished building it due to the strong demand in the area. I was tempted to sell to reinvest the proceeds in the stock market, which was just starting to pick up after a sharp sell-off. In addition, I expected property prices to pull back by around 20 per cent after the boom. However, I decided to draw down the available equity with a loan instead to avoid transaction costs and capital gains tax. This is how the two options would have panned out.

The property rose 130 per cent from $245 000 to $570 000. It then dropped by 25 per cent to around $450 000 at the bottom of the next cycle.

### Draw down equity
Cost price = $245 000
Initial equity = $50 000
Initial debt = $195 000
Required equity = $114 000 (20 per cent × $570 000)
Available equity = $261 000 ($570 000 − $195 000 − $114 000)

### Sell and buy back
Buying costs = $4000*
Selling costs = $12 000

## Drawing down equity is usually better than selling and buying back (cont'd)

Capital gains tax = $77 000 [48.5 per cent × 50 per cent ×
($570 000 − $12 000 − $245 000 −
$4000 + $10 000**)]

Proceeds = $286 000 ($570 000 − $12 000 −
$77 000 − $195 000)

The sell and buy back option appears to provide $25 000 more cash. However, I have to take into account the entry cost into the real estate market at a later date. Assuming I can purchase the same property at its low of $450 000, I would incur:

Acquisition costs = $17 000 (stamp duty and conveyancing cost)

Thus, the sell and buy back option only gives an additional $8000 in cash. The real amount is lower because I am unlikely to be able to buy the property back at its low, and would incur higher acquisition costs.

From a profitability perspective, the sell and buy back option gives away $106 000 ($12 000 + $77 000 + $17 000) in selling costs, capital gains tax and acquisition costs.

The draw down equity option gives $120 000 back to the market at the lowest price ($570 000 − $450 000). So at the lowest price, the sell and buy back option is $14 000 more profitable. However, there is very little chance of buying the property back at its low, so in reality the draw down equity option is at least as profitable as the sell and buy back option.

If the property value only increased by 100 per cent to $500 000, the sell and buy back option gives a similar amount of extra cash like before ($11 000), but is $39 000 less profitable.

In summary, the sell and buy back option gives slightly more cash. However, it is less profitable except when there are strong capital gains and strong pullbacks in prices (and provided you can time the highs and the lows).

Note that the sell and buy back option is more attractive if you are on a low marginal tax rate (all other things being equal), such as in retirement, or do not incur any capital gains tax, such as on your principal residence. However, if you are on a low marginal tax rate throughout your career, investing in real estate will be a less attractive option in the first place.

* Stamp duty on the land and mortgage stamp duty; conveyancing was free; I ignore the capitalised interest while building (it was only a few thousand dollars as construction was quick and interest rates were low).

** Cost base reduced by building depreciation deductions of $2500 per annum (2.5 per cent per annum on building cost of approximately $100 000).

# Sell if long-term demand declines

One exception to 'avoid selling if possible' is if you see signs of long-term demand for homes declining in your area; in this case, sell as soon as you can in an orderly manner. It usually starts with the loss of a key employer in the city or the decline of its key industry, resulting in a gradual decline in the population. For example, Cleveland in the United States made headlines during the subprime market collapse with its high number of foreclosures. After World War II, the city's population peaked at over 900 000. Today there is around half that number. The decline resulted from the slump in its steel mills and manufacturing industries, and the population shift to the suburbs. In 2007, one in ten homes were vacant.

When long-term demand declines, your yield suffers on both fronts. Firstly, as demand falls so will the price of real estate, so you will face capital losses for many years. Instead of doubling every seven to ten years, prices could fall from six digits to five digits — that is, from the hundreds of thousands of dollars to the tens of thousands of dollars — over many years. The capital losses result in a negative yield, which reduces the value of your equity (see chapter 10, 'Bringing it together').

Secondly, the decline in demand will result in high vacancy rates, so your rental yield will also fall. Eventually the property will remain vacant as houses in the area become vandalised and are boarded up. So you will lose an important source of funding for your property (the tenant), which results in the loss of your second source of funding (the Tax Office), and you will have to service the property yourself.

# If you get a great offer

Sometimes you might get an offer to buy your property that is too good to refuse. Examples include synergistic purchases *above market value* by a developer to consolidate land for higher usage, or the next door neighbour who wants your property to build a tennis court or own the whole floor in an apartment. This is similar to a takeover in the stock market. As an added bonus, these types of purchases usually occur at the top of the cycle. In these situations, which you need to assess on a case-by-case basis, you are probably better off selling the property because the pull back in prices will far exceed what you give up in transaction costs and capital gains tax.

Sometimes you also have to take into account the impact of not selling. For example, if you choose not to sell your house to the developer who is building the block of apartments next door, your property will end up being surrounded by blocks of apartments, which would significantly reduce its value. So instead of making a windfall gain, you suffer a loss by not selling.

## When to sell: the Selling Zone

If you ever need to sell a property, the best time to do it is during the Selling Zone, during the late uptrend and distribution stage when market value is greater than intrinsic value (see figure 20.1). Timing is also crucial here. If you miss the boat, you could face a price reduction of 20 per cent from the highs. Many people make the mistake of holding out too long, only to see prices go down rapidly. While it is easy to indentify the Selling Zone after the event, you can estimate it in real time as the period after three to four years of consecutive growth in prices of 10 to 20 per cent per annum growth.

Figure 20.1: only sell when market value > intrinsic value

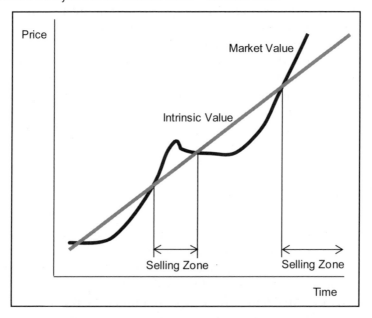

### If you have to sell, do it in the Selling Zone

One of my friends was forced to sell his property after his marriage broke up. Fortunately, this was in early 2003 in Sydney, when the market was nearing its peak (though obviously no one knew for sure at the time). However, after he sold it, property

> prices in the area kept on rising, and he was filled with remorse. I tried to console him by explaining that I had stopped buying real estate in Sydney three years earlier because it was too hard to find any value in the market and that his timing was spot on. Five years on, prices in the area have still not recovered their 2003 value and my friend is glad he sold in the Selling Zone.

Unfortunately, many people are forced to sell at the wrong time. Instead of selling at the top of the cycle, they buy at the top of the cycle, and when interest rates rise or their circumstances change they are forced to sell as prices pull back. Others do not have to sell right away, but end up selling in frustration after buying near the top and then seeing prices move sideways for many years. In both situations, the sellers end up selling during the Buying Zone instead of the Selling Zone. Selling real estate can be a catch-22 situation. When you have to sell, it is at the wrong time. But if you can afford to wait for the right time to sell, you are better off holding on to the property forever.

# How to sell

If you choose to sell your property the most important decision is whether you use an agent or do it yourself. Next, you have to set the price and advertise to find buyers, show them the property, and finally get them to pay their highest price.

## Agent vs DIY

The cost of using an agent to sell a median three-bedroom house in Australia is around $9500 to $14000 (using the typical agent's commission of 2 to 3 per cent on a median price of around $470000). On top of this, you have to pay for advertising and marketing costs that vary from $500 to thousands of dollars. If you have the time and do not mind dealing directly with buyers, you might be able to save yourself a lot of money. The key to selling successfully yourself is to find enough buyers so that the property sells itself. The risk is that you do not get the highest price for the property, compared to what an agent would, or it does not sell at all.

> They key to selling successfully yourself is to find enough buyers so that the property sells itself.

Even if you decide not to use an agent, you should still invite a few agents to give you a listing presentation so you can borrow some ideas on how to sell your property. It will also provide an independent check of your starting price. The following steps are for the sellers that choose to use an agent, although most of it will also be relevant to the DIYers.

## Independent valuation

The first step is to get an independent valuation of your property. Explain to the valuer that it is for selling purposes and to give you the best estimate. In particular, look at the sales comparisons used to value your property. This valuation has two purposes: to help you set the selling price in conjunction with the agent and to avoid the agents that over-quote to win your business.

## Listing presentation

Next, invite all of the major local agents to give you a listing presentation where they walk you through the sales process they will use to sell your property. You are effectively interviewing them for the job of selling your property. An agent has two goals with the listing presentation: firstly, to win the listing, and secondly to set the selling price and adjust it according to market conditions to achieve a sale. That is, the agent not only wants to win a listing, but to win a listing that can be sold.

The listing presentation begins with the agent getting to know you, and in particular why you want to sell (they will usually insist that both decision-makers are present). The agent might not ask this directly, and instead casually ask, 'Where are you going?' He or she wants to assess how serious you are with the sale, and how easy it will be to make the sale. For example, if you recently bought somewhere else you will be very keen to sell and will probably be amenable to a reasonable selling price. But if you are just testing the market you are probably not in a hurry to sell, if at all.

The agent will also enquire about what you want to do with the sales proceeds to find out your needs and your emotional buttons and to take your focus off the price of the property. Later on, he or she will gently push those buttons if needed to steer you in a particular direction. A good way for the agent to break the ice and build rapport is to ask to inspect the property. It is your pride and joy and you can probably talk about it forever. Do not be surprised if you get plenty of compliments on the property.

The agent will then get down to business and recommend either a private treaty sale or taking the property to auction, and follow up with a marketing plan to find buyers. Eventually the agent will arrive at the two dreaded price questions: how much he or she thinks the property is worth and how much he or she charges (because this is where agents are most likely to lose the listing). At the end of the listing presentation, the agent will try to 'close' the sale by asking you to sign a listing agreement giving the agent exclusivity for at least 60 days. Do not sign anything until you hear from the other agents. Finally, do not just rely on the testimonials that the agent puts forward as they are all bound to be positive, but ask for a list of past sellers and randomly call them. Also, ask each agent about competitors and what he or she thinks of them.

## Private treaty or auction

The key difference between private treaty sales and auctions is how the price is initially set and adjusted. Private treaty sales usually start with a high price and this reduces to the *highest selling price*. Auctions, on the other hand, start with a low price and this increases to *just above the second highest selling price* because the winning bidder only has to pay above the second highest bidder, and not his or her *maximum* price. Auctions also reveal the seller's minimum price—the reserve price— whereas private treaty sales do not.

Furthermore, with private treaty sales the price is set in private, while for auctions it is set in public. Therefore, with private treaty sales, if you really want the property you have to put forward your best offer because you cannot see what your competitors are offering. However, with auctions you only have to beat the next highest bidder, because you can see his or her price. So in theory private treaty sales should achieve a higher selling price than auctions.

However, the public price-setting of auctions can also be their strength under certain circumstances. All that is needed are two bidders that get carried away in the heat of the moment and pay over their limit. However, if there are insufficient bidders, such as at foreclosure sales during the accumulation stage of the market, the property might be undersold.

Your choice of sales method should be partly based on the predominant sales method in the area because it is the approach that buyers in the area are most familiar with. For example, auctions are the norm in the inner city suburbs of Sydney and Melbourne, while private treaty sales are more common in the outer rings and the smaller capital cities. However, at the very upper end sales are by private treaty. You should also take into account the unique features of the property, such as water views, which are more likely to result in emotional bidding at an auction. Finally, you should consider the stage of the property cycle that you are selling into. You will usually get the best results with auctions during the uptrend of the property cycle, especially in the frenzied later stages when novices enter the market.

## Setting the price

Agents dread the 'How much is my property worth?' question because it is usually where they lose the listing. So most will go to great pains to point out how other agents overinflate what they think they can sell the property for to win the listing, and then tell you how much they think it is worth. Some might skirt the issue and say that the property is worth what a buyer will pay. Keep pressing until the agent gives you a price or a price range, even if you are taking the property to auction. Then ask the agent to justify the price by showing you supporting sales evidence.

With private treaty sales, the most effective approach is to set a starting price 5 to 10 per cent above market value for the first few weeks. That is when the property receives the most interest. You might be fortunate enough to find a buyer that develops an emotional attachment to your property and buys with their heart instead of their head. For example, they think that only the rooms in your house are big enough to live in (as did one of my friends). If there is no sign of interest at that price, do not wait too long to adjust the price to a more realistic level. Otherwise, the property becomes stale and buyers will avoid it because they think there is something wrong with it or that you are asking too much.

I don't recommend advertising a property without a price, or saying that the price is negotiable because you will end up with a lot of bargain hunters making low-ball offers that waste everyone's time. Even serious buyers will start with a low offer if you do not specify a price. In addition, the uncertainty around price will put some buyers off. You increase your chances of getting a good price if you make it as easy as possible for buyers to buy. I also do not recommend specifying a price range, because the buyers will automatically focus on the bottom of the range and you might as well specify that as your asking price.

Sometimes you might get a good offer early on. While you should not accept the first offer you receive, it is important to remember that sometimes the best offers occur early, when interest in the property is at its greatest. Sellers sometimes become overconfident when they get a good early offer, and end up holding out too long for better offers. Some might even wait for more offers to justify paying the agent's commission. The commission is a sunk cost (paid in arrears), so it should not enter your decision-making process. Instead, you should consider how the offer compares to your valuation and your expectations, where you are in the property cycle, and whether you think prices will soften in the near future.

The equivalent of the starting price for an auction is the price guide. One of the biggest complaints buyers have is the extent to which some agents underquote the price guide for a property. Although illegal, some agents still quote a high price to sellers and a much lower price to buyers. If you get a huge turnout to the first open inspection, there is a good chance that the agent underquoted the price guide. Baiting buyers with a low price will attract more interest, but is counterproductive because it mainly attracts bargain hunters who will not be able to afford to pay the reserve price. You are better off setting the price guide near your reserve price. That way the buyers that you attract will be able to afford your reserve price. If you get no interest, it might indicate that your reserve price is out of line with the market.

> Baiting buyers with a low price will attract more interest, but is counterproductive because it only attracts bargain hunters.

You also have to set the reserve price for your property, which should be based on your independent valuation. In particular, you should be clear about how flexible you can be with the reserve price so that you are not rushed into making a decision on auction day. For example, if the bidding stops $9000 below your reserve price, what will you do?

## Finding buyers

Buyers generally select an area first and then start looking for a property in the area. In addition, most buyers live in or around the area, and they come into the area buy. So the focus of your marketing should be in the area around your property. The most common ways of finding buyers are:

- sign boards
- window displays in the agent's office
- advertising on real estate websites such as Domain and realestate.com.au
- advertising in the local newspaper
- advertising in the agent's in-house magazine
- the real estate office's buyer enquiry database
- letterbox drops in the local area.

## Advertising and marketing

Be wary of paying for advertising that is of marginal value in finding buyers. For example, a small advertisement in the local newspaper with the details of your property and a photo is sufficient and will generate the same number of enquires as a full-page spread. The agents prefer the big spreads because it promotes their profile to other sellers. In addition, advertising in the local newspaper is more cost-effective than advertising in the daily metro newspaper because it focuses on the area where the buyers are looking. You should also investigate cheap advertising methods such as letterbox drops in the local area promoting the sale of your property, which can be very effective but are often neglected by agents.

> Be wary of paying for advertising that is of marginal value in finding buyers.

When the agents go through their marketing plan, ask them what the marketing cost covers and then ask them for a breakdown of the source of their buyers. (If the agent does not track this statistic, you should question his or her competence.) This will help you understand how the agent finds buyers and whether you can trust this person to put your interests first. For example, if only 10 per cent of the agent's buyers come from newspaper advertising, yet the agent is asking you to pay $1500 in marketing costs, half of which covers newspaper advertising, then it is clearly not the most effective use of your marketing spend. Also, make sure the agent passes on all rebates (volume discounts) from the newspapers and real estate websites.

Advertising and marketing costs are payable irrespective of whether your property sells or not. You might be able to avoid this situation by negotiating a 'no sale, no fee' arrangement with the agent. Make sure there are no hidden charges. The downside of this approach is that the agent will do everything possible to condition you to a lower selling price to ensure a sale so that he or she does not have to foot the marketing costs. You might be better off paying for the advertising and marketing costs yourself and having the agent work for you, instead of the buyer.

Some agents deliberately omit the address of the property and the floor plan in the advertisement. They reason that this will encourage buyers to contact them so they can qualify the buyers and deal with their objections. Unless your property has some unique features, I would discourage this marketing approach on the premise that you get the highest selling price by making it easy for buyers to buy. For example, when I do online inspections to buy a property, to save time I usually avoid the agents that use this sales method.

# Choosing an agent

After you have sat through all of the listing presentations, you will have a good understanding of the sales process. Each agent will recommend a sales method and marketing campaign to support the sale, including the advertising and marketing costs. You will also have the answer to the two price questions: how much the agent thinks the property will sell for, and how much they charge.

There are two main steps in selling a property:

▶ Finding genuine buyers in a cost-effective way.

▶ Getting the highest price from the buyers.

So the agent to choose is the one that is most likely to find the most genuine buyers in a cost-effective way, because it is much easier to achieve the second step if you find more genuine buyers in the first step. However, it is not as straightforward as it sounds because you have to distinguish form from substance. For example, an agent that spends a big chunk of your money advertising in the daily metro papers will generate a lot of publicity, but this can actually be counterproductive by attracting mainly sticky beaks. Similarly, an agent that underquotes the price guide by 20 or 30 per cent will generate a huge turnout at the open inspection, but this does not guarantee strong bidding at the auction because the reserve price will be more than what many of the bidders can afford.

> Choose the agent that is most likely to find the most genuine buyers in a cost-effective way.

Start with what each agent thinks your property is worth. With your independent valuation and the other agents' valuations, you will have a good idea of the market value of your property and which agents provided realistic estimates. Discard the low ones because these agents are either not confident of getting you market value or are conditioning you to a lower price, and reject the high ones that are overinflated to win your listing.

Next, compare the marketing plans. There will be many elements in common with the agents, such as advertising in the local paper and the real estate websites. Note any points of difference that could help you find more genuine buyers and get a higher price. You should avoid the agents that charge a large marketing levy just to build their profile. Not only does it waste your money, it can also be counterproductive in finding genuine buyers.

Then consider price. You should avoid the agents that charge next to nothing, such as a flat 1 per cent commission. The income is insufficient to run a profitable real estate sales business, and they will have to cut corners to survive. This makes it very difficult for you to get a good price for your property. However, there is no correlation between the highest commission rate and the highest selling price. Similarly, the agents that make the most sales will not necessarily get you the highest price. These agents might just be good at making listing presentations and building rapport with sellers, while the properties sell themselves.

If the remaining agents all use a similar marketing approach but one charges a commission rate that is out of line with the others, ask this agent to justify it. The agent might respond by claiming to be the best negotiator and that you actually end up paying less because he or she will be able to get you a higher price. However, all the agents claim to be top negotiators who can get the highest price. When an agent claims to be the best negotiator or that he or she will get you the highest price for your property, ask him or her to demonstrate these attributes. If the commission is a sticking point, see if the agent is prepared to accept a sliding scale commission instead of a flat commission, so that the agent only gets paid the extra commission if a higher price is achieved.

Finally, select the agent that you feel most comfortable with and have the most confidence in. Do not just rely on your gut feel, but take into account the testimonials and feedback of past sellers.

## Sales commission

Agents usually charge a sales commission of 1 to 3 per cent of the selling price, plus advertising and marketing costs. For more expensive properties the commission rate will be lower. The commission is typically shared between the listing agent (the agent that persuades you to sell your property with the agency) and the selling agent (the agent that persuades the buyer to buy your property). In many situations, the listing and the selling agent are the same.

If you ask agents to reduce their sales commission, some will tell you that they do not negotiate their commission, and that any agent prepared to discount their commission would do the same with the selling price of your property. Others will appeal to your sense of fair play and ask whether you were prepared to take a pay cut at work, because that is what you are effectively asking them to do. Regardless of what the agents say, remember that you are negotiating from a position of strength because there are many agents competing to list your property, and only be prepared to pay a higher commission if the agent can justify it.

## Exclusive listing

You should give the agent an exclusive listing for six weeks (the agents will typically ask for 60 days). It is long enough so that the agent will invest the necessary time and effort to market the property and find you a buyer, but not too long for him or her to just sit back and wait for a buyer to turn up. If the agent does not perform to your satisfaction, you can take the property to another agent after the expiry of the listing agreement. If you choose a shorter period, you reduce the risk of being tied to an underperforming agent. However, there will be less incentive for the agent to find you a buyer, and you could end up with a self-fulfilling prophecy.

Make sure you negotiate everything you need before you sign the listing agreement, when your bargaining power is strongest. After you sign the listing agreement, the balance of power shifts to the agent. The agent has exclusivity over your property for the term of the listing agreement, and if you are under pressure to sell—maybe because you have already bought elsewhere—the agent will exploit this to try to achieve a sale before the listing agreement expires.

Some sellers think they might be able to sell faster or get a higher price if they use more than one agent. However, there are two reasons why you should never multi-list your property. Firstly, the agents will put less effort into selling your property compared to their exclusive listings because there is no guarantee that they will be paid, or they might have to share the commission with another agent. Secondly, buyers can play off the agents against each other to pay the lowest price. The agents will do all they can for the buyer so that they can make the sale before the other agents and so will effectively work for the buyer instead of you.

## Presentation of the property

If you want to get the highest price for your property, you need to present it in the best light. This increases the chances of buyers developing an emotional attachment to the property because when buyers purchase a property for emotional reasons they are prepared to pay much more than they normally would. A furnished property is much more welcoming than an empty one, so ideally you should sell your home first before you buy another one. That way, you save on the cost of hiring furniture. In addition, there will be less pressure on you to accept any price to achieve a quick sale.

Start from the outside:

▸ mow the lawn

▸ prune the shrubs

- tidy the garden

- remove any rubbish

- give the fence and front door a fresh coat of paint to improve the property's street appeal.

Inside the property:

- consider repainting the walls and ceilings to give the property a new look

- steam-clean the carpets

- wash/dust the curtains/blinds

- throw away junk to de-clutter the property and give the impression of more space

- remove cigarette, pet and food odours

- patch up cracks, fix leaking taps and creaking doors, and so on

- make sure everything is sparkling clean, especially the kitchen and bathrooms because this is where women focus first and they usually have the final say.

The agent will be able to provide specific guidance for your property. You should also attend a few open houses around your area to get some ideas. For more expensive properties, you might want to consider hiring a home stylist whose services range from advising on basic presentation to project managing the furnishing of your property (including plant hire for the garden). The cost, including furniture hire for four weeks, can reach up to the tens of thousands of dollars.

For open inspections, choose a time that presents your property in the best natural light. Also consider noise, traffic and so on. During the open inspection:

- Draw the curtains to let in as much light as possible. If the living areas are south-facing, turn on the lights as well.

- Buy freshly cut flowers to brighten up the property.

- Some sellers also use the aroma of brewing coffee or a baking cake to make buyers feel at home.

## Reducing the price

On average, it takes one to three months for a property to sell in the capital cities, depending on the state of the market. However, if you hold out for a high price, it could take much longer. The biggest risk for sellers is that market conditions change and prices start to fall. When this happens, the best course of action is to adjust the selling price to the market or take the property off the market.

The problem is that things are not as straightforward as this. Throughout the sales process, agents will condition you to accept a lower price so they can sell the property quickly and easily and get paid. When the agent tells you that there is no buying interest at the current price and that you should consider reducing the asking price, you have to distinguish between agent conditioning and a genuine change in market conditions. By law, the agent is required to pass on all offers to the seller, so you will have a gauge of buyer interest. You should supplement this by keeping track of the trend in sales statistics in your area, such as the number of properties listed for sale on the real estate websites and the number of sales and auction clearance rates, to help you make your decision.

You face a similar situation if you auction your property and the bidding does not reach your reserve price, only it will be much more stressful. As the bidding slows down the agent will pressure you to lower the reserve price by pointing out that this is all the market is prepared to pay. If the property is passed in, you face more pressure to negotiate with the highest bidder to reach an outcome to justify the expense of the marketing campaign. However, this is a sunk cost, a cost that has already been incurred and cannot be reversed, and therefore should not affect your decision-making process.

The only factor you should take into account is the stage of the property cycle and whether you expect prices to fall further. If you think that prices are temporarily weak, for example because of the onset of winter, then take the property off the market for a few months and then sell it as a new listing, perhaps with a new agent. Otherwise, you should revise your expectations and accept a lower price before prices fall even further.

### Don't hold out for too long

A Bronte cottage on sale for $1250000 received an offer of $1650000 six months before, which was rejected because the seller wanted $1750000. This is a $500000 or 30 per cent reduction on his original asking price, and a $400000 or 25 per cent price reduction on the offer that he received, in six months.

# Part V: Making money in real estate

When you ask property investors how they make their money in real estate, some stare at you blankly, while others whip out a property investment analysis computer model, input a few garbage assumptions (such as a capital growth rate of 10 per cent per annum) and show you an unrealistically high internal rate of return and explain that this is how they do it. Most people do not understand how real estate works as an investment. This section explains the common investment strategies used in the real estate market and how I make money in real estate using the value approach. I then wrap up by explaining the stages in the development of a property investor. This section contains many of the **SYSTEM T™** concepts and terms, which you might need to refer back to.

# 21  Common real estate investing strategies

Over the past few years, a number of real estate investing strategies have been advocated. Real estate books used to focus on negative gearing. As rental yields dropped, the focus shifted to finding motivated sellers or positive-cash-flow properties. At the top of the last cycle, the popularity of renovation shows on TV gave rise to the renovation approach to making money. However, the market conditions no longer support any of these investing strategies. (As the focus shifts to a particular strategy, the demand from investors bids up the price on those properties, while the prices of the other properties fall due to the lack of demand, so there might be scope to make money by adopting a strategy opposite to the rest of the market.) I use the value approach to investing, which is commonly used in the stock market but has not been explicitly applied to the real estate market.

## Negative gearing

The aim of negative gearing is to buy high-growth properties that pay a low rental yield. The loss you make on the property reduces the tax payable on your other income. You make your money from the tax savings and the excess of the capital gains in future years over the income loss in the initial years. Since the tax losses feature prominently in the initial years, it is a strategy aimed at high-income investors. You are very silly if you just use this strategy for the tax benefits because it is pointless to spend $1 to save slightly less than 50¢ in tax. Most investors are smarter than this, and invest for both the tax benefits and future capital gains. However, their poor timing with this strategy (paying inflated prices in the later stages of the property cycle) leads to no capital gains for a long time, and so it reduces to a tax-reduction strategy. Negative gearing fell out of favour as rental yields fell over the last five years and it became unsustainable.

## Motivated sellers

The idea behind this strategy is to find sellers that are 'motivated' to sell, such as a deceased estate, divorced couple or bank foreclosure. They want to sell quickly and might not be concerned about getting the highest price. If you low-ball enough of these sellers you will be able to buy a property for below market value. You make your money when you buy.

The problem is that sellers and buyers are much more sophisticated nowadays. With the amount of information available, you would expect every seller to know what their property is worth, and even if there were some that did not know and are desperate to sell, you are still competing with other buyers who know what the property is worth. So your chances of being able to buy a property significantly below market value are very slim. In fact, I have never managed to do this. Furthermore, even if you manage to buy below market value, you could still be paying above intrinsic value (the true worth of the property) and so you might not be getting the bargain that you think you are.

## Positive cash flow

The aim of this strategy is to only buy properties that pay a high rental yield so that the rent from the property is more than sufficient to cover the interest cost of the mortgage and holding costs. A property with these characteristics is self-sustaining; you do not have to contribute any money after you buy it, and you make your money from the positive (that is, residual) cash flow each year. Many authors recommend a 10 per cent rental yield as the secret formula to success.

Positive-cash-flow properties were common in the 1990s, but they are mostly gone now. The demand from investors has bid up the price of these properties and they are now negatively geared. So investors that want positive-cash-flow properties have had to resort to buying in the regional areas or mining towns, or selling wraps and lease options to unsophisticated buyers to improve their cash flow.

Investing in the regional areas and mining towns as a workaround is very risky because these areas are dependent on one industry or employer. If this employment source leaves the area or the cycle turns, you face a collapse in prices and rents. In addition, the wide availability nowadays of non-conforming loans, such as low-doc loans, has made selling wraps and lease options much more difficult. However, the main drawback of a positive-cash-flow strategy is that it pays a high income but has low capital growth and therefore the after-tax returns are lower than a negative gearing strategy, all other things being equal.

# Renovation

The 'reno' strategy involves buying a run-down property and renovating it to re-sell at a profit. You make your money from the increase in value of the property less renovation costs. The problem with this approach is that it does not work when property prices are falling or moving sideways, and probably does not work in rising markets either when you take out the gains due to the market. This approach might have been feasible in the past when run-down properties sold at a discount to market value, but nowadays investors have bid up the price of these properties, so you are starting from behind. In addition, most investors do not have the expertise to undertake such projects.

# Value

My value approach to investing in real estate involves buying only when market value is less than intrinsic value. If this criterion is satisfied, I pay market value for a property. I make my money from spending time in the market and timing the market (the difference between intrinsic value and market value). This universal strategy applies to all investment markets because it is based on general investing principles. In fact, investors such as Warren Buffett have used it successfully in the stock market for over 50 years. It is also timeless. As long as the real estate market is driven by fear and greed, prices will overshoot their intrinsic value, so there will always be opportunities for value investors to make money.

Value investing also makes sense. We all love to go shopping when there is a sale. Yet we do not automatically apply the same principles when the property market is having a sale because no one tells us how much a property is worth. This leads on to the last point. Value investing requires hard work. Anyone can inspect properties; it is much harder to do research.

# 22 How I make money in real estate

I make money in the real estate market by firstly spending time in the market. This is what investing in real estate is about. I augment my returns by timing the market with my buying. I only buy when market value is less than intrinsic value. This is what value investing in real estate is about.

## Yield vs costs

Your reward for spending time in the real estate market is the difference between the long-term yield and the cost of investing in real estate. Most people fund real estate with a combination of debt and equity. The cost of investing in real estate is the cost of the debt and the cost of the equity. For simplicity, I will assume that the cost of equity is the same as the cost of the debt. Over the long term, real estate has returned around 10 per cent per annum, and will probably provide a similar return in the future. Over the last 50 years, interest rates (measured by the standard variable rate) have fluctuated between 5 and 17 per cent per annum. Over the last 10 years, they have averaged around 7 per cent per annum and will probably fluctuate around this level in the future.

Therefore, over the long term we are comparing a yield of 10 per cent per annum with interest rates of 7 per cent per annum. Assume that the 10 per cent yield consists of capital growth of 6 per cent and a rental yield of 4 per cent (the split will vary with the particular property). We have seen before that 1 per cent of the capital growth is due to the capital injection by investors for new buildings, alterations and additions. Therefore, the net capital growth is only 5 per cent per annum. Furthermore, the net rental yield is typically 70 to 80 per cent of the gross rental yield, so a gross rental yield of 4 per cent per annum reduces to a net rental yield of approximately 3 per cent per annum.

So in reality we are comparing a net yield of 8 per cent per annum with interest rates of 7 per cent per annum, to give a *margin* of 1 per cent *of the property value.* For a property funded with 20 per cent equity and 80 per cent debt (a magnification ratio of 5), equity earning a return equal to the cost of debt of 7 per cent per annum plus 1 per cent of the property value gives a return on equity of 12 per cent per annum (7 per cent + 5 × 1 per cent). Over the long term, the returns from investing in real estate are satisfactory, and comparable to the returns from investing in shares.

> Over the long term, the returns from investing
> in real estate are satisfactory.

There is no guarantee that future yields and interest rates will turn out as expected. However, the long-term margin will probably be around 1 per cent of the property value. If it is negative, investors will shift their funds to the other asset classes, causing property prices to fall, which boosts future yields and restores the margin to its long-term level. Similarly, if it is much greater than 1 per cent, then investors will shift their funds from the other asset classes into real estate, causing property prices to rise, which reduces future yields and restores the margin to its long-term level. Depending on the timing of your purchase, over the medium term the margin can be a bit more than 1 per cent (Buying Zone) or a bit less than 1 per cent (Selling Zone).

Figure 22.1 (overleaf) shows my estimate of the *actual* yields for median Sydney houses compared to the standard variable rate over the last 28 years. (I have subtracted 1 per cent from the capital growth rate to allow for construction costs and assumed that the net rent is 75 per cent of the gross rent.) In some years, the yield was much higher than the standard variable rate (1985 to 1988 and 1996 to 2003), while in others it was less than the standard variable rate and even negative. If you had bought in the Buying Zone (1984 to 1986, 1992 to 1994 and 1997 to 1999, based on fundamental analysis), you would have enjoyed strong capital gains for a number of years after your purchase. In contrast, if you had bought at the top of the cycle in 1988 and 2003, you would have suffered large capital losses for a number of years after your purchase.

Figure 22.1: Sydney median house net yields vs standard variable rate[1]

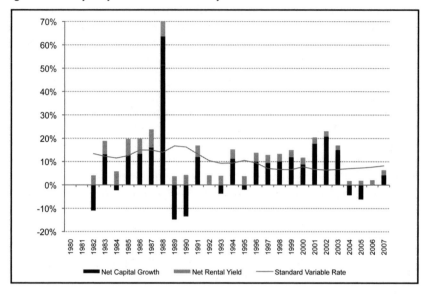

Over 1982 to 2007, the average net yield was 10.4 per cent versus an average standard variable rate of 10.2 per cent, giving a margin of just 0.2 per cent. (The margin was less than 1 per cent because the starting yield was negative; prices fell by 10 per cent in 1982.) You would have achieved this margin if you had bought a median house in 1981, which was in the Selling Zone. You get a very different result if you purchased three years later. Over 1985 to 2007, the average net yield was 11.2 per cent versus an average standard variable rate of 9.9 per cent, giving a margin of 1.3 per cent. You would have achieved this margin if you had bought a median house in 1984, which was in the Buying Zone.

For a property funded with 20 per cent equity and 80 per cent debt (a magnification ratio of 5), the difference in a margin of approximately 1 per cent of the property value (1.3 per cent – 0.2 per cent) is equivalent to a 5 per cent difference in the return on equity, which is significant.

If you cannot obtain a standard loan and have to pay 2 per cent per annum above the standard variable rate, you turn a margin of 1 per cent into –1 per cent (1 per cent – 2 per cent), and your return on equity reduces to 2 per cent per annum (7 per cent – 5 × 1 per cent). You are better off renting and investing the equity and cash savings each week (from not having to pay the interest on the mortgage less the rent) in an online savings account earning close to 7 per cent per annum, or in another asset class such as shares.

While the margin is small, there is some scope for increasing it through lower interest rates, since no one pays the standard variable rate anymore (0.5 per cent), and depreciation tax benefits (0.5 to 1.0 per cent). However, for investors with multiple properties in a state, land tax reduces the margin by approximately 0.5 per cent.

The levers you have to maximise the margin between yield and costs were discussed in part IV. They include:

▸ *Property management.* Make sure that you charge up-to-date market rents and try to sign fixed-term leases that do not expire over December–January, to minimise your vacancy rate. Also, regularly check that your loans have one of the lowest interest rates in the market.

▸ *Renovations.* Undertake cosmetic renovations that are rental positive, such as installing a split-system air conditioner. Focus on the boring things that can make you money and avoid the sexy things that can cost you money.

▸ *Property development.* This is an advanced strategy for improving your yield (both capital growth and rental yield). However, it is risky, and you should only undertake development opportunities as they arise and not actively pursue them.

▸ *Selling.* Avoid selling if possible; otherwise, try to sell in the Selling Zone.

Some people might also be tempted to use the **SYSTEM T™** magnification lever to improve their yield. For example, if you overextend yourself and fund the property with 10 per cent equity and 90 per cent debt, pushing the magnification ratio from 5 to 10, you increase your return on equity from 12 per cent per annum to 17 per cent per annum (7 per cent + 10 × 1 per cent). This is not a good idea because it reduces the security of your investment. It is better to make a satisfactory return, instead of overextending yourself to try to achieve a better return and going broke.

# Buy when market value < intrinsic value

You can augment the margin that you earn from spending time in the market by timing the market. If you only buy when the property market is in the Buying Zone — that is, when market value is *less* than intrinsic value — then you can make a *one-off* return of up to 20 per cent of the property value, relative to intrinsic value. There are also one-off acquisition costs of around 5 per cent of the property value (stamp duty, conveyancing and loan costs), so the one-off return reduces to up to 15 per cent of the property value. For a property funded with 20 per cent equity and 80 per cent debt (a magnification ratio of 5), this gives a one-off return on equity of 75 per cent per annum (5 × 15 per cent).

Time in the real estate market provides a satisfactory return. Timing the market turns a satisfactory return into a very good return. However, if everyone followed my value approach at making money in real estate and timed their buying, it would remove the cycles from property prices, market value would closely follow intrinsic value, and we would lose the one-off return from timing the market. Let's hope everyone doesn't catch on!

Timing the market turns a satisfactory
return into a very good return.

Note that if you buy when market value *equals* intrinsic value you are automatically starting from behind by 5 per cent of the property value or 25 per cent return on equity (5 × 5 per cent) due to the acquisition costs. If you are silly enough to buy at the top of the market, and pay 20 per cent *above* intrinsic value, you are automatically starting from behind by 25 per cent of the property value or 125 per cent return on equity (5 × 25 per cent). This is significant because the return on equity from spending time in the market is only 12 per cent per annum. That is, when you buy at the top of the market, you automatically give away 10 years' worth of returns (125 per cent ÷ 12 per cent).

The levers you have to maximise your return from timing the market are discussed in part III. They include:

▶ *Research*. Spend the bulk of your time researching when, where and what to buy and how much to pay, instead of attending open inspections.

▶ *Inspection*. Ask the four key questions and look for the issues not evident in the advertisement to aid your decision-making process.

▶ *Valuation*. Determine the market value of each property you inspect so you can snap it up if the price falls to your valuation, or move on to the next property if it doesn't.

▶ *Getting to yes*. Use the buying strategies and tactics to buy the property for the lowest price.

# 23 The development of a property investor

It usually takes at least 10 years to become an experienced property investor, because that is how long a property cycle typically lasts. As you make your way through one property cycle, you will start to understand whether your past investing results were due to skill or luck, and whether your investing strategy is sustainable over the long term.

Most real estate investors develop along the following path:

▶ *Renters (30 per cent of all properties in Australia) and people living at home (this includes people saving for a deposit on their first home):* with the increase in property prices over the last 10 years, an increasing percentage of generation Y are likely to remain renters for life. There is nothing wrong with this situation if you provide for your retirement through superannuation and direct shares or managed funds outside of superannuation.

▶ *Homeowners:* your focus is to pay off the mortgage as quickly as possible. The advantage you have over renters is that the mortgage forces you into a regular savings program to pay for a growth asset that can be used to (partially) fund your retirement when you downsize. Over time, your home also provides the equity for you to piggyback into your first investment property. Unfortunately, many people are content to remain at this level, having achieved the Great Australian Dream of owning their own home.

▶ *First-time property investors:* most of you already own your own home and have taken the first steps with a negatively geared investment property. You realise that you do not have to wait until you have paid off your home to purchase another property and will build your wealth faster than the homeowners. You have not been through one property cycle yet, and depending on when you made your purchase are either looking to buy as many more properties as you can to retire in a few years (during the uptrend) or questioning your decision to invest in real estate (near the top of the cycle). Some of you in the former category are at risk of over-committing yourselves as the property cycle peaks, and face bankruptcy when the market turns, while some of you in the latter group will sell out too early, just before the market picks up again.

▸ *Experienced property investors:* you own a portfolio of properties and have been through more than one property cycle. You do not get overly excited when the market rises strongly or question the merits of investing in real estate when it corrects and moves sideways for years. You have perfected a cookie-cutter system for investing in real estate that involves buying real estate at the opposite time to when novices are buying, and never selling. Many of your properties are positively geared and you regularly draw down the equity on these properties to buy more properties.

In my experience, the development of an investor is similar to the development of a professional such as an accountant, lawyer or doctor. It involves a number of years of learning, followed by years of practical experience and professional development (continuous learning), and you only become proficient after around 10 years. That is how it worked for me, and I have been told that I am a quick learner. (It does not have to strictly follow this order; for example, some investors jump into the real estate market right away and learn on the run and some people work and study at the same time.)

Unfortunately, many novice investors do not see it this way. Instead of trying to learn the fundamentals of investing and then working hard to apply the principles, they think that they can shortcut the development process if they can unlock some secret that will give them an edge over everyone else, and they are willing to pay thousands of dollars to learn these 'advanced strategies'. In addition, they tend to bite at strategies that involve taking advantage of other people, such as finding motivated sellers and using wraps and lease options, because that is how they think you make money in real estate.

However, if you look at the successful long-term investors you will notice that they do not rely on any advanced investment strategies for their success. No, just a boring buy-and-hold strategy, combined with a lot of hard work called research. So the main difference between novice investors and experienced investors is that the novices look for a shortcut that will give them an edge but does not require much work, while the pros use a basic strategy that anyone can apply, but requires hard work.

> The main difference between novice investors and experienced investors is that the novices look for a shortcut that will give them an edge but does not require much work, while the pros use a basic strategy that anyone can apply, but requires hard work.

If the advanced strategies really worked, the experienced investors would not bother with all the hard work and they would be the first ones to use them. Similarly, if shortcuts were possible in the real world, then brain surgery students, for example, would not bother spending years learning and practising. They would just pay a few thousand dollars, take the advanced course and start operating the next day.

Until you move beyond this *shortcut mentality*, you will not be able to make any serious money from investing. I know, because I was at this stage many years ago. To move past this level, you have to acquire enough basic investing knowledge to distinguish between misinformation and hype and the investing principles that really work (see **SYSTEM T**™). Only then will you start to make money because:

▸ you will stop wasting your time and money searching for the Holy Grail of investing

▸ you have acquired a BS detector to protect yourself from being ripped off by scammers and spruikers

▸ you will really be investing (spending time in the market) instead of trying to make a quick buck.

# Appendix: Comprehensive buying example

## Background and research summary

I decided to re-enter the Sydney real estate market after a seven-year break in the middle of 2007 because a number of the inner city suburbs in Sydney were in the Buying Zone. In addition, I wanted to rebalance my investment portfolio after the strong run in the stock market since 2003, to an asset class that was out of phase with it (see 'Out-of-phase markets' in chapter 5). Table A.1 lists each step of the buying process in this example, and its duration.

Table A.1: purchase steps

| What | Duration |
|------|----------|
| Research | 1 month |
| Inspections | 3 Saturdays |
| Offer | Monday morning |
| Acceptance | Monday noon |
| Exchange of contracts | Monday afternoon/night |
| Building and pest inspection, lender valuation | That week |
| Unconditional | Following Monday |
| Settlement | 5 weeks later |

I focused on three suburbs characterised by rejuvenated old houses on large blocks of land where the median price was around $1300000. I had a budget of $1500000 to $1600000 to buy either a home or another investment property. I ended up inspecting 15 properties over three consecutive Saturdays, made two offers on my target property and bought it the following Monday. Figure A.1 (overleaf) shows the locations of 10 of the properties that I inspected (the other five were on the west side). The rectangle bounded by the highway and main road is the blue-ribbon area of three adjacent suburbs. The railway line runs parallel to the highway and buses stop along the main road. The CBD is to the south of the diagram. The east side of the highway is more expensive than the west side. Table A.2 (overleaf) lists these properties, with my summary of the features of the property and the original asking price.

Figure A.1: locations of properties for sale

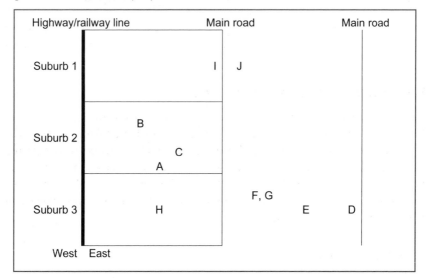

Table A.2: features of properties for sale

| House | Location* | Land | House | Condition | Asking price |
|-------|-----------|------|-------|-----------|--------------|
| A | BR 2/3 | 840 m² | Large | Above average | $1.7–$1.8m |
| B | BR 1/3 | 440 m², slope | Medium | New | High $1.3m |
| C | BR 2/3 | 920 m², slope | Medium | Average | Auction |
| D | MR 6/3 | 595 m² | Medium | Average | Auction |
| E | 5/3 | 700 m² | Medium | New | > $1.5m |
| F | 4/3 | 969 m² | Medium | Average | Auction |
| G | 4/3 | 930 m² | | Land value only | $1.25m |
| H | BR 2/3 | 723 m² | Medium | Above average | Auction |
| I | MR 3/3 | 745 m² | Medium | Average | > $1.38m |
| J | 4/3 | 935 m², slope | Small | Below average | $1.1m |

\* BR = blue-ribbon area; MR = main road; fractions refer to the distance from the highway/railway line as a fraction of the width of the blue-ribbon area.

## Valuation

After going through all of the recent sales that I could find and talking to a few agents, I determined the following reference points: the market value of an 800 m² block of land was around $1 100 000, and the depreciated value of a 'medium'-sized double-brick house in average condition was around $500 000. Note that in this area a 'medium'-sized house consisted of four bedrooms plus study, separate lounge and dining room, family room and two or three bathrooms.

Table A.3: my valuation of the properties for sale

| House | Location | Land | House | Condition | Asking price | Valuation |
|-------|----------|------|-------|-----------|--------------|-----------|
| A | BR 2/3 | 840 m² | Large | Above average | $1.7–$1.8m | $1.6–$1.7m |
| B | BR 1/3 | 440 m², slope | Medium | New | High $1.3m | < asking price |
| C | BR 2/3 | 920 m², slope | Medium | Average | Auction | $1.5–$1.6m |
| D | MR | 595 m² | Small | Below average | Auction | $0.8m |
| E | 5/3 | 700 m² | Medium | New | > $1.5m | $1.5m |
| F | 4/3 | 969 m² | Medium | Average | Auction | $1.6m |
| G | 4/3 | 930 m² | | Land value only | $1.25m | $1.1m |
| H | BR 2/3 | 723 m² | Medium | Above average | Auction | $1.6m |
| I | MR 3/3 | 745 m² | Medium | Average | > $1.38m | $1.2–$1.3m |
| J | 4/3 | 935 m², slope | Small | Below average | $1.1m | $0.95m |

Using this information as a starting point, I valued each of the properties using a combination of the summation and the comparison method, as follows (see table A.3):

▸ I started with Property G, a run-down two-bedroom house on a large block of level land outside of the blue-ribbon area. The asking price should only reflect the land value. I always start with the sales of land first to use as or check my reference point. Property G had just come on to the market so the vendors started with a 'high-ball' asking price. Although Property G fell outside the blue-ribbon area, its value was offset by a bigger land size, so I valued it at $1 100 000. The house had to be knocked down and there was the opportunity cost of building (at least $100 000 in interest for a year), but this is offset by my ability to put my own stamp on the property.

▶ Property A was a double-storey Federation house that had been on the market for six months after being passed in at auction, and it recently moved to another agent. Property A was located around 10 minutes' walking distance from the railway station. The land size was only slightly bigger than my reference block, so I valued it at $1 100 000. The house was large with five bedrooms and a study, a separate lounge and dining room, two family rooms and three bathrooms. Other significant improvements included landscaped gardens and outdoor areas. Property A was larger and in better condition than my reference point, so I valued it at $500 000 to $600 000, giving it a total valuation of $1 600 000 to $1 700 000. This was below the asking price range of $1 700 000 to $1 800 000. Property A was purchased in the early 1980s, renovated and extended, and a second storey was added three years ago, so its last sale price was not relevant.

▶ Property B was a near new double-storey house that had been on the market for a while, but the vendors did not seem to be in a hurry to sell. A possible reason was that they paid $1 375 000 for it in February 2005 and were asking for nearly $1 400 000 to recover their purchase price (they would still lose over $60 000 in stamp duty plus transaction costs). Property B was in an excellent location but the land was only half of the normal size for the area because it was part of a dual occupancy subdivision. In addition, the land sloped down from right to left and was terraced at the back. The house was only four-and-a-half years young and medium sized with a separate living and dining room, four bedrooms, a family room and two bathrooms, so I valued it at $500 000. However, there were no recent dual occupancy sales in the area to value the land. So to see if the property was worth buying, I worked backwards from the asking price of $1 400 000 (the sellers were not motivated, so there is not much scope in negotiating the price down), and subtracted the value of the house of $500 000, to give a price of $900 000 for the 440 m$^2$ block. This was too expensive compared to the $1 100 000 market value of 800 m$^2$ blocks.

▶ Property C was a split-level house built in the 1950s, situated near Property A. The land was slightly larger, but this was offset by it not being level, slopping down from right to the left, so I valued it at $1 100 000. The house was medium sized with separate lounge and dining rooms, four bedrooms, two family rooms and two bathrooms, and in average condition. However, the building quality was not up to the standard of the older properties, and it was not well designed (one of the family rooms was put downstairs almost as an afterthought to provide access to the backyard), so I valued it at \$400 000 to \$500 000, giving Property C a total value of \$1 500 000 to \$1 600 000. It was going to auction but did not have any unique features, so the bidding would probably be sensible. A pre-auction offer around the middle of my valuation range would probably have secured the property. On the other hand, if there was a lack of interest at the auction it might have been possible to buy it for a lower price after it was passed in.

▸ Property D was a single-storey Californian bungalow on a main road, far away from the blue-ribbon area. The block was smallish, and based on similar sales on main roads, but adjusting for the smaller size, I valued it at \$500 000. The house was small, with only three bedrooms, separate lounge and dining rooms, two 'utility' rooms (too small to be bedrooms) and two bathrooms. In addition, the house was in below-average condition, especially the kitchen and bathrooms, and the flow of the rooms was poor, so I valued it at \$300 000, for a total valuation of \$800 000. Property D was a mortgagee auction.

▸ Property E was the type of house that you can easily fall in love with and overpay for. The sellers purchased it not too long ago, completely renovated it and added a spectacular kitchen and family room extension, so the last sale price was not relevant. It was situated away from the blue-ribbon area and the land was at the smaller end for the area, so I valued it at \$900 000 to \$1 000 000. Although in brand-new condition, the single-storey house was medium sized, with separate lounge and dining rooms, three bedrooms and a study, family room and three bathrooms. I valued it at \$500 000 to \$600 000, giving a total valuation of around \$1 500 000. The vendors were looking for a price 'over \$1 500 000'.

▸ Property F was another single-storey Californian bungalow outside the blue-ribbon area. The block was larger than normal, which offset its location, so I valued it at \$1 100 000. The house was medium sized with separate lounge and dining rooms, four bedrooms and a study, a family room and two bathrooms. It was in average condition, with a new kitchen but original bathrooms. I valued the house at \$500 000, giving a total valuation of \$1 600 000. Property F's last sale price was not relevant; it was bought in 1989, and had since been extended and renovated. It was going to auction with an initial price guide of 'above \$1 350 000', which increased to 'above \$1 400 000' nearer to the auction date, based on the number of enquiries. The agent clearly underquoted this property to attract bidding interest, and this resulted in a huge turnout at the first open inspection.

▸ Property H was a single-storey Federation house situated in the same position as Property A, but in an adjoining suburb. Although it was in a closer suburb to the CBD, the land was at the smaller end for the area, so I valued it at $1 000 000 to $1 100 000. The house was medium sized with separate lounge and dining rooms, four bedrooms and a study, a family room and two bathrooms, and in above-average condition. The property also included a pool, which together with the house I valued at $550 000, for a total value of $1 600 000. This property was also up for auction.

▸ Property I was another single-storey Californian bungalow that had been on the market for a while. The sellers were looking for offers above $1 380 000. It was located inside the blue-ribbon area, but just one house away from the main road. A similar-sized block on the main road had a market value of $600 000, so the value of the land was probably $700 000 to $800 000. The house was medium sized with separate lounge and dining rooms, four bedrooms and a study, a small family room and two bathrooms, and in average condition, so I valued it at $500 000, giving an overall valuation of $1 200 000 to $1 300 000. It last sold for $865 000 in January 2001.

▸ Property J was a double-storey house built in the 1960s, situated just outside the blue-ribbon area. The block was large, but sloped steeply up the back. The land had a valuation of $650 000 based on the recent sale of the two houses next door (the valuation was so low because only half of the land was useable). The house was small with an L-shaped lounge and dining room, four small bedrooms, a sunroom and a bathroom, and in below-average condition. I valued the house at $300 000, giving a total valuation of $950 000, compared with the asking price of $1 100 000. Property J had not traded for a long time.

## Getting to yes

Once I had determined a valuation for each property, I proceeded to make offers on the properties that had been on the market the longest. There was no point in making offers on the properties that had just listed with an asking price significantly above my valuation because the sellers were probably starting with a 'high-ball' price to see if there were any buyers that had a special reason for buying their property. I also assessed my likelihood of success with the private treaty negotiations from the agent's feedback on my initial offers to see whether I should put in pre-auction offers on the properties that were going to auction. I had to be very selective in making a pre-auction offer because it meant incurring building and pest inspection costs and tying up my funds for a few days.

Table A.4 shows how the final price for each property compared with the initial asking price and my valuation.

Table A.4: final price of the properties for sale

| House | Location | Land | House | Condition | Asking price | Valuation | Final price |
|-------|----------|------|-------|-----------|--------------|-----------|-------------|
| A | BR 2/3 | 840 m² | Large | Above average | $1.7–$1.8m | $1.6–$1.7m | $1.62m |
| B* | BR 1/3 | 440 m², slope | Medium | New | High $1.3m | < asking price | $1.35m |
| C | BR 2/3 | 920 m², slope | Medium | Average | Auction | $1.5–$1.6m | $1.51m |
| D | MR | 595 m² | Medium | Below average | Auction | $0.8m | $0.825m |
| E | 5/3 | 700 m² | Medium | New | > $1.5m | $1.5m | $1.57m |
| F | 4/3 | 969 m² | Medium | Average | Auction | $1.6m | $1.62m |
| G | 4/3 | 930 m² | | Land value only | $1.25m | $1.1m | $0.97–$1.13m |
| H | BR 2/3 | 723 m² | Medium | Above average | Auction | $1.6m | $1.66m |
| I | MR 3/3 | 745 m² | Medium | Average | $1.38m | $1.2–$1.3m | $1.32m |
| J | 4/3 | 935 m², slope | Small | Below average | $1.1m | $0.95m | Withdrawn |

* Still on the market one year later with a new agent.

I approached each property as follows:

▸ I considered Property G due to my experience in buying land and building houses, and estimated that the total cost of building would be around $1 900 000 ($1 100 000 land + $700 000 construction cost + $100 000 opportunity cost; note that the construction cost is significantly higher than the depreciated value). This did not compare favourably with Property A. In addition, the asking price was too high at the time, so I decided to wait until it dropped further before making an offer.

The asking price of Property G quickly fell to $1 195 000, then $1 145 000, and it eventually sold for $970 000 to $1 130 000, which confirmed my initial valuation.

▸ Property A was my first choice based the property's location, size and condition. However, at $1 700 000 to $1 800 000 I was prepared to walk away from it. At the first open inspection, I found out that the owners were selling for 'asset realisation' reasons, and made an offer on Monday of $1 600 000, which was at the bottom of my valuation range. The agent knocked back my offer and told me that I needed to be closer to the asking price range. This was a promising development because it meant that the sellers were prepared to go below $1 700 000 (which was within my valuation range) and that no one else had offered anything higher. I was going to ask the agent how much closer I needed to be at the next open inspection. I was only prepared to go up to $1 680 000 (yes, I increased my budget, like many people do) because I had another attractive alternative.

Interestingly, I noticed that although Property A had been with the new agent for only three weeks, very few people attended its open inspection compared to Property F, when Property A was a better property in nearly every way. Property A had become stale by being on the market for too long. Some buyers might have avoided the property, thinking that there was something wrong with it or that the vendors were asking too much. I found out later that the agent had suggested to the vendors to take the property off the market for a month or two, so that it could come back on the market as a new property, but they were in a rush to sell.

At my second open inspection, which I attended by catching the train and walking to the property, I discovered another buyer in animated discussion with the agent. Out of nowhere, the agent announced that a price 'over $1 618 000' would secure the property. Interestingly, when the agent asked the other buyer how much he thought the property was worth, he instinctively low-balled with $1 580 000. Obviously there was no need to introduce competition so I stayed in the background.

When everyone had left, I asked the agent why the sellers had the sudden change of heart, and was told that they had an offer of $1 618 000 and had decided to sell now for that price. The agent then threw time pressure into the mix by claiming that the buyer, who was with the previous agent, was expected to come in at this price on Tuesday, but any price above it would secure the house.

Inexperienced buyers might call the agent's bluff and come back with something like, 'that's still too high', and then say they have to check with their partner to counter the time pressure. However, I immediately saw value in the revised price, which was towards the lower end of my valuation range. On the spot I decided to accept the asking price, and asked if I could pay a holding deposit (I always bring a chequebook to open inspections if I am looking to buy). The agent had not been prepared for this and did not know what to do, so he told me to wait until Monday so he could check with the vendor's solicitor.

I might have been able to negotiate the sellers down closer to $1 600 000 (by suggesting they split the difference between $1 600 000 and $1 618 000, for example), but thought that at $1 618 000 the pool of potential buyers for Property A would more than double. If other buyers entered the negotiations, the price could quickly rise back near $1 700 000, especially given the shortage of quality properties for sale in the area at that time. When I did a cost–benefit analysis — save $9000 (or a bit more) but risk paying up to $80 000 more — it was clear that I should not bother haggling.

In case I had fallen in love with the property and was not being objective, I checked with another agent to get an independent view. I had made the point of seeing her property late on Saturday because the property was selling for mainly land value (not Property G). Although I ended up rejecting the property, I had a long chat with the agent who provided valuable information about land prices and building costs in the area. On Sunday I gave her a call and asked what she thought of Property A. She was familiar with the property but clearly unhappy with my question, and grudgingly said it was a bargain. I also spoke to a different agent who was not familiar with the property but did an 'internet valuation' that came in at $1 600 000 to $1 700 000.

At 10.00 am on Monday I put in a formal offer for $1 620 000 that expired at 5.00 pm that day. An hour later the agent told me that my offer had been accepted. (If I did not know the value of the property, I would have been worried about paying too much because the sellers did not try to get me to raise my offer — see 'Psychology of negotiations' in chapter 15.) The agent seemed to be serious about the time pressure. His assistant drove for an hour to hand-deliver the contract to me to sign and collect two personal cheques, one for 0.25 per cent of the purchase price and the other for the balance of the 10 per cent deposit. That night, after calling me to confirm that I wanted to proceed with the purchase, the agent took the contract to the vendors to exchange contracts. So after two weeks of inspections, I was able to close the deal on Property A.

▸ I decided not to make an offer on Property B because I did not think that the asking price was close to market value. As it turns out, Property B was still on the market 12 months later with a different agent and a $50 000 reduction in asking price.

▶ Property C fitted nicely within my budget. However, it will always sell at a discount to the older properties because the building quality was not up to the standard of the older properties. There was a moderate amount of interest in Property C because it was at a lower price point for the area, without any significant defects (such as being on a main road), so I did not think that I would be able to buy it at a sufficient discount and decided not to pursue it.

Property C sold at auction for $1 510 000, which was within my valuation range. As I expected, it sold for a sensible price because it did not have any unique features.

▶ Property D was the worst house on a good street. I did not want to live on a main road and so rejected it as a home. The rental yield was very low because the property was on the main road, and unless the traffic was diverted elsewhere I saw no reason why it would appreciate in value faster than any of the other properties. So I also rejected Property D as an investment property because the yield would have been poor unless I could buy it at a discount to market value, and there was not much chance of that as it was a mortgagee auction. Property D sold for $825 000 at auction, slightly higher than my valuation.

▶ I was very impressed with Property E. It had a higher proportion of its value in the house (which depreciates over time) than most of the other properties. This was not a major concern if I was going to live in it because it is pointless living like a hermit in a shack on a huge block of land and letting your children enjoy the fruits of your labour. The main concern I had was with the price. The asking price was higher than my valuation, and when I asked the agent what 'over $1 500 000' meant, she replied that she already had an offer of $1 520 000. Property E also had some minor issues that detracted from its value for me. Firstly, it was located outside of the blue-ribbon area, which meant that the only transport to the city was by bus, which was located over 15 minutes away. Secondly, at the open inspection I noted that the large setback (the distance of the building from the boundary of the property) of the house left only a small backyard. As a result, I decided not to pursue Property E, but placed it on my watch list in case the interest in it dropped.

There was a private bidding war for Property E and it sold shortly after for $1 570 000.

▶ Property F was my second choice. I would have put in a pre-auction offer near $1 600 000 for Property F if I felt that I did not have any chance of securing Property A. The disadvantage with this arrangement was that I could only put in one offer, so to maximise my chances of securing the property I needed to submit my best offer or close to it. Furthermore, the pre-auction offer precluded me from negotiating on the other properties due to my commitment to this one, yet there was no guarantee that the seller would accept my offer or that someone else would not submit a higher offer.

When I spoke to the agent afterwards, he indicated that anything near $1 600 000 would have been a very good offer. Eighteen buyers registered and the auction was competitive. The final price of $1 620 000 was nearly a street record. Coincidentally it was the same price I paid for Property A. The selling agent thought that I got a better deal on Property A, and 'that's why you should always sell at auction.'

▸ Property H would have been one of my top three choices but I did not have my finances finalised before auction date, when it sold for $1 660 000.

▸ When I first inspected Property I, the first thing I did was to walk outside and stand there for 10 minutes to get a feel for the traffic on the main road. The traffic was heavy, even though it was 11 am. For some reason, none of the other people inspecting the property considered doing this. When I went inside, I opened the windows in each room, and the traffic noise was intrusive. However, my biggest concern was that the vendors were asking way too much for the property. They were pricing it more like a property away from the main road, even though it was just one property away, and this was why I decided not to pursue the property.

After a few months, the sellers reduced the asking price for Property I by $100 000 to offers above $1 280 000. It eventually sold for $1 320 000.

▸ I told the agent for Property J that the asking price was not realistic and asked him what price the vendors were prepared to accept for the property. He replied that they were flexible, but indicated that the price needed to be closer to $1 100 000 than $1 000 000. This was significantly more than my valuation and the vendors were not prepared to budge from their position, so I decided not to pursue the property.

The asking price for Property J briefly dropped below $1 100 000, but then increased by $40 000 to $1 140 000 after some nearby competition sold. It was withdrawn from the market six months later.

## Closing the deal

After checking the contract for Property A for any non-standard items, I exchanged contracts right away and paid a non-refundable deposit of $4050 (0.25 per cent × $1 620 000), due to the possibility of another buyer entering the fray the next day. My solicitor confirmed that the contract was standard; that is, there were no special conditions for the sale. Since a second storey was recently added to Property A, the solicitor confirmed that the builder had homeowners warranty insurance and the council compliance certificate was satisfactory.

The building and pest inspection cost me $350 and $160 respectively. The building inspection report concluded that the property was in above-average condition for its age and construction. The main problems it pointed out were:

▶ Some rising damp was evident at the base of the family room wall and it recommended installing or replacing damp-proof course material.

▶ Some areas in the subfloor did not have ant capping, which deters termites and facilitates detection during inspection.

▶ Drainage on the right-hand side of the property was inadequate and drains should be installed. This was evident after unusually heavy rainfall.

The pest inspection report found no active timber pests. However, there was evidence of moderate inactive (past) termite damage under the floor of the study, which was originally the veranda. The vendors confirmed that termite activity was discovered 23 years ago when they extended and renovated the house, which they treated chemically. (There is usually a sticker in the meter box to indicate recent treatment, with information such as chemical used, date applied and life expectancy of the treatment.) They also cleared the subfloor area of timber as a preventative measure.

The lender's valuation of Property A was in line with my purchase price and the report concluded that the purchase price represented fair market value. However, the valuation appeared to be conservative because the sales evidence used (Properties 1, 2 and 3) was not only a long way outside the blue-ribbon area, but two were on the much cheaper west side (see figure A.2). Property 1 was superior with a price of $1 700 000 (double the land size, four bedrooms), while properties 2 (four bedrooms) and 3 (three bedrooms) were inferior with prices of $1 510 000 and $1 400 000 respectively. The three comparison properties were sold six and five months before.

Figure A.2: location of comparison properties

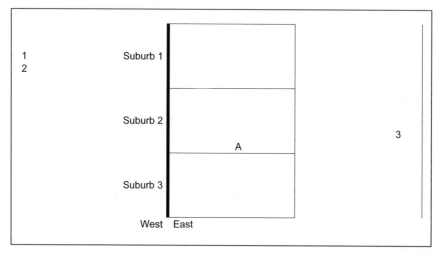

After the satisfactory building and pest inspections and unconditional loan approval from my lender, I paid the balance of the 10 per cent deposit of $157950 (9.75 per cent × $1620000) before the expiry of the cooling-off period. At settlement, I paid the balance of the purchase price of $1460000 (90 per cent × $1620000). My final inspection was very quick.. The sellers left the property in pristine condition, with appliance manuals, touch-up paints and spare light bulbs. They also left instructions on how to use the various electrical items, together with warranty information and contact details.

After each purchase, I review my results against my expectations at the start. What did I do well and what were the opportunities for improvement? I was pleased with the efficiency of my purchase. All up, it took only a month and a half from research to exchange of contracts, including three Saturdays of inspections. There was no doubt that I needed a little luck to secure the property at such a good price so quickly. However, given the same opportunity, most people would have hesitated or tried to get a better deal and lost the property to the other buyer, confirming the adage: luck is what happens when preparation meets opportunity. By doing thorough research, I had a good idea of what the property was worth, and when the opportunity to buy it within my valuation range arose I acted without hesitation.

The selling agent told me afterwards that the property had originally been passed in at auction in the 'high 1s' (that is, almost $2000000), and the sellers had subsequently knocked back offers of 1.8s and 1.7s. When I spoke to the previous agent, he would only confirm that he had an offer of $1710000. (He took over from another agent in the agency so it is possible that there were higher offers.) He was bemused by what happened because he had a buyer with the same offer, confirming what the selling agent had said.

As it turned out, the vendors had high price expectations and waited too long to adjust to the market. Over the course of six months, the property became stale and the offers gradually reduced in value. The vendors changed agents to see if they could bring in new buyers, and three weeks later accepted a price of $1 618 000 offered by a buyer introduced by the previous agent. The sellers wanted to give the new agent the first right of refusal, which gave me the opportunity to pay $1 620 000 and buy the property.

The property market in the suburb that I bought in was in a state of frenzy four months later. For example, a couple paid $1 975 000 at auction for a property similar to mine, $325 000 above the reserve price. The agent, who originally quoted a price of above $1 500 000, and then above $1 600 000, thought that $1 650 000 to $1 700 000 would have been a stretch and was very surprised at the result. The strong market was causing buyers to push the price of similar properties way over the reserve price because many of them had missed out over the past few months.

This was the reason why I acted so decisively when the asking price for the property dropped to $1 620 000. The uptrend in the suburb had already started, and I had an opportunity to buy a good property at an accumulation-stage price because there was virtually no competition. If the vendors had decided to take the property off the market for a few months and then auctioned it again in late spring, it could have fetched 10 to 20 per cent more. A novice buyer, on the other hand, might have started with a low-ball offer of, say, $1 450 000 (a 10 per cent discount to the selling price). The agent would probably have laughed at this, and not given the person the opportunity to match the other buyer's offer when it arose.

# Glossary

| | |
|---|---|
| **auction** | The public sale of a property to the highest bidder. |
| **blue-chip shares** | The shares of large, well-established companies that have a strong history of paying dividends. |
| **buying off the plan** | Entering into a contract to buy a property, usually an apartment, before it has been built. |
| **Buying Zone** | When the market is having a sale and market value is less than intrinsic value. This is the only time you should be buying real estate. |
| **company title** | The ownership of real estate through ownership of company shares, which entitles the owner to exclusive possession of a 'unit' of the property. Changes in occupancy must be approved by the company. |
| **comparison rate** | The true interest rate on a loan taking into account the upfront costs and ongoing fees. Also known as the average annual percentage rate (AAPR), it allows borrowers to compare loans with different interest rate and fee structures by showing the actual total cost for a standard situation. |
| **contract of sale** | A written agreement of the terms and conditions of the sale of a property. |
| **contrarian** | An investor who does the opposite of what most other investors are doing, such as buying when others are selling. |
| **conveyancing** | The legal process of transferring the ownership of a property. |
| **cooling-off period** | The statutory period after exchange of contracts where the buyer can cancel the contract unconditionally for a small penalty. |
| **cross-collateralisation** | When two or more properties are used as security for a loan. |
| **debt service ratio** | The measure of a borrower's ability to service a loan, calculated as the ratio of loan repayment to serviceable income (a percentage of salary and rent). |

| | |
|---|---|
| **deposit bond** | A guarantee that the deposit will be paid at settlement (for an off-the-plan purchase). |
| **depreciation** | The write down of the original cost of the building, capital works or fixtures and fittings by a specified percentage each year to reflect wear and tear. |
| **development application** | The application to council for consent to carry out development. |
| **diminishing value method** | The depreciation of a constant proportion of the remaining value of the item each year. |
| **dollar cost averaging** | The investing of equal amounts of money at regular intervals (in shares and managed funds) to reduce the average cost by acquiring more shares/units in periods of lower prices and fewer shares/units in periods of higher prices. |
| **dual occupancy** | Two dwellings on one lot. |
| **duplex** | A single building on one lot that is up to two storeys in height and contains two attached dwellings. |
| **easement** | The right to use someone else's land for a specific purpose, such as a government authority running mains, drains and water pipes through private property. |
| **exchange of contracts** | The vendor and purchaser each sign a copy of the contract of sale and then exchange these documents to enter a legally binding contract. |
| **exclusive listing** | When only one agent is appointed to sell or lease a property. |
| **fittings** | The items attached to a property, such as light fittings. |
| **fixtures** | The items fixed to a property, such as kitchen cabinets. |
| **flip** | To buy a property and quickly sell it. |
| **for sale by owner (FSBO)** | A real estate sale without an agent. |
| **gazumping** | When the vendor verbally agrees to sell the property to one party, but then sells the property to another party on more favourable terms. |

**hedge**
An investment that cancels out the risk, and return, of another investment.

**intrinsic value**
The long-term value of a property based on the net present value of future cash flows.

**lease option**
A lease with the option to buy the property. Note that both the selling price and the rent are significantly higher than what you can get in the marketplace.

**lenders' mortgage insurance**
Insurance that protects the lender if the borrower defaults on the mortgage and the property is sold for less than the outstanding amount on the loan. The borrower remains liable to the mortgage insurer for the amount it has to pay the lender.

**loan-to-valuation ratio (LVR)**
The ratio of the loan to the value of the property securing the loan.

**low documentation (low-doc) loan**
A loan for borrowers who cannot provide proof of income to qualify for standard loans.

**magnification ratio**
The ratio of the value of a property to the value of the equity. It measures the extent of leverage and risk.

**margin of safety**
The difference between the intrinsic value of a property and its market value. When you buy a property at a discount to its intrinsic value, you build up a buffer against future adverse returns.

**mark to market**
To assign a value to an investment based on the current market price for that investment.

**market value**
The price, or value ascribed by the market, of a property. Where a property is untraded, it is estimated as the amount a willing and knowledgeable buyer would pay to a willing and knowledgeable seller for the property in an arm's length transaction.

**median price**
The middle price when prices are arranged from lowest to highest; it is the representative price in an area.

**multi-listing**
When more than one agent is appointed to sell or lease a property.

**negative cash flow**
When the rent plus tax credit does not cover all cash expenses and interest and you have to put money into the property.

| | |
|---|---|
| **negative gearing** | When the rent does not cover all the expenses and interest and you make a loss on the property. Negative gearing can be with negative cash flow or positive cash flow. |
| **open for inspection** | When an agent opens up a property for inspection by prospective buyers at a specified time each week for around an hour. |
| **opportunity cost** | The cost of pursuing one course of action in terms of the foregone return that could have been earned on an alternative course of action. |
| **owners' corporation** | The body comprising all the lot owners in a strata scheme that administers, manages and maintains the common property. It was formerly known as the body corporate. |
| **passed in** | Not sold at auction because the bidding did not reach the reserve price of the property. |
| **piggyback** | The use the available equity in an existing property as a deposit for a new property. |
| **positive cash flow** | When the rent plus tax credit covers all cash expenses and interest and the property puts money in your pocket. |
| **positive gearing** | When the rent covers all the expenses and interest and you make a profit on the property. Positive gearing is always with positive cash flow. |
| **prime cost method** | The depreciation of a fixed amount over the effective life of the item each year. |
| **private treaty** | The sale of a property through private negotiation, usually via a real estate agent. |
| **rescind** | To cancel a contract. |
| **reserve price** | The lowest price at which the vendor is prepared to sell the property at auction. |
| **Selling Zone** | When market value is greater than intrinsic value (the opposite of the Buying Zone). If you have to sell a property, this is the time. |
| **setback** | The distance of the building from a boundary. |
| **settlement** | The final stage of the buying process when the buyer pays the balance of the contract price to the vendor and takes legal possession of the property. |

| | |
|---|---|
| **standard variable interest rate** | The banks' reference rate that applies to fully featured loans. |
| **strata levy** | The quarterly contributions paid by lot owners to the owners' corporation in strata schemes to fund ongoing maintenance and recurring expenses (administration fund), and major maintenance expenses and expenses of a capital nature (sinking fund). There are also occasional special levies to fund unplanned expenses. |
| **strata title** | The ownership of a 'unit' of a property (block of apartments, townhouses, and so on) based on the subdivision of the property into lots and common property. The lots (apartments, garages, and so on) are owned by the owners, and everything else is common property (driveways, gardens, stairs, and so on) that is owned by the owners' corporation, which comprises all the lot owners. |
| **subdivision** | The division of a parcel of land according to council approval into separate lots, each with a separate title. |
| **SYSTEM T**™ | The investment framework that forms the foundation of every buying and management decision I make with my real estate portfolio. It stands for security, yield, spread, time, equity, magnification and tax. |
| **Torrens title** | The ownership of land by registration with the Land Titles Office. |
| **two-tier marketing** | Selling real estate to out-of-area investors for a higher price than the locals. |
| **variation** | The addition to, deletion from, or alteration to a building contract. |
| **wrap** | A form of vendor financing where the vendor sells the property and provides financing to the buyer. Note that both the selling price and the interest rate are significantly higher than what you can get in the marketplace. |
| **zoning** | The classification of land in a municipality into areas to regulate use (such as residential, business and industrial), density (from single houses to high-rise apartment buildings), building dimension, arrangement and design. |

# Resources

## My website

▸ *I Buy Houses* book: <www.ibhb.com.au>

My website contains the most up-to-date links and other resources.

## General

▸ Australian Taxation Office: <www.ato.gov.au>

▸ Defence Housing Australia (DHA): <www.dha.gov.au>

▸ First Home Owner Grant: <www.firsthome.gov.au>

▸ Real Estate Institute of Australia: <www.reiaustralia.com.au>

## State/territory buying and selling real estate and renting handbooks

▸ Australian Capital Territory: Office of Fair Trading: <www.fairtrading.act.gov.au>

▸ New South Wales: Office of Fair Trading: <www.fairtrading.nsw.gov.au>

▸ Northern Territory: Department of Justice—Consumer and Business Affairs: <www.nt.gov.au/justice/>

▸ Queensland: Residential Tenancies Authority: <www.rta.qld.gov.au>

▸ South Australia: Office of Consumer and Business Affairs: <www.ocba.sa.gov.au>

▸ Tasmania: Consumer Affairs and Fair Trading: <www.consumer.tas.gov.au>

▸ Victoria: Consumer Affairs: <www.consumer.vic.gov.au>

▸ Western Australia: Department of Consumer and Employment Protection: <www.docep.wa.gov.au/consumerprotection/>

## State or Territory Office of Revenue

▸ Australian Capital Territory: <www.revenue.act.gov.au>

▸ New South Wales: <www.osr.nsw.gov.au>

▸ Northern Territory: <www.nt.gov.au/ntt/revenue>

▸ Queensland: <www.osr.qld.gov.au>

▸ South Australia: <www.revenuesa.sa.gov.au>

▸ Tasmania: <www.sro.tas.gov.au>

▸ Victoria: <www.sro.vic.gov.au>

▸ Western Australia: <www.dtf.wa.gov.au>

## Banks

▸ ANZ: <www.anz.com.au>

▸ Commonwealth Bank: <www.commbank.com.au>

▸ NAB: <www.nab.com.au>

▸ Westpac: <www.westpac.com.au>

## General insurers

▸ Allianz: <www.allianz.com.au>

▸ Insurance Australia Group: <www.iag.com.au>

▸ Suncorp: <www.suncorp.com.au>

## Credit information

▸ Mycreditfile: <www.mycreditfile.com.au>

## Loan comparison

▸ CANNEX: <www.cannex.com.au>

▸ InfoChoice: <www.infochoice.com.au>

▸ Moneymanager: <www.moneymanager.com.au>

## Maps

▸ Google Maps: <maps.google.com.au>

▸ Whereis: <www.whereis.com>

## Real estate sales

▸ Domain: <www.domain.com.au>

▸ realestate.com.au: <www.realestate.com.au>

## General data

▸ Australian Bureau of Statistics: <www.abs.gov.au>

▸ Reserve Bank of Australia: <www.rba.gov.au>

## Real estate data

▸ Australian Property Monitors: <www.apm.com.au>

▸ Real Estate Institute of Australia: <www.reiaustralia.com.au>

▸ Residex: <www.residex.com.au>

▸ RP Data: <www.myrp.com.au>

# Notes

## Chapter 2

1   Australian Bureau of Statistics, *Year Book Australia 2002*, Labour,
    Special Article. 'A Century of Change in the Australian Labour Market'.
2   Real Estate Institute of Australia.

## Chapter 4

1   Australian Bureau of Statistics, *Building Activity, Australia*
    (Cat. No. 8752.0).
2   Productivity Commission 2004, *First Home Ownership*, Productivity Commission,
    Report No. 28, Melbourne, p. 16, to 2004; Real Estate Institute of Australia
    after 2004. Australian Securities Exchange.
3   Productivity Commission 2004, *First Home Ownership*, Productivity Commission,
    Report No. 28, Melbourne, p. 16, to 2004; Real Estate Institute of Australia
    after 2004. Australian Securities Exchange. Australian Bureau of Statistics,
    *Consumer Price Index, Australia* (Cat. No. 6401.0).
4   Real Estate Institute of Australia.
5   Real Estate Institute of Australia.
6   Population statistics sourced from Productivity Commission 2004, *First Home
    Ownership*, Productivity Commission, Report No. 28, Melbourne, pp. 61–70.
7   Australian Bureau of Statistics, *Year Book Australia 2006*, Chapter 5 Population.
    <www.abs.gov.au/AUSSTATS/abs@.nsf/Latestproducts/A49FFD794E07339FC
    A2570DE00060B35?opendocument>
8   Australian Bureau of Statistics, *Census of Population and Housing: Selected Social
    and Housing Characteristics, Australia, 2001* (Cat. No. 2015.0).
9   Note that wages refer to gross wage before tax. Typically, one-third of gross
    wages go to the Tax Office, another third on living expenses, and the
    remainder covers housing costs. So in effect median house prices are currently
    around 24 times $(8 \div \frac{1}{3})$ the average housing allowance.
10  Australian Bureau of Statistics, *Australian Social Trends 1998*, Work — Paid
    work: Trends in women's employment (Cat. No. 4102.0), and Australian
    Bureau of Statistics, *Labour Force, Australia* (Cat. No. 6202.0).
11  Productivity Commission 2004, *First Home Ownership*, Productivity Commission,
    Report No. 28, Melbourne, p. 16, to 2004; Real Estate Institute of Australia
    after 2004. Australian Bureau of Statistics, *Average Weekly Earnings, Australia
    1941–1990* (Cat. No. 6350.0) and Australian Bureau of Statistics, *Average Weekly
    Earnings, Australia* (Cat. No. 6302.0). The average earnings are male total
    earnings (not seasonally adjusted) because the ABS did not start collecting
    female earnings until the 1980s.
12  Productivity Commission 2004, *First Home Ownership*, Productivity Commission,
    Report No. 28, Melbourne, p. 16, to 2004; Real Estate Institute of Australia
    after 2004. Australian Bureau of Statistics, *Average Weekly Earnings, Australia
    1941-1990* (Cat. No. 6350.0) and Australian Bureau of Statistics, *Average Weekly
    Earnings, Australia* (Cat. No. 6302.0). <www.rba.gov.au/Statistics/Bulletin/
    F05hist.xls>.
13  Productivity Commission 2004, *First Home Ownership*, Productivity Commission,
    Report No. 28, Melbourne, p. 17.
14  Productivity Commission 2004, *First Home Ownership*, Productivity Commission,
    Report No. 28, Melbourne, p. 126.
15  Real Estate Institute of Australia.

16    Australian Bureau of Statistics, *Consumer Price Index, Australia* (Cat. No. 6401.0).
17    Real Estate Institute of Australia.
18    Real Estate Institute of Australia. <www.rba.gov.au/Statistics/Bulletin/F05hist.xls>.
19    Real Estate Institute of Australia. <www.rba.gov.au/Statistics/Bulletin/F05hist.xls>.

## Chapter 5

1    <www.buffaloflipping.com/Learn.htm>.

## Chapter 6

1    Productivity Commission 2004, *First Home Ownership*, Productivity Commission, Report No. 28, Melbourne, p. 16 and <www.asx.com.au>.
2    <www.rba.gov.au/Statistics/Bulletin/F05hist.xls>.
3    Real Estate Institute of Australia.
4    Real Estate Institute of Australia. <www.rba.gov.au/Statistics/Bulletin/F05hist.xls>.
5    Hence the capital growth rate is slightly higher than 5 per cent when the relative rental yield is 60 per cent and slightly less than 5 per cent when the relative rental yield is 40 per cent. However, for simplicity I have assumed that the capital growth rate is equal to 5 per cent in both cases.
6    Real Estate Institute of Australia.

## Chapter 8

1    <www.rba.gov.au/Statistics/Bulletin/F05hist.xls>.

## Chapter 12

1    Real Estate Institute of Australia.
2    RP Data.
3    RP Data.
4    <maps.google.com.au>.

## Chapter 14

1    For example, in New South Wales go to <lpi-online.lpi.nsw.gov.au>.

## Chapter 16

1    See <www.fairtrading.nsw.gov.au/corporate/publications/ftr10conveyancing.html> for an example.

## Chapter 22

1    Real Estate Institute of Australia. <www.rba.gov.au/Statistics/Bulletin/F05hist.xls>.

# Index